Why do I say these things?

Jonathan Ross

BANTAM PRESS

LONDON · TORONTO · SYDNEY · AUCKLAND · JOHANNESBURG

TRANSWORLD PUBLISHERS
61–63 Uxbridge Road, London W5 5SA
A Random House Group Company
www.rbooks.co.uk

First published in Great Britain
in 2008 by Bantam Press
an imprint of Transworld Publishers

This book is substantially a work of non-fiction based on the life, experiences and
recollections of the author. In some limited cases names of people, places,
sequences or the detail of events have been changed solely to protect
the privacy of others.

A CIP catalogue record for this book
is available from the British Library.

ISBNs 9780593060827 (hb)
9780593047262 (tpb)

Addresses for Random House Group Ltd companies outside the UK
can be found at: www.randomhouse.co.uk
The Random House Group Ltd Reg. No. 954009

The Random House Group Limited supports The Forest Stewardship
Council (FSC), the leading international forest-certification organization. All our
titles that are printed on Greenpeace-approved FSC-certified paper carry the FSC logo.
Our paper procurement policy can be found at www.rbooks.co.uk/environment

Typeset in 12/17pt Bell by
Falcon Oast Graphic Art Ltd.
Printed and bound in Great Britain by
CPI Mackays, Chatham, ME5 8TD

2 4 6 8 10 9 7 5 3 1

Mixed Sources
Product group from well-managed
forests and other controlled sources
www.fsc.org Cert no. TT-COC-2139
© 1996 Forest Stewardship Council
FSC

To Jane, and Betty and Harvey and Honey,
who are all that matter.

Contents

Acknowledgements

This book was first promised almost ten years ago, so I offer both thanks and apologies to Larry Finlay for the long wait. Thanks also to Susanna Wadeson and her team who helped decipher my ramblings on tape before we committed them to paper, guiding me gently in the right direction without judging. And thanks to Suzi Aplin and the talented and patient people who work on my various shows and who must have grown tired of hearing me say I couldn't make a meeting because I had to work on 'the book'. Thanks also to David Baddiel and Jimmy Carr and Victor Hillman for not blowing my cover when we were playing tennis after I had managed to avoid a meeting, claiming I needed to work on 'the book'.

Thanks to Shaun, Frasier and Jim for making me laugh, and to Jez for pretty much the same but for longer. And to Fiona and Andy and Chrissie and Jerry and Lou and Lesley over at Radio 2.

My agent, despite all the odds, is also my friend. Addison – thanks for always being there, even when you're not.

Thanks to Robert for keeping the computers working, to Sam for getting the kids from school, and Lillya, Catherine, Tommy and Paul for loads of other things. Thanks to Andy for watching my front, and Dave, David, Stephen and Ian, aka Four Poofs and a Piano, for watching my back. Thanks to Danny and

Damon and Joe, at the other office. Thanks to Mr Pickle, Captain Jack, Sweeny, Princess, Yoda, Cupcake and Spider, for keeping me company on the couch.

Thanks, finally, to all the Little People, without whom *The Wizard of Oz* would have been nowhere near as much fun.

WHY DO I SAY THESE THINGS?

Why *do* I say these things? It's a phrase which I've moaned to my wife on any number of occasions over the twenty or so years we've been together, and a phrase which I used with my friends and family before Jane and I found each other. A phrase which, over the years, has shifted from being a genuine question to a rhetorical one, until now it's more of a groaning statement of defeat. I've lost count of the number of times that I've inadvertently insulted a guest on one of my shows, or given away just a little too much about my sex life while making a speech at a charity fundraiser. And so, unable to control my loose tongue and rambling brain, I have instead tried to channel them and turn this mental tic to my advantage.

Oddly, for someone who is virtually unembarrassable, I still feel some things are best kept to yourself, which is why this book is not my autobiography. My life has had a lot of fun moments and a few dramatic ones, but mostly it's been fairly straightforward – at least that's how it seems to me – and of course it's still going on. Maybe one day, when I'm winding things down on the career front, I will write that book. That's if people still seem interested enough, and my kids have grown up enough not to be shocked when they find out that Dad's done all the same stupid things and made the same mistakes that they will one day. Nor is this one of those books that recounts every meeting the writer's ever had with a famous person, predictably retelling the event so that they always come out on top. And it's certainly not a collection of short stories, or a guide to anything useful or interesting, like finding the right pension, or how to meet the perfect partner. Which leaves us with the question of exactly what this book is.

I wanted it to be the story of how I regained consciousness in the Pacific Ocean, more dead than alive. Nursed back to health by a friendly sailor, I had no inkling of who I really was, the only clue being the number tattooed on my arm which led to a safe deposit box in a Swiss bank. There I discovered a gun, money and a number of different passports. But who am I? Jason Bourne, the lethal killing machine, or mild-mannered David Webb, family man and college professor? But dammit, that didn't happen to me, and it's already been done. So I decided to write about a bunch of stuff that really has occurred. A bunch of stuff that I think you'll find funny, or interesting, or both. The sort of stuff that I ramble on about in between the records on my radio show, or sometimes crowbar into the talk show between guests. The sort of things that have occasionally resulted in my getting told off by my wife or kids or the people I work for, but more often lead to people telling me that they liked hearing it. That's what I went for in the end. Hope you enjoy.

I DATE-RAPED MYSELF

Filming a documentary on the woefully neglected topic of Mexican wrestling movies some time around 1989, I found myself landing in Mexico City itself. It's not a place I'd recommend for a fun tourist break, not least because, aside from the pollution and the overcrowding and the mind-boggling traffic jams and the violent crime, landing there is a bitch. We flew in on a turbulent day, and our approach entailed flying over a mountain range. The abrupt shifts in air pressure led to an effect that I believe pilots refer to as shearing, while we passengers chose more colourful phrases like 'Oh fuck, we're all going to die.'

Only a handful of my fellow travellers seemed unconcerned by the improvised rollercoaster approach to the runway, even when a stewardess fell into someone's lap and several bags exploded, piñata-style, from the overhead lockers. I assume the ones who kept their cool were either regulars, who had experienced this often and knew it was par for the course, or drug mules, so intent on not drawing attention to themselves that they would have stayed in their seats, staring straight ahead and minding their own illegal business, even if the tail had fallen off. Never yet having smuggled drugs, I can only imagine how keenly having a condom filled with cocaine working its way through your lower intestine must focus your attention. However, now I think of it, surely they would have been smuggling drugs out of the country rather than into it. Perhaps they were lost or stupid drug mules. I added that qualifying 'yet' in the sentence about me smuggling drugs because you never know what the future might hold, and I don't want to make rash promises now that I might have trouble keeping later in life.

Even though we were down Mexico way to work, we squeezed in a few afternoons off, one of which we spent at the amusement park that could be seen from my hotel-room window. The hotel was new and super-modern and incredibly tall and seemed to have been built exclusively out of glass. Lovely to look at from the outside, rather terrifying to sleep in, especially on the fifty-ninth floor during an electrical storm. The funfair, however, was great, and while enjoying the rollercoaster, an old-fashioned johnny made of wood apparently built in the fifties then left alone to acquire the appearance of elegant decay, which looked as if it was rarely if ever troubled by pesky safety checks, I had something of a minor epiphany. I love being scared when it's safe, but loathe the reality of actual fear. The swoops and drops that I willingly permitted the rollercoaster to hurtle me through were fun, because I expected them and had signed on for the experience. But encountering more or less the same sensations unexpectedly in a plane or a tall glass building made me sweat and pray to all the gods I've flirted with over the years and promise I'd never put myself in the same situation ever again.

Seeing as much of the build-up to visiting Mexico City involves people finding different ways of telling you you might not make it back alive, you'd have thought a bumpy landing and some lightning would have been easily shrugged off. It's not as if I hadn't tried to prepare myself for the worst. I had packed some shabby clothes for our trips out of the city, having been warned that we should try our hardest to look poor. Compared to today, I suppose I was poor back then, having a mortgage that kept me awake at night and not for a moment believing I had any long-term career prospects on television, and therefore worried about how I would support my family once the bubble burst. But compared to some of the actual live Mexicans I saw there, of course, I was rich beyond comprehension.

Driving out to a big wrestling event that was taking place in what I remember as being a very, very large barn with seats, we saw many people who were proper, raggedy-arse, cartoon poor. That's not to say they didn't look nice. In fact, compared to the way poor people look nowadays they looked fabulous – traditional-style clothing that had been patched and repaired and was still authentically of the region, straw hats, babies tied on to their bodies with lengths of colourful cloth – nice friendly eye-candy-style poverty. None of the truncated limbs or festering sores that India is so rightly famous for, nor the starving, fly-covered African-style poverty that frankly no one can enjoy driving past, however quickly. This was old-school, 100 per cent charming poverty – picturesque and life-affirming and, most importantly to those with a purist approach to travel, indigenous. Not like today, when no matter where you look you're likely to see people wearing hand-me-downs and cast-offs from the West. There were some pictures printed recently showing the survivors of an earthquake somewhere so far away I can't even remember its name. Along with the usual sporting brands of shirts, shorts and baseball caps that had been handed out to the survivors, one of them, a very old man, was wearing a *Little Britain* T-shirt with Daffyd, the only gay in the village, on the front. That's just cruel, isn't it? Surely he had suffered enough already.

Like many of you, I'm sure, I sponsor some charmingly poor families in picturesque but underprivileged parts of the world. As part of the deal for setting up the standing order that ensures they receive a set amount each month, enough to help the village educate their kids and keep fresh water coming, they send you a picture of the families you are sponsoring, sometimes with a note from the children. It's very sweet, and helps to keep you involved enough not to cancel the standing order in a year's time when you get bored with the concept of sending money to strangers.

But in one of the pictures they sent me, alongside the adorable children living in a tiny house made of clay, trying their best to smile and look cute for the rich but possibly fickle stranger half a world away who helped pay for the village well, you can make out an elderly family member sitting in the background. He's wearing a hooded sweatshirt that someone, somewhere, must have bought after going to see Bucks Fizz play live. Oh, the humiliation. I've tried to make out who was supporting them, and it might have been Dollar, but the old man is sitting at a funny angle and there's a crease in the shirt. And while I'm on the subject, would it not have been a good idea for them to clean up a little before the photo was taken? I don't expect it to look like a *Hello!* spread – Mustafa and Kemel show us around their charming mud hut – but surely they could have used one of their dodgy T-shirts to wipe the table and give the windows a clean? There's no better use for a Curiosity Killed the Cat sleeveless tanktop than a little light hovel dusting.

Anyway, the Mexicans we met were mostly poor, but fabulously friendly, and I fell in love with them, imagining how rich and fulfilling my life would be if I came back to live here. This is something I normally do when I encounter a new country with a new language and a new history. I get overly excited and start making all sorts of stupid pointless promises that I never manage to keep. I convince myself I will return with the whole family within six months. I just know that, this time, I really will go to the absurd trouble of learning the language fluently, and when I reappear, those people to whom I stammered an unconvincing 'Good morning' or 'How much is that?' in native will be delighted and impressed that the handsome gringo who they secretly recognized as being somehow better than all the other tourists is now virtually one of them.

With that in mind, and considering myself virtually a proper Mexican by day three, I took great care to ensure that my mementoes reflected my status. I managed to collect a vinyl box set of Mexican revolutionary songs, certain that I would soon be an expert not only on the war against the Americans but, more specifically, the folk music of the period. Almost twenty years on I still have that box set, still unopened. I also bought some Frida Kahlo postcards, some Day of the Dead figures with which to decorate my soon-to-be-Mexican-themed house, and an over-large sombrero. This was purchased only as an ironic joke, but I soon grew to hate it as I couldn't pack it in any of the cases I had, so I wound up wearing it on the flight out of the country, looking like the biggest, stupidest tourist in the history of tourism.

It was later stolen from my hotel room in Los Angeles. I often wondered about that and have concluded that it might have been taken by a furious Mexican employee convinced I was taking the piss. The chance of someone actually wanting or needing a giant sombrero so much that they would take the risk of stealing it and then smuggling it out of a hotel is too remote even to contemplate, so I have surmised it was hidden in the dirty laundry, then taken downstairs and destroyed, while every single Mexican employee in the hotel cheered and danced around it.

But the most interesting thing I picked up in Mexico City and took back over the border into America was a stomach bug, the worst stomach bug I have ever had, and this is coming from someone who managed to contract a mild form of dysentery whilst canoeing just outside Seattle, a story I will save for another time. I can even pinpoint the exact meal that I got it from, and I really do have no one to blame but myself. It was our last night there, and we had been careful not to drink anything but bottled water or – as was more often the case – beer. But after a few days of this we had begun to think we were being stupidly, needlessly cautious. After all, we had toughened up our systems with junk food from the four corners of the globe. Our national dish was chicken madras. We were confident we could handle anything the Mexicans cared to throw at us. And so on the last night, while eating in a fabulous restaurant that had a live band and a dance floor where people twirled one another around as the rest of us chowed down chimichangas, we asked for a dish that you could only get in Mexico. Mexican food that you'd never see in a so-called Mexican restaurant anywhere else in the world.

The meal we were served and, crucially, ate, was lamb that had been wrapped in banana leaves and buried underground for three days before cooking. Essentially we ate a reincarnated meal, the Jesus of main courses. It probably tasted lovely. I can't remember, because doubtless I was drunk on tequila by the time it was served. But I ate it, and nothing bad happened. For about twelve hours.

Then, like a blip on a weather radar that signals a hurricane is on the way, while we were on the plane back to Los Angeles, I farted. This was no ordinary fart. This was the kind of fart that caused my fellow passengers to look at the doors and wonder whether it really would be such a bad idea to open them at twenty thousand feet. Was the worst that could happen likely to be any more terrible than remaining in this fouled environment? Because this was the Adolf Hitler, the Genghis Khan, the Osama bin Laden of farts. (Although technically the events in this anecdote took place before Osama's acts of lunatic extremism earnt him a place on that list, and he was probably still living it up as a stupidly rich hypocritical Saudi playboy at the time. But it seems right and just to name a disgusting, stomach-churning bowel-burp of wind after him.)

Somehow the pilot managed to land the plane despite the wailing of his passengers and the greenish fug that hung in the air. Somehow I managed to retrieve my bags and waddle my way to a taxi, where I lay in the back shivering and holding my buttocks together with superhuman willpower. Somehow I managed to check into my room and, after an hour or so spent sitting on the toilet, crying, while my sphincter tried to pass my lungs into the bowl, I climbed into bed.

Before I did, I raided the emergency medical kit a doctor back in the UK had given me, for just such a situation. He had been one of the cheery souls who had prophesied my probable death in Mexico City. To try to prevent this, he had supplied me with syringes and dressings, swabs and antiseptic wipes, powder that dries up large wounds and is normally only supplied to the SAS to be used if they get wounded behind enemy lines and can't find a medic, and a whole pharmacy worth of pills for almost every eventuality. For the current situation, which I brilliantly self-diagnosed as extreme nausea and diarrhoea brought on by massive stupidity, he had included some pills which are now quite infamous for their association with date rape but that back then no one had really heard of – Rohypnol. He had suggested I should take one if necessary, but I felt so utterly, utterly miserable I took two, possibly three, and went to bed.

I must have slept for about twenty hours. When I awoke, or tried to wake, I was just about aware that there were other people in my room, concerned people. One might have been the director of the programmes we were filming, another might have been a representative of the hotel. I think a third person, out of focus in the background, might have been wearing my sombrero. They were talking to me and trying to work out what was going on, and whether or not I needed a doctor. I was later told that I had been adamant that I was a doctor and the situation was under control. They phoned the doctor whose number had been included in the pack. I suspect he was a little disappointed that I hadn't been killed in a knife fight or caught leprosy so he could have written 'I warned him' on the death certificate, but instead he reassured them that I had done the right thing and just needed to sleep it off.

Over the next couple of days I drifted in and out of consciousness, often half aware that someone was looking at me or, on one occasion, poking me in the side to see if I would make a noise. It was the weirdest sensation. The harder I tried to wake myself up, the more thought I put into even lifting my head from the pillow, the more impossible it seemed, and the effort would then send me back into a deep sleep. I remember occasionally having enough energy and presence of mind to drag myself to the toilet, where I would sit for a while, passing water and toxic air with fabulous urgency but never really feeling any better. On one occasion I even fell asleep on the toilet, and only woke when I fell off and hit my head. That's about as pitiful a position as you can be in – waking up on a toilet floor with your pants down, dribbling and trying to stay awake long enough to either get back to bed or back on the loo, knowing that you only have yourself to blame.

Eventually the Rohypnol wore off, as did the diarrhoea. I had an upset stomach for about another week though, so it didn't give up without a struggle, and although many of the odd promises I made to myself during my trip to Mexico were soon forgotten, I have kept one. I have never again eaten lamb that has been wrapped in banana leaves and buried for three days underground. Never even been tempted.

MY GREATEST ACHIEVEMENT

ere's a dull question for you. What makes a man a success? When called to account for your life, what will you look back on and say was your greatest achievement? Unless you're Nelson Mandela or Gandhi or Mother Teresa, or even someone not so universally easy to approve of, like Harold Wilson or Joseph Stalin, chances are you won't have made a global impact, so the answer will probably have something to do with your kids or your community. You might even have saved a few lives, which is terrific and more than I've ever done, but if so it's likely to be because you're a fireman or a lifeguard or a doctor, so although it's still a fabulous achievement it's sort of predictable. No, a better question, one which throws up a few more interesting responses, is what do you remember most fondly? It's worth giving this some thought, otherwise on your deathbed you might start ruminating on all the time-wasting afternoons you spent playing Solitaire on your laptop, or filling in sudokus, convinced that you were doing yourself a whole lot of good in staving off senile dementia, but knowing deep down you just wanted that incredibly brief moment of triumph when you fill the last box with the right number. So for your own sake, start drawing up a mental list of all the really cool, memorable moments so that you will at least be able to check out with a smile on your face, instead of lying there cursing the fact that you wasted hundreds of hours reading Jackie Collins and probably entire days searching for your glasses or keys.

I have mine ready, and they might surprise you. I have, of course, enjoyed many successes as an adult, both in my personal and professional life. I've won awards, met the Queen, had dinner with David Bowie. All lovely experiences, but not as exciting as you might hope. And to be honest with you, most of my professional accomplishments have pretty much occurred by accident. I worked in TV for about six or seven years before I started presenting programmes, and right from the start I was lucky enough to have my name in the title of the show. A little later, I remember my mum getting quite excited when she saw a dodgy BBC sitcom in which a young male character of about thirty complained to his partner that he didn't feel as if he'd achieved anything in his life, commenting bitterly that Jonathan Ross had been a household name by the time he was thirty. It's a weird feeling, hearing your name used as a yardstick for precocious success when you don't really feel you've done that much to deserve it, so I didn't really get that excited by it, or at least not as excited as by other things I've done – the more straightforward, simple-minded pleasures of my youth. Maybe being of an impressionable age has more to do with it than the actual value of the modest feats I achieved, but whenever I think about what has made me happiest or proudest in my life, the first thing that comes to mind has nothing to do with fame, or even family. No, it is the moment I discovered I could do a forward roll.

I was about six or seven and on my way to school in Leytonstone. I was actually born in Camden Town, in north London, but when I was about two my parents moved out to Leytonstone, where they could afford a bit more space for their expanding family. East London wasn't seen as particularly nice, or fashionable. Then, as now, there were little pockets in the east and south-east of the city that were quite charming and pleasant, and others that were a bit dodgy, and Leytonstone, I guess, came somewhere between the two. It was nice enough and I have very good memories of growing up there.

Initially, we had the bottom floor of a house, and eventually my parents managed to buy the top floor from whoever lived above us. Just as well because by then our family had swollen from being the two grown-ups and three boys to include three more small, runny-nosed children dressed in hand-me-downs. If we'd all stayed on the one floor it would have been like the family in *Charlie and the Chocolate Factory*, but after we took over the whole house we had enough room for my sister – the only girl – to have her own room. I still shared with my four brothers, but we had just about enough space to grow up still liking each other. The house was near to a patch of open ground known as Wanstead Flats, which wasn't what you'd call attractive, bordered as it was on our side by two enormous ugly tower blocks with equally ugly names – John Walsh Tower and Fred

Wigg House. Once you crossed over the Flats you could get to a much larger spread of natural parkland and, beyond that, Epping Forest, so it was a kind of stepping stone out of the concrete jungle towards greener pastures. And we were literally just around the corner from my first school.

I started in the infants at about five, and later progressed to the junior school; then it was Norlington, followed by Leyton County High School for Boys, which had a sister school for girls. Much to my delight and amazement, I discovered not so long ago that in the mid-1980s they renamed Leyton County High School for Girls as the Winnie Mandela High, in honour of the great Nelson Mandela's wife at the time, and then, when she was publicly shamed and convicted of fraud, they changed it back again to Leyton County High.

Anyway, back to my thrilling feat, and the first time the ability to perform it revealed itself to me. I don't want to give this too enormous a build-up as of course it matters a lot more to me than to you, and it's not as juicy as me telling you about the night – or afternoon – when I lost my virginity, or the time I found myself in a gay nightclub in Madrid late at night and very much alone. But the forward roll still figures as a big deal in my memory bank, and I find myself thinking of it and smiling probably once a week, even though it was decades ago and I've since learnt to do far more complicated manoeuvres.

My brothers had already left for school but I was running late for some reason. I was a sweet little boy then – I didn't start getting ugly until I was about eleven, and as a five-year-old you'd have wanted to scoop me up and cuddle me hard. Little shorts, bare knees, dinky socks, probably brown shoes done up with a buckle, and, I imagine, a little school cap. Yes, we wore caps. At least I think we did – I'm old enough now to find it difficult to distinguish real memories from invented ones. I raced off to catch up with my brothers and as I rounded a corner I tripped on a step or an uneven bit of pavement. As I lost my footing I remember thinking, Oh my God, I might die and never get my own chat show. Actually I don't remember quite that, but I'm sure I anticipated a grazed knee at the very least. But instead of throwing out my arms, as I fell I somehow managed to tuck my body into a small ball and execute a forward roll off my right shoulder, before springing to my feet again and carrying on running. Without even breaking stride.

I cannot begin to describe how excited I was. I already harboured great ambitions to be, if not an actual superhero, then special in some unspecified way, and this seemed to me a very necessary and valuable first step in that admirable if fuzzy ambition. But try as I might to replicate this particular stunt, I never managed to pull it off quite as successfully again. Even today I'm sometimes tempted to go out into the garden and give it a shot, and I often throw myself on to the bed in a peculiar way which my wife has learned to ignore, but I know that whatever the result, it would never be the same as that first perfectly timed, gracefully fluid movement. It was an instinctive reaction, cat-like, flawless, perfect. And without the stimulus of the danger and the adrenalin that kicked in, I've never been able to match it. Oh, and even better, my cap stayed on. At least I think it did . . . No way could I do that again.

One childhood skill I *was* able to hone and which, once again, I look back on with great pride, was jumping on and off

the old London Routemaster buses with the necessary speed and judgement. They had an open platform at the back with no door, just a pole to hold on to, so you could leap on board while the bus was moving, grabbing the pole to haul yourself in.

They were beautiful, those buses, and I miss them. But is it because they really were as lovely as I remember, or is this just another example of nostalgia clouding your judgement as you get older? Is it the buses I miss, or the past? I wonder if today's kids will ever feel as nostalgic for the ugly utilitarian boxes that ferry them around. Back then, as well as being prettier, buses seemed to be fewer and further between. I was forever going to the end of my road in the hope of catching the number 262 only to wait half an hour before two or three turned up together or, worse still, to see one pulling away from the bus stop.

The 262 took me from Leytonstone to where my best friend lived, a Spanish boy called José Roman Martinez Diaz, though he called himself Joe Martin at school. If you were the only Spanish kid at school in east London in the 1960s you'd probably have done the same. I'm still in touch with him from time to time. We bonded over our shared love of comics and because no one else wanted to be seen talking to such obvious losers, a status we inverted and wore like a badge of pride. But if I missed the bus to Joe's it was a royal pain in the arse. I'd have to either wait half an hour for the next one or set off on the boring thirty-minute walk to his house. Pretty soon I got in the habit of jogging the full length of my road down to the bus stop, so that if I did just miss the bus at least I didn't beat myself up for having missed one that I *could* have been on if I hadn't walked. On those occasions when I arrived, probably breathless, just as the bus was taking off, I'd try to find a little pocket of untapped stamina and run full pelt to catch it and bound aboard. Using the rudimentary physics at my fingertips, I'd anticipate the speed and trajectory of the bus, sometimes from behind, sometimes as I ran alongside it, and launch myself into the air, hoping to hit the open space between the pole and the back end. I missed only once that I recall, bouncing back on to the pavement and having a very sore arse and back to show for it. Usually I managed it, and on one spectacular occasion the bus and I were moving at such a lick that I was forced to do a small, tucked-in forward roll as I landed on the platform, jumping straight back to my feet.

You must by now have surely guessed that this is right up there in my all-time list of favourite moments, along with that first forward tumble with my cap on. But where did that athleticism go? How did the lithe suppleness of youth disappear so completely that these days, rising from my armchair too swiftly after watching *The Antiques Roadshow* causes me to let out a small, involuntary half-gasp, half-moan – a real old man's noise.

Before we leave the buses, I have remembered that while jumping on to a Routemaster was fun, jumping off one was even better. As the saying goes, we had to make our own fun in those days, and buses were more than just a mode of transport, they were also a thrilling source of entertainment. If there was a bunch of you going somewhere together, getting on and off the bus gave you the opportunity to play a game involving great skill and foolish courage. Picturing ourselves as cowboys riding a freight train heading across the old west, we'd all race to catch the bus as it picked up speed and the last person to get on – in other words, the person with the most courage and precision, who waited till the last possible moment – was the winner, or at least, gained the most kudos, since there was no prize as such. Occasionally somebody wouldn't make it and he'd be left standing in the road, forlorn and out of breath. Occasionally we'd lose him altogether, but there was usually a chance he'd be able to sprint to the next stop before the bus pulled away, especially if there was a queue of people waiting there who took their time to get on. I say 'him' because, with the exception of my sister and her friends, who rarely played with us because they were quite a few years younger, we had next to no deliberate contact with girls until way after puberty. Why would we need them when we had buses?

The most fun to be had was in the getting-off procedure. This time the game would be reversed, and the bravest person was the one who jumped off first. The bus might still have been doing maybe twenty, twenty-five mph, and whichever one of you had the most to prove or most needed the confidence boost that winning gave would try to hit the ground running, invariably too soon to pull it off, and instead go arse over tit.

The best and most dramatic accident caused by this game occurred on our way to the swimming baths over in Leyton. We were on a number 10 bus – oh, friendly companion to the 262, how I miss you! One boy leapt off very early. Really very, very early indeed, earlier than I had seen anyone try to disembark before. You could see from the second he hit the ground that even though his legs were pumping and his arms were flailing he had absolutely no control over himself, and there was no way he was going to stay upright. With his face red, his legs churning comically fast and his arms shooting up and down and sideways, he looked a bit like a turkey trying to take off. The bus slowed down quite gracefully while he kept running, virtually alongside us now as we cheered him on, until he slammed face-first into a concrete lamp post. He didn't pass out, which meant we still got to go swimming, but he did lose three, possibly four teeth in the process. They really should bring those buses back.

I KISS MY DOGS, EVEN THOUGH THEIR BREATH SMELLS BAD

It's often been said that I'm far too kind-hearted a person. Mainly by me, I'll admit, but I pride myself on being super kind to all the little creatures that wriggle and walk and hover and limp – especially the limping ones. Why, just the other day I stopped halfway through a game of tennis to pick up a lady-bird I had spotted on the ground and place her safely on a nearby leaf. I'm fond of all living creatures – even the ones I eat, though like most non-vegetarian animal lovers I pretend not to know too much about what is on my plate and how it got there. I circumvent this apparent contradiction quite happily via the assumption that people like Gordon Ramsay would probably be out there killing pigs and sheep and cows anyway, just to prove how manly they are, so I might as well put the end product to some good use. Some delicious good use, with potatoes and salad.

Of course, I draw the line at eating domesticated animals, but were I to get especially peckish we have plenty to choose from.

Over the past twenty years our family has managed to acquire quite an impressive menagerie. We have had approximately seven or eight cats, some of whom are still with us in various stages of domesticity, with one or two being almost completely feral and only hanging around for the food and because they fancy their chances with the fifteen or twenty fish we have in the small pond at the end of the garden.

It's hard to grow especially fond of fish, isn't it? I wonder if we'd spend more time with them if we could breed a fish with fur, and maybe extend the fins so they look a bit cuter, more like little arms and legs. But then they'd look like frogs in fur coats, which in turn I suspect would resemble German businessmen from the 1930s as portrayed in cartoons, and so the fish would be no better off, really.

We also used to have six ferrets, which make adorable pets. Highly recommended if you like the idea of having a very thin fur ball to tickle. They also play with each other in a very cute way, sort of frolicking and dancing around like animated draught-excluders. We no longer have them because three died and the one girl escaped, and you need a female with every small group of boys, to keep them in order. So we had to either start again with a new bunch or hand them back to the rescue centre we got them from, which we did. We still have our python, Ken, but Dave the iguana died just before Christmas. As I'll explain later, Dave was actually a Davina, but I'm pretty certain that our confusion regarding her gender had nothing to do with her death. She was just old. We currently also have seven dogs. Too many for any sane household, but fun in a noisy, smelly way. They have somewhat ousted the cats from the house, though, who now live down the end of the garden in the flat that is currently occupied by my wife's dad, in a weird little commune. Only cats and old blokes allowed.

I love our cats, even if the wilder ones only crouch and hiss when I go in to feed them. The cat commune started with Merlin, an incredibly handsome and seemingly very intelligent beast. He was Bengal, a type which I think are cross-bred from some kind of North American wildcat, like a lynx, and a domesticated cat. The offspring are tame enough to keep as pets but still look very strong and rather like mini-leopards.

Merlin used to follow us around when we went for walks in the garden. We had a picnic once, just Jane and me and the kids and Merlin. He looked so splendid lying in the sun that I took some pics of him, and we all talked about how lucky we were to have him. I told the children that the nice thing about cats is that they are quite sensible and can live for ten or fifteen years easily, so he would still be part of the family when they were grown up. You can probably guess where this is heading. About two weeks later he was run over by some twat in a Porsche speeding past our house, who just drove off callously. I've never much cared for Porsche drivers anyway – Porsches seem to be the cars most beloved by flash types with absolutely no taste – and this confirmed my low opinion of them. Merlin was in such a bad state that I was in tears as I rushed him to the vet, and I was amazed that he pulled through. They're a strong breed, Bengals, and although we were delighted to have him still with us, in some ways we all wished that he had just died quickly and painlessly. The damage done to him made the last two years of his life pretty uncomfortable. He'd lost an eye, his palate had been split in half and wouldn't heal, which meant he couldn't chew solid food – we had to mix up some sort of liquid stuff for him, and a lot of what he tried to eat just got stuck in the hole in the roof of his mouth – and gradually most of his fur fell out. Towards the end he looked like a small, partially furred version of the Elephant Man. We still all gave him loads of attention, and allowed him to limp up on to our laps while we watched TV. I hope he didn't notice that we were no longer quite as thrilled to have him there as we used to be. The once proud and glossy cat that we used to practically fight to grab and stroke had been replaced by a mangy, one-eyed, drooling thing that occasionally would look up to you with his one good eye and sneeze, showering cat snot and watered-down meat paste over your face. He's gone now, but I knew I'd never feel quite as fond of another cat.

We persevered, though. Our second Bengal cat was Ophelia, who begat Suji – Japanese for 'stripy' – who begat Electro Girl. Ophelia is long gone, and we never found out what happened to her. Maybe when our dogs started to arrive she went off in a huff and moved in with somebody else, or maybe she suffered the same fate as Merlin. Suji and Electro Girl are still around. Both are very pretty cats, although Electro Girl has a tiny black smudge on her nose, which makes her look like a very half-hearted Hitler impersonator.

What is it with cats wanting to look like Hitler? On paper it seems like an unlikely mix, but there are loads of them out there. There's even a website that parades a whole gallery of Kitlers – cats and kittens who bear a passing resemblance to old Adolf. Some of them have clearly been worked on by their owners to enhance the look, which, when you think about it, is a pretty odd thing to do to a pet.

I'd recommend owning a few animals to anyone with a family. They are a great practical help when it comes to teaching children some of life's valuable lessons. One of the first things kids learn from them is how to be kind to smaller, weaker beings than themselves, which, with luck, will nip any bullying tendencies in the bud. It's a terrible thing, bullying: it upsets me if I see it going on or read about some poor kid who's been horribly picked on at school. Having a sweet little puppy or kitten or hamster to take care of at a young age, and learning not to be rough with it, sows the seeds of consideration for others. Having said that, we did have a hamster once, which, while never deliberately manhandled, was the victim of an accidental act of violence that changed the course of its life, unfortunately not for the better.

We purchased Fluffy for our eldest daughter, Betty, when she was about two, thinking it would be nice if she had a little pet to stroke. This was before the cats and the dogs and the iguana, which wouldn't really have been a great pet for a small girl anyway. Betty loved Fluffy but, being a toddler, she was a bit too young to understand the difference between a pet and a toy. One day we had Fluffy out on the dining table and were giving him some little hamster treats when Betty suddenly made a grab for him and pulled him towards her with such force that he went flying off the table and landed in a small heap on the floor. Of course we were panic-stricken and overcome with guilt, blaming ourselves for not having anticipated Betty's lunge – what were we *thinking of*? But Fluffy, miraculously, seemed fine so we put him back in his cage, calmed down and forgot about it.

Fast forward six months, and we noticed that Fluffy had taken to doing an unusual and very impressive trick. So impressive we used to say to people, 'Come over and see our hamster. You won't believe what he can do.'

He'd come out of his little sleeping area, ready for a spot of exercise, and rather than run around in his wheel, he'd pull himself up on to the bars of the cage by his arms – or front legs, I suppose they are on a hamster – climb up the side and swing from the roof of the cage like a miniature monkey. It was brilliant, and we were delighted and proud to have what was probably the most talented hamster in the world. It was quite some while before we found out (we'd taken him to the vet because he was looking a bit peaky) that at some stage in the past both his back legs had been rather badly broken and had never healed properly. So he had been dragging himself around on his front legs all this time because they were the only fully working limbs he had. We were horrified, but the vet assured us he was in no pain – well, he probably had been at the time, but he wasn't any longer – and that in compensating for his disability he had developed quite extraordinary upper-body strength, like a lady weightlifter.

We now have two pet pigs in the garden called Piggy-Pie and Sugar-Pie. They are Pennywell Miniatures, and when we bought them – suckered in by a picture we saw in the paper of a baby pig sniffing a buttercup – we were told they would grow no larger than a small dog. Piggy-Pie now weighs about three hundred pounds, so either the man who sold them to us was being a little casual with the truth or he's seen some bloody enormous corgis. Morrissey came round for dinner one night – you know, the pop star – which was lovely, and he seemed very pleased that they were never going to be eaten. 'Two were saved,' he said, rather gloomily, no doubt thinking about all the others who weren't. I didn't eat pork for nearly a week to show my solidarity. I have also secretly been hoping he will write a song called 'Two Were Saved' and dedicate it to me.

Pigs are fine, if smelly, and cats are lovely, and snakes are beautiful, but it's our dogs we love the most, and boy do they love us back. Someone told me they once saw a sign in a pet shop – PUPPIES FOR SALE. THE ONLY LOVE MONEY *CAN* BUY – and it's sort of true. Of course you have to be nice to them, but they are a cheap date – stroke them a few times and feed them and don't be mean and they'll roll right over and show you their privates. They're so eager to please, so desperate for your company and so delightfully reliant on you. You only have to go out for half an hour, and the minute you walk back in, they go nuts. Many's the occasion somebody in our family has been head-butted by Yoda, our young Boston terrier, always so hysterical with joy when we return after having been away for all of fifteen minutes that he tries to knock us out to show his love. It's as if dogs just can't believe their luck. We should learn from them, of course. They live in the moment, they don't get bogged down with the minutiae of day-to-day existence; while they're awake they just want to eat, sleep or fuck. Rather like the French.

We had a dog when I was a kid, a kind of half-breed mongrel called Trog. She was called Trog because I was given the job of naming her as a puppy when I was about six, and I christened her after my favourite character from *Pogles' Wood*, one of those sweet black-and-white TV puppet programmes that were popular in the 1960s, owing to the fact that they were just about the only thing there was to watch if you were a child. I can't imagine how modern kids would deal with the kind of suffering we had to put up with: just two TV channels, neither of which ever showed anything except well-meaning stuff made by elderly people in business suits. But anyway, one of the characters in *Pogles' Wood* was Tog, which – rather ironically, bearing in mind that I would later earn a certain degree of notoriety for my inability to pronounce the letter R – for some reason I interpreted as Trog.

So we had a dog called Trog, which was actually a pretty cool name when you think about it – sounds like a slightly wild yet still friendly caveman. She was black and white and fat and a little on the plain side. But she was always popular with male dogs in the neighbourhood because she was so easy. She would have it away with anyone. I don't know what my parents could have been thinking, but they never had her spayed, so every so often she would go crazy and we'd suddenly find loads of randy mutts hanging around outside the house. They were a bedraggled crew, too. Leytonstone, not being a particularly well-heeled part of London, was the kind of place where people ended up with scabby old dogs they'd just sort of acquired, partly as status symbols, partly as guard dogs, I guess. And then there were the strays. But what they all had in common was that they were ferociously horny.

It was terribly embarrassing when you were bringing friends back from school, walking home to find a pack of slavering mongrels sitting outside your house with their lipsticks out. I'd have to run the gauntlet with my mates, muttering apologetically, 'Don't mind the dogs. Trog's on heat.'

One got inside once, but we managed to chase him straight

out into the garden and hoicked him over the wall. Trog did not take kindly to being kept indoors while her fan club sat outside barking, and she would try to escape on a regular basis. So you had to be very diligent about shutting the door after you. Which is probably why one of my enduring childhood memories is of my father shouting, 'Shut the bloody *door!*'

It wasn't just because of Trog. It was also because he was a money-conscious, working-class dad with six kids who were always leaving doors open and letting out the heat, so even inside the house, 'Shut the *door!*' was a familiar refrain, occasionally accompanied by a slipper flying towards your head if you were the one who'd forgotten. A soft slipper, as he was a very kind father. But with excellent aim.

Inevitably Trog would sometimes escape, and as a result we grew up with a lot of puppies, as well as a lot of stress brought on by trying to keep the dog indoors. If there is such a thing as an exhibitionist dog, then Trog was one.

I'm no expert on the mechanics of mating dogs, but as you probably know, once they are in the throes of passion, they get physically locked together and it's very hard to separate them. The only way you can do it is to give them a shock to the system. And it's no good just shouting something about mortgage rates going up or pouncing on them and yelling 'BOO!', you have to give them a real jolt. The traditional method is to throw a bucket of cold water over them, and we found this to be the most effective solution. In fact, it became quite a sport for us and we'd take it in turns to do the honours, because in a weird kind of way we quite enjoyed it. True, it was embarrassing, but at the same time it was fun being the centre of attention.

I remember being given the job one Sunday when Trog had chosen to entertain one of her many gentlemen callers in the middle of a football field where a local amateur-league match was in progress. The players were obviously quite amused, as well as a little irate, to find two dogs fornicating on their pitch and the game had more or less come to a standstill. I'd probably been picked because it was me who'd let Trog out in the first place. Anyway, after assessing the situation, I ran back home, filled a bucket with cold water and returned to the scene. I walked slowly across the pitch and, to a cheer from the admittedly small crowd of football supporters, upended it over the dogs, who separated, shook themselves and ran off, as did I to a round of applause. Ah, show business.

Yet given those emotional scars, it's probably not surprising that I've made sure that all the dogs we have now get neutered – well, all but one, at the moment. Two of them are most peculiar, it has to be said. Mr Pickle, my beautiful but slightly fat and very, very greedy pug – he looks a little bit like a retarded seal when he sits down – really is the stupidest dog I've ever known. I love him tremendously but there's no getting away from his brainlessness. He's always getting stuck in things, and he'll nod off, still sitting upright, on the edge of the couch and just keel over on to the floor. You hear a snore and then a loud bang and there he is, lying down on the floor wondering what's happened.

'You fell asleep sitting up on the corner of the couch, you idiot,' I admonish him. 'Not even lying down. Lie down! There are cushions here, too.' But no, he carries on sitting up straight and dozing off where he is. He's just too lazy and too stupid to move.

Mr Pickle gets on very well with Sweeney, my wife's tiny-weeny Brussels Griffon. He's a sweet little rusty-coloured dog, with an underbite that makes his chin jut out. He reminds me of how George Michael looked in those paparazzi snaps when he fell asleep in his car after smoking too much skunk or whatever it was he owned up to, only slightly prettier. And like George Michael, he seems to prefer same-sex relationships. Sometimes you'll see him playing with Mr Pickle, and they'll start off in a joshing manner, tussling and shoving each other, but then everything goes a bit quiet and if you glance over at them you'll catch them casually licking each other's crown jewels, trying to make it look like an accident when you know full well it was always on the agenda. I don't want to be the mean grown-up who tells Sweeney and Mr Pickle they have to stop, but frankly it's not nice if you're trying to eat a sandwich or something. So you have to go, 'Come on, boys!' and try to distract them with their slipper.

Sometimes I feel I spend more of my life looking at dogs' privates than I care to, especially those of the small and short-haired varieties of dog, whose arses are on permanent display. Often a dog's arse is the first thing I see in the morning and the last thing I see at night. But you learn to live with it.

It would be easier if they wore clothes, and I must admit I have once or twice dressed mine up. I have a strange and in-explicable desire to put my pug in lederhosen. There's something about his little round face and his little floppy chops that gives him a slightly Germanic or Austrian air. One summer, I did tell the children I was planning on shaving him and taking him round Europe with us in a baby-carrier, claiming he was a little Deutsche boy I'd adopted. They were very taken with the idea – but then we found out we'd have to get a dog passport for him to leave Britain, which would involve six months of tests and what have you, and it all seemed too problematic, thankfully, to justify a moment of racist whimsy. So we left him at home and let him keep his hair.

Being the greediest dog (I think pugs are just naturally prone to greediness), Mr Pickle loves his breakfast and he loves his tea. He doesn't get a meal in the middle of the day, and you just know he bears a grudge about that. He sits there while we're having lunch and you can see how furious and perplexed he is that we're allowed another meal and he isn't. I can almost imagine him cursing the fact that he's a dog and we're people. Cursing the fact that he doesn't know how to open the fridge on his own. Cursing the fact that even though he jumps up at the table repeatedly, we make him get down. 'What is it with them? Sometimes they love me; sometimes they have me on their lap and stroke me, sometimes they even let me on their bed to sleep next to them. They cuddle me, they kiss me, they seem to adore me, and yet if I try to get on to the table it's "Get down! No food for you! Bad boy!" All I want is a little bit of steak, or chicken, or pie, or . . .'

Very occasionally we might give him a scrap, but we try not to do it too often because it encourages him, and because he's fat. Fat, as they used to say, as butter. He's like a little black shiny bowling ball, or a fur-covered Space Hopper. We have to keep him on a diet or he'll have a heart attack, but still he sits there stubbornly. Recently, when we were enjoying a proper lunch, he came up with a good tactic, which was to put me off my food. To disgust me to the point where I either had to banish him from the room and remove him from his torment or give him something to make him stop what he was doing. He was sitting right in my line of vision as I ate my lunch – scallops, as I recall, which is not a dish you'd think a dog would particularly fancy, but I suppose it was the spicy aroma that enticed him – anyway, he was sitting right in my line of vision, and he produced a little erection and just sat there rocking backwards and forwards, rubbing himself against the slightly rough texture of the couch. The glint in his eye told me, 'OK, if I can't have any food, I'll have to take my pleasure elsewhere, and if, in doing so, I ruin your enjoyment of whatever those round, meaty white things are on your plate, so be it.' So Mr P scored a major point there. I gave him a scallop and sent him on his way. Which was probably not a good idea, because all I was doing was rewarding his bad behaviour. I only hope the kids don't ever resort to that kind of blackmail, or my father-in-law.

Although we could do without the kind of sex education offered by the likes of Sweeney, Mr Pickle and Trog, there is another important fact of life children learn from pets: mortality. I say this, but to be honest I haven't quite come to terms with it yet myself and I've seen loads of things die. I'm still banking on scientists developing a way of prolonging people's lives. Or some people's, at any rate: hopefully multiple BAFTA winners like me will be first in the queue with their families, but others will be there, too, I'm sure, if they've got enough cash or have friends in the government. We might end up being around for two or three hundred years, you never know.

I'm quite convinced that somewhere in the world there's an island or remote region we don't know about that is full of really, really old people. Somewhere with lots of comfy chairs and opiates where everyone just lies around all day doing drugs and watching the sunset. But theoretically at least, the death of pets can help children come to terms with that big inevitable full stop waiting at the end of the sentence for us all. Hamsters and gerbils and mice die – very sad. Goldfish and terrapins die – very sad. You bury them in the garden or flush them away and call it a burial at sea. They're not difficult to dispose of, which is just as well, as neither hamsters nor gold-fish have a very long life expectancy. But bigger creatures can be more of a problem.

Those ferrets, for example. When they die, being a little bigger than a mouse or even a pet rat, if you have such a thing, they aren't something you can flush away, and you have to give some thought to how and where you bury them, as you don't want them being dug up by a passing dog or cat. So when the first of our ferrets turned up its toes we decided to bury it in its own coffin.

We have a friend who does odd jobs for us – actually, he used to be a fireman who helped us out in his spare time. He's not a fireman any more, but he still comes round occasionally to lend a hand. Anyway, at that time we had an odd-job fireman. And one morning I greeted him with, 'I've got a very odd job for you today. I need you to build a coffin for a ferret.' So he made us a coffin for our ferret and it was very nice, quite big and surpris-ingly heavy. But by the time we put the ferret into it, he was stiff as a board and no longer looked much like the friendly pet the children had loved. In fact, he now looked like a shrunken version of some really scary monster from a horror movie. We had to nail down the lid pretty hastily. So that was a lesson for the kids, and a lesson for the grown-ups: when a pet dies, get rid of it sharpish. Don't delay the funeral until rigor mortis has set in, or your children will be terrified and just fear the inevitable even more.

Yes, from cradle to grave, pets are great teachers. From their pets, our kids will learn that it is not socially acceptable to whip out your old man at the dinner table. They will learn, I trust, that it's not acceptable to mount each other – well, not each other, obviously, but their sexual partners – in the middle of a football match. They will learn, too, how wonderful it is to have friends around you; cuddly, friendly friends. Not people, necessarily, because people can be quite annoying, but unquestioning, loyal friends who are happy to sit adoringly at your feet while you're watching TV and keep you warm.

Fame: Getting There's Easy

If there's one question that I get asked more than any other, it would have to be 'Why are you wearing that?' – often followed by 'at your age'. It's a query I generally choose to interpret as being affectionate rather than aggressive. I think people tend to regard my wardrobe malfunctions as an inadvertent idiosyncrasy rather than a challenge or threat, and that's a relief. But apart from queries about my rather spectacular dress sense, the other question I encounter a lot is 'What's it like to be famous?' It's a strange one to deal with, as it supposes that you still have enough of a grasp on what life was like before you were hit by this particular life-changing truck called Fame to make a valid comparison and report back from the front line. Or should that be accident site?

But I don't get asked it as much as I used to. I guess that is because by now people are used to seeing me on TV and we have that weird relationship where they feel they know me without actually knowing me, if you know what I mean, and so the question probably seems less relevant.

Scarily, there are now young adults walking around unaided, old enough to vote and fornicate and generally carry on under their own steam, who were born *after* I first appeared on my own talk show. These poor souls have never known a time when I wasn't available for the home consumer on radio or television at least once a week for most of the year. To them I have always been famous, and to everyone else the novelty wore off long ago, which might explain why I rarely get asked about fame any more by the curious or the needy or any wannabe celebrities out there. It's a bit like having been dead for a long time. When you first die some people imagine you're still hanging around, soaking up the last little dregs of life before you head off into eternity. That's when people go to mediums to try and have one last chat with you.

I'm convinced people go to mediums more readily if their loved one has only recently passed on rather than twenty years down the line. The conventional wisdom seems to be that there's more chance of the supposed psychic reaching someone who's freshly dead than someone who's been cold for donkey's years. Personally I think that's a mistake. Here's my theory. Kicking the bucket and shifting over to the other side, where Doris Stokes rules the roost and everyone wanders around naked with wings, or bright red with pitchforks, must be rather like getting a divorce and moving to a new town and a new job. You still remember the people you left behind, hopefully with some fondness, but you have to put it all behind you if you are going to start afresh. Certainly the first few months will be spent settling in and bedding down, learning the shortcuts on your drive to the celestial office, trying to remember all the lies you told about yourself in the first week to make you seem braver and sexier then you ever really were in the other place. You might even have claimed to have had a cool nickname, like Foxy or Snake, and that takes some remembering. Take it from old Ho' Pants here. But you certainly aren't going to be rushing to the phone every time someone calls up asking where you left the insurance forms or whether or not they were the love of your life. Leave it a year or two, that's my advice. Then when your dearly departed has got bored with the novelty of being able to fly, or listening in on every conversation happening on Earth simultaneously, they might be prepared to hover back over for a chat.

But to answer the question, the truth is that fame is almost definitely not what you'd expect it to be at all. The change in your life and situation and the effect of your being well known on those around you is gradual, and the changes take place so slowly that you don't tend to notice them until years have gone by. Plip, plop, plip, plop, like water dripping on limestone, form-ing a little puddle, then a deeper bowl, and finally the original slab is no longer recognizable, having been either transformed into a unique tourist attraction that will survive for decades or completely washed away. Christ, I'm deep. Actually, to go off briefly on a small tangent, typing the words 'plip, plop' there reminded me of a very fine joke that the very fine comedian and comic actor Paul Whitehouse once told me. Can you name the French man who invented the sandal? Philippe Pheloppe.

So, that feeling of being famous takes a while to kick in. You do feel slightly different eventually, but only because of the way you get treated by others. The way you feel about yourself doesn't really change, but the way that others react to you and deal with you certainly does. In many ways this is very pleasant, and in other ways it's kind of peculiar and occasionally a little bit unsettling. I'm certainly not complaining – I probably enjoy being famous as much as anyone possibly can, but it is weird to go through life with most people already having a firm opinion of whether or not they like you before you've even walked into the room.

One of the nicest things about being on TV and consequently being famous is that you're treated politely, even by people who don't like you very much. And I'm not so far gone that I can't appreciate there must be plenty of people out there who, on the basis of my TV and radio work, can't stand the sight or sound of me. I know for a fact that not everyone's completely in love with me and my output. That's an odd phrase – 'me and my output' – it sounds like a porn movie for a very niche audience. Not a bad name for a band, either.

I have a small collection in the back of my head of weird things people have said over the years that would make great titles for books or names for popular indie bands. 'My life is bubbles' is one that I have earmarked for my autobiography if I ever get the urge to write it. That was said by my youngest daughter when she was about four, playing in the garden as we blew bubbles towards her. Lovely, isn't it? And for a band, how about 'The Maybe Elvis Toenail'? I encountered that gem while filming a documentary for Channel 4 called *Viva Elvis* in which I met up with a whole load of Elvis impersonators – let's use the collective noun 'a thrust' of Elvises. Or Elvii. While in

Gracelands we hooked up with a devoted fan of the late King who had honoured him with a small museum. Most of what she had was fairly pedestrian, but in a frame on the wall was a toe-nail clipping she had surreptitiously retrieved from the shag pile while on a guided tour of Gracelands with a posse of other Elvis fans. It may or may not have grown on Elvis's foot, so in the interests of accuracy and full disclosure the sign underneath read 'The Maybe Elvis Toenail'.

But if we assume that there are plenty of people out there – many of whom I meet and interact with on a day-to-day basis – who *don't* enjoy my work, or just don't like me and think that the way that I carry myself on television is irritating and obnoxious, then I am even more convinced that fame creates politeness in people. Because almost completely without exception I am treated with great courtesy or open displays of affection.

It's like when someone meets a very old person, or a member of the royal family. Trust me, unless you're a rabidly fervent republican, when you meet a royal you're suddenly going to forget all those opinions you've rattled on about in the pub for years and you will find yourself bowing or curtseying and saying, 'Yes, Your Majesty.' That's the power of being on stamps and five-pound notes and giving a speech on the telly each Christmas for you. It's also how I imagine being a judge might be – everyone's polite and gracious because they never know when they might need a favour from you. So if you're royalty or a member of the judiciary or just plain famous then you find yourself having a pretty easy ride through life.

Let me give you some specific examples. For starters, you'll get slightly better service in a bar at a crowded gig. That's an interesting way of telling whether or not you're truly famous. You manoeuvre your way to the front and eye the harassed barman, who is looking out at the sea of people all holding a tenner out, hoping to be served next. Now the first rule of working behind a crowded bar is not to make eye contact. That creates a bond and makes it harder to carry on as if everyone is equal.

According to several quite comprehensive magazine articles I have read on the subject, if you ever find yourself in the unhappy situation of having been kidnapped by a serial killer who intends to make you his next victim, the thing to do is to make him – or her, I suppose – think of you as a person, a fellow human being. Then it will be much harder for them to kill you and wear parts of your body as a hat. So it is with bar staff. If you penetrate their icy professional demeanour and get them to regard you as a fellow traveller on life's highway, with hopes and dreams and the not unreasonable desire to get a bloody drink before the band come one, then you're in with a much better chance than the stranger next to you who might still wind up being worn as a hat by the bartender. If he or she is also a serial killer. But if the bar staff spot a famous person they can't help but make eye contact, and eye contact means that you will definitely be served next, or next but one at the latest.

I don't know if fame would help with the whole kidnapped-by-serial-killer scenario I threw into the mix there, but it probably wouldn't hurt. You might be killed a little bit more quickly and kindly if you're famous. And only worn as a hat to extra-special occasions. That's the way fame works – people give you a little bit of extra leeway.

Another perk of fame that at first seemed incomprehensibly cool was going out to the West End and getting into nightclubs free. Previously, not only was it a matter of having to pay to get in, but you weren't even certain you were going to be allowed in. Especially looking the way I used to look. So to suddenly find them hustling me to the front of the queue, opening the door for me and sending over a free drink – man, I felt like I'd died and gone to heaven.

Here's another example. These days I'm quite happy to pay the full fare when I travel, but for many years I used to rely on the charity of airlines as much as any other freeloading celebrity and would often buy a ticket in the class below the one I actually hoped to travel in, on the assumption that if there was space in the comfy haven of First Class then they would upgrade me. And more often than not they did. I might even be safe in saying that once my shows started getting a decent-sized audience I never once found myself sitting on a plane where there were seats in the class above that were empty without being offered the chance to sidle up the aisle and park myself with the rich people. Only if the people working the plane were British, of course. No one else on the planet knows or cares who the hell I am, and they wonder why I keep dropping hints about extra legroom.

Of course, even when they know who you are and like you, it isn't guaranteed. The only way you know for sure that you'll be sitting up front is if you pay for it. I've got to the stage in my life now where I rather enjoy treating myself, so I happily part company with an absurd amount of cash just to get a nice wide seat with a bit more space around it that folds flat at bedtime on a long haul.

But being famous creeps up on you. I remember when I began doing my first television talk show, *The Last Resort*, which started in January 1987 – alarmingly twenty-one years ago as I write this, which is both rather difficult and rather depressing for me to get my head around. It was my first concerted effort to be a TV performer, and there's rarely a day goes by when I don't thank my good fortune that it panned out the way it did. That's not to say that the show necessarily deserved to be a hit. Some weeks were terrific, but others were bloody awful. To be honest with you, I think we got away with a lot simply because there was no one else attempting a show like it, certainly not a young bloke, clearly with working-class roots, who also dressed a bit peculiar and spoke funny. Maybe they could sense my nerves and gave me the benefit of the doubt.

Young people certainly didn't wear designer suits when I first started, in fact no one on TV did, remarkable as that seems now. I don't know where they bought their suits back then but they never seemed to be in fashion. Or to fit. I suspect the older ones were passed down from presenter to presenter, like shiny, cherished heirlooms. But I put the success of the show mostly down to a series of lucky accidents. I couldn't talk any differently than the way I did, no matter how hard I tried, and I had no idea that my difficulties with the letter R would become a weird sort of trademark – part impediment, part catchphrase. The suits weren't a deliberate ploy on my part to try and get noticed either, it's just that I'd always wanted to have a few really nicely made suits and had never been able to afford them before. Now here I was, doing a TV show, and discovering to my delight that there was a clothes budget for the presenter. It wasn't a huge amount – about fifteen hundred pounds for the whole series. You can do the basic sums required here to work out that it didn't buy me a suit a week. I think it bought me two new ones and a bunch of shirts and ties and a pair of nice black shiny shoes. Things have shifted again since then and the younger presenters on the hipper shows don't really want to wear suits any more. Nowadays the fashion is for skinny jeans and T-shirts with the names of cool-sounding old bands like Kiss and the Ramones and Led Zep on, but for a while after I first started doing it you couldn't channel hop without seeing some gormless young berk like Andrew O' Connor or Shane Richie in a shiny red or purple mohair two-piece gurning away. My sartorial gift to the nation, for which I apologize unreservedly.

You may well be familiar with the school of thought – or theory, rather – called the Kübler-Ross model, that outlines the universal processes that people supposedly use to deal with grief. It suggests that there are five stages: denial, anger, bargaining, depression and acceptance. Well, I would like to put forward my own model for the five stages that people go through in finding fame, losing it, then finding it again. They are: desire, entitlement, bargaining, depression and – yay, for symmetry – acceptance. Pay attention, class.

First up, desire, to demonstrate which I shall recount the tale of my first-ever autograph. Not the first one I ever got, which may well have been Cliff Richard, so please let's not dwell on it. No, the first one I ever gave.

I was delighted when this happened. It was January 1987 and I was walking down South Molton Street after the second episode of *The Last Resort* had gone out on Channel 4. When it first began we recorded the show on a Friday evening at around seven, then tidied it up with a perfunctory edit before transmitting the finished item at twelve thirty. We didn't expect, or get, a huge audience, but it was certainly getting noticed. But it hadn't in any way changed my life, including my financial situation – which was fine, but I was hardly rolling in it and not yet in the market for a £500 suit. So I was window shopping, when a guy came up to me and started chatting. My initial thought was that I had yet again been mistaken for a young gay man on the lookout for some action. It happens far less frequently these days now that I am – how shall we say? – more solidly built. But back then I was a slip-thin youth with a quiff staring through the windows of flamboyant menswear emporiums, so I brought it on myself really. If we have time, I'll tell you later about the time I was chased by a young Chinese fella in a multi-storey shopping mall in Hong Kong and wound up playing a weird sort of hetero/homo hide-and-seek. And maybe also about the time I was chased around a desk by a toothless old queen in Scotland while researching a documentary on the Edinburgh Festival. Happy days.

Anyway, this particular guy wasn't one of those not-so-particular gays. After some small talk concerning the possibility that the monocle might make a reappearance on the catwalks of Milan, he said, 'Are you the new guy on TV?'

Reader, it was only because I had the presence of mind to grip the store's railings that I was prevented from swooning like a Jane Austen heroine finally getting a dance with a legitimate prospect. To be recognized! By a stranger! In the street! In this particular street! It was all too heady a combo. Some further small talk ensued, during which he might have pointed out that the show was almost quite good, but he certainly wasn't what you would consider lavish in his praise. So I was all the more surprised when he concluded with 'Can I have your autograph?'

Now, although I had been quite looking forward to being recognized, maybe chatted to and so forth, I hadn't expected this. Maybe it's because I've never been much of an autograph hound myself. I did once shout out 'Dustin!' very loudly when I was working part-time as a decorator in Chelsea and we drove past the great Dustin Hoffman on the King's Road. That was an exciting moment, even for him, I imagine. He jumped a bit, but then we were hurtling past at considerable speed and as I'd leant from the window to shout I was probably only about seven inches from his right ear. But even had we been walking, I don't think I would have asked him to sign anything. The reason the autograph scenario sticks so firmly in my mind, I think, is that as soon as this guy asked me to sign my name he was treating me differently from the way he would treat anyone else he might have been having a conversation with.

I can't remember what I wrote, but I do remember that it was that request, that moment, that made me feel like I was famous, like I had jumped over the rope that normally keeps people off the red carpet. It wasn't appearing in magazines or being invited to parties by people I'd never met to celebrate the launch of products I didn't use. No, it was being asked to scribble something friendly but meaningless on a piece of paper that did it. And I knew at that moment that despite having rattled on previously about not caring whether I became famous or not, and how I wanted to do this show because I simply liked the idea of making a good TV show, I had been lying, as much to myself as to others. I wanted to be famous – and the moment I gave that first autograph I realized I was on my way.

The depressing thing – or one of the depressing things – about fame is how quickly you get used to it and start to take it for granted. It's like a beautiful view in a new house or a spell of unexpectedly nice weather. At first you can't quite believe your luck, but after a while you only notice it when it's not there, and even then your reaction isn't that you were lucky to have had it at all, but rather how unfair it is that you can't enjoy it every day, for ever. Which brings us to stage two: entitlement. I don't have a lot to say about this stage as it's self-explanatory really – but it takes a while to get there. I must have been on TV fairly solidly for about six or seven years before I mistakenly began to feel it was a right rather than a privilege.

When I first started doing *The Last Resort* I spent most of the time in front of the audience in a state of panic. But despite that the show took off and it did pretty well. But although there were one or two shows in the first series that were really good, on the whole I knew that it wasn't consistently of the standard it should have been. And consistency, I believe, is what distinguishes an amateur from a professional. A lucky amateur can occasionally deliver a professional performance, but a professional can always entertain. They might be in a bad mood, it might have been a slow news day, there might be a small audience, the guests might not be as interesting as they should be, the country might have just gone into a recession or war, but still you'll find something to talk about with the guests and spin out into stories that will be entertaining for the audience, and with any luck you'll make them forget about the horrible things and have a nice time.

Back then, however, it was more luck than judgement with me. The show that probably worked the best was episode fourteen of the first series. The line-up was fantastic: we had Terry Gilliam, Dawn French and Tom Jones – and Tom Jones sang. Now at the time, booking Tom Jones seemed to the people in the office to be a bit of a strange gesture because Tom Jones was almost a figure of fun, in that he was a Vegas-style performer who had lost touch with the younger audience. But I had been a fan of his ever since I was a kid. I've always loved his voice. 'It's Not Unusual' is one of my favourite pop records of all time. I love 'What's New Pussycat?' too – it's an odd song, in fact it doesn't even really sound like a song, it's more of an exclamation that punctuates a movie. And the movie's fabulous, in a very sixties way.

I remember once being off school sick, as a kid, and finding that my mum and dad had a Tom Jones album and playing it again and again and again, and just loving it, lying in my room in my stripy pyjamas belting out 'What's New Pussycat?' without the faintest idea what it meant or where it came from, but just bloody loving it. I'd always loved his image, too – he was one of those macho showbiz stars from the sixties you don't really see any more – hairy-chested monsters, like Sean Connery and maybe George Lazenby, who were like cartoon versions of macho men.

Anyway, for all those reasons I really wanted to have him on the show. We didn't expect him to want to do it as he was such a huge star and the show was seen as something of a curio, but I think Tom's son, Mark, had just taken over as his manager and he had his eye on repositioning Tom for a younger audience. That's how, even though he was booked to be here in the UK to appear on *Sunday Night at the London Palladium* with Jimmy Tarbuck, he also got roped into appearing on *The Last Resort*.

Back then I tried to meet the guests before they came on the programme, partly so that I wouldn't be overawed when they finally walked out in front of the cameras. We duly trotted along to meet up with Tom during the rehearsal – which in itself would have been more than enough for me, frankly. I can barely convey what a dynamically exciting moment for me it was to meet Tom Jones. I couldn't believe it. Tom motherfucking Jones! I could barely have been any more excited if Batman or an alien had been there. But it was the real deal – Tom Jones was sitting there in front of me, chatting away. And he was nice as pie – 'Hello, boy' – you know, in a thick old Welsh accent. His son was sitting there as well and we talked about the show.

One of our policies on the programme was that, whenever possible, we had guests doing a cover version if they wanted to sing, rather than performing their new single. Which was fine in its way, although it was a little hit and miss. Some weeks you'd have someone great doing something great and it was a treat, and other weeks you'd have someone great doing something awful and it was a wasted opportunity, and yet other weeks you'd have someone not so good doing something that just didn't work, and that was a *terrible* way to end the show.

So we mentioned this to Tom and he said that he'd recently started doing a few current numbers live as part of his show, one of which was 'Dance Hall Days' by Wang Chung, and another of which was 'Kiss' by Prince. I was there with a friend and associate at that period, Graham K. Smith, who was in charge of the music for the show – he is now a big television executive and has been involved with any number of fine shows over the years. He's worked a lot with Vic and Bob and Jools Holland and many other people who came to prominence at about the same time as me. We immediately pressed for Tom to do 'Kiss', both being huge Prince fans as well. And he said (in exactly the same Welsh accent he'd used earlier), 'OK, no problem, I'll work it out.'

What a night. He performed it with our house band, Nick Plytas and Ecstasy, and it blew everyone away. It also helped bring about the Tom Jones renaissance, as the show was watched that night at home by Anne Dudley, from Art of Noise. She loved it and they contacted Tom afterwards and got him to record their version of the song, which went straight into the charts when it was released, putting Tom in touch with the younger audience Mark had been hoping for when he allowed him to come on the programme.

Dawn French was a brilliant and funny guest too – you couldn't hope for a better guest on a talk show. When she wants to be funny, you just have to sit back and relax and enjoy it. And Terry Gilliam was perfect for us, because Monty Python was still recent enough for him to seem very fresh and exciting, and of course he's not only a very funny man but a brilliant director, which gave us something more to talk about than just performing comedy. So more by good luck than judgement we delivered a remarkable show, unlike anything else on at that time, and the audience we got for that show reflected its success – we had

3.9 million watching, which for Channel 4 at the time was just astronomical. That's why I remember it, and I knew we were heading in the right direction.

A couple of months later, Tom Jones's son got back in touch and asked if I would come along and introduce Tom on stage – he was performing at the Albert Hall. Strangely, I remember nothing of the actual performance, but I clearly remember walking offstage, and seeing Jimmy Tarbuck beckon me over. I was a bit nervous, because there seemed to be this feeling that I was part of the new wave of alternative comics on TV – and I wasn't, of course. I'd never appeared as a comic, and even though I shared some of the sensibilities of the Comedy Store crowd, I disagreed with other things – like the fact that they were supposedly opposed to old-style humour, like Benny Hill. I grew up loving comics like Benny Hill and the Two Ronnies and still do today. So I didn't feel in any way opposed to Jimmy Tarbuck, although I can't say I was a huge fan of his because I'd never really seen him do his stand-up.

Anyway, he called me over and said, 'They like ya.' At the time I thought these words of wisdom seemed a) a bit creepy and b) a bit condescending, but I now realize exactly what he meant. Which is that there is a sort of indefinable, un-quantifiable something in some performers – I'm not saying I have it, though Jimmy was kind enough to suggest that was the case. You can certainly see it in some people – Ant and Dec, for example. You can see it in Simon Amstell and Russell Brand. Ricky Gervais has it. Catherine Tate has it. I've always thought Danny Baker has it, but he often forgets to bring it with him to the studio. These people have a certain something and people respond well to them. People like them. They like seeing them on screen. So what Jimmy meant was, 'You might not know this yet, but you've got a career here if you want it.' And then he delivered a body blow: 'Getting there's easy, but staying there's hard.' By which I presume he meant that getting that first burst of attention because you're the new kid on the block is pretty easy, providing you're in the right place at the right time and you put in a bit of work, but *staying* there – maintaining people's interest and keeping them involved and watching you on TV – that, my friend, is hard. Of course, I now know how right he was, but at the time, with a newly growing sense of entitlement – after all, hadn't Tom Jones just asked me to introduce him on stage? – I dismissed it as showbiz nonsense.

Another quirk of fame is the spurious connection you have with other famous people and they with you. If you're in a crowded room with lots of people and another famous person comes in, if you meet their eye and they meet yours, you're kind of obliged to nod to each other. It's strange. Even people you don't really like or know. I remember early in my career I went over to America to make a show about obscure film-makers called *The Incredibly Strange Film Show* – and to this day I'm still very glad that I managed to get that particular show off the ground. My best friend at the time, Alan Marke, who was also the co-founder of my company Channel X, was with me. We went all around America together while we were filming, and we ended up going to Los Angeles to interview Russ Meyer, the king of the nudies, aka the Farmyard Fellini, the man who specialized in featuring fabulously pneumatic women in his movies. At the time I think I loved the women more than the films themselves, although it's hard to resist their raw power and their unembarrassed, straightforward love of the subject.

So we were in Los Angeles and I was with my lovely girl-friend, Jane, who wasn't yet my wife. I had just turned twenty-seven and she would have just turned seventeen, which is obviously a marvellous thing and I wish I'd enjoyed it even more than I did at the time. While we were waiting for our car outside the Mondrean Hotel in Los Angeles, someone else pulled up and it turned out to be Chris Quinten – Brian Tilsley from *Coronation Street*, who'd left the show to go and make his fortune in America. At the time he was a big tabloid name in the UK, and there was a degree of interest as to whether or not he'd make it out in the USA. We didn't know Chris, but we were a long way from home and he was what passed for a familiar and friendly face. He had seen some of my shows and got out of his car. I said, 'Oh hello, you're that *Coronation Street* bloke,' and he said, 'Yeah, you're the Channel 4 bloke. There's a party going on tonight up in the hills, if you fancy coming along.' He was dating a woman called Leeza Gibbons at the time, who was on an entertainment news show in America.

So we were thrilled and quite excited – or at least I was. I don't think Jane was particularly. She was a little bit wary. She tended to base her friendships on people she actually liked and had something in common with, whereas I hadn't yet learnt that golden rule and was quite happy to try and be friends with any-one just because they were on TV. Shallow, I know, but I'm delighted to say I've learnt nothing over the years and will still gladly invite complete strangers round for dinner who I've only met for sixty seconds but I quite like their record, or book, or hat. Jane dreads it when I start a sentence with 'I've invited some people for dinner' because it will inevitably be people she either doesn't much like or has never met.

So we went up to this party, and I remember realizing we'd made a mistake as soon as I spoke to Chris for a while, as I had absolutely nothing in common with him. Not that he wasn't a friendly bloke – just a bit odd. The moment I realized that was when he introduced me to a writer who he claimed was going to write a movie built around him. The plan was to launch him as a big star in the USA. He was, as I said, a nice enough bloke, but I thought it improbable that this writer could turn him into a Hollywood star. And later in the evening, presumably to fill a lull in the conversation, he leapt up and grabbed hold of a beam in the front room and did twenty pull-ups in front of everyone. This was in the middle of a crowded room, while fully clothed people were just milling around, dipping celery in cheese and drinking wine. Sadly for Chris, neither the pull-ups nor the writer managed to help him crack America.

The Last Resort had been a big hit for me and for the company I had started with my friend. But after series four, despite it continuing to get pretty good ratings, we agreed with Channel 4 to stop. This wasn't an agreement reached in a sane or sensible way; we all just sort of decided to try something new. It's indicative of the charming nature of television back then, at Channel 4 in particular, that the real or perceived success of a show wasn't really that much of a factor when it came to commissioning stuff. Looking back, we probably stopped making *The Last Resort* a little too soon, especially as we had no idea what to put in its place. Now, if I had genuinely only wanted to make shows I was proud of, I'd have done nothing until I had thought out a new show, with a sense of identity and purpose, to bounce back with. But I had grown accustomed to having my face on TV, and the money that comes with it, and so I fronted a number of different programmes, none of which were really that interesting and none of which really worked, before eventually agreeing to split from the company I had helped start and consequently had felt obliged to stick with.

If we want to stick with my five-stages routine this would be the bargaining stage, especially as I wound up working for ITV, a company that's never felt right for me. Too blatantly commercial and mainstream to really suit my tastes or skills, especially back then. I appeared in *Fantastic Facts*, a sort of trivia-based entertainment show that I've almost completely forgotten, and then *The Big Big Talent Show*, notable only because a pre-teen Charlotte Church came on to introduce her aunt. Imagine what a pisser that must have been for her aunty. Just before you try out for a spot in the final, the world's most talented juvenile comes on and blows everyone away.

Anyway, this unhappy and unproductive period inevitably led to stage four: depression. I was stuck in a groove, basically drinking too much and spending my earnings none too wisely. I wanted to keep making shows because I didn't know what else to do, and because I thought I needed to keep earning the sort of money I had grown accustomed to. But earning that money by making shows I didn't care about made me far unhappier than being broke ever could have done. I also missed being respected for what I did. Even when we'd been producing shows that were, according to the viewing figures, failures on Four, we were still making stuff that we would have watched. But the shows for ITV were rubbish.

One night I was out at a hip place in town called the Atlantic with Jane and a bunch of friends when a young guy came up to me, quite full of himself. 'Excuse me,' he said – and I immediately assumed he wanted an autograph or something – 'Excuse me, but didn't you use to be Jonathan Ross?' Not a bad line – not an especially original one, but seeing as he was saying it to my face you can't fault the timing. And he was right. Standing there, overweight from booze, looking forward to another night of getting off my face in an expensive restaurant, paid for by churning out rubbish that I had no respect for, why should others respect me? Yes, I did 'use to be Jonathan Ross'. I did use to be someone who made a certain kind of show. Even though the bloke who said it was clearly an obnoxious twat, and he almost certainly didn't mean to be anything other than unkind and make his mates laugh, he actually did me a favour.

There was a moment of low-level epiphany and I realized more keenly at that point than ever before the wisdom of the great Jimmy Tarbuck's words when he said, 'Getting there's easy, but staying there's hard.' I had found it surprisingly easy to get there, but staying there had meant gradually losing sight of what I had enjoyed doing and why I had started doing it, with the result that I was now making the kind of rubbish that I had started out deliberately mocking. Ah, the wisdom of Tarby, a veritable showbiz Buddha.

So we finish with acceptance. I'd found it pretty easy to get to a position in show business where I felt my shows were watched but could have been fronted by anyone. So I backed off and stopped doing shows for no reason other than cash. I started doing radio, not least because Chris Evans, who had always liked what I did, had shrewdly spotted that I was floundering, in danger of dying on my back on a beach somewhere. Radio helped me get my foot back in the door. It was while I was at Virgin with Chris, who encouraged me to do more or less what I wanted, that I really learnt to trust my own judgement about what works and what doesn't.

Again, I was inspired by a greater talent than my own. Just as my talk show had been based on the American-style comedy shows, in particular the *Late Show with David Letterman*, my radio show was an attempt to create something as personal and quirky as the programmes that both Chris and more pertinently Danny Baker produced. The show worked on Virgin, and I eventually agreed after being courted for several years to take it over to Radio 2, which coincided with me turning up on a regular basis on the comedy sports quiz *They Think It's All Over* on BBC1.

That was a liberating and fun experience. I got to extemporize and ad lib and mess around to my heart's content without being the host. I never felt that the success or failure of the whole thing rested on my shoulders, so I could be as good as I could without worrying. It was far less money than I would have got for hosting talent shows on ITV, but it was actually fun, and I wasn't embarrassed by what I was doing. I need to thank the writers Jez Stevenson and Shaun Pye here, as they wrote a mountain of jokes for me, to help me seem both funny and vaguely interested in sport, essential requirements for a comedy sports quiz.

From there I side-stepped into hosting a show called *It's Only TV But I Like It*, and finally, after I'd dropped several hints, the

BBC finally came around to the idea of me hosting a talk show again, and Friday Night with Me began around 2001. It wasn't an immediate hit, and we had some teething problems, but by the second series we were heading in the right direction, and from series three we started beating most shows up against us in the ratings. Weird that it took me twenty years to go from being a flash in the pan to learning how to do the show I always wanted to do, the show I more or less started with, in a way that works and is reliably entertaining and is popular with a huge share of the audience.

Acceptance, baby, as Tom Jones might have said in his Vegas period. Accept who you are and what you want to do and try your best to stay true and do it, and the rewards will come. And so will the awards. I never won anything much to speak of in the early years. I didn't expect to, really, although I thought some of the shows I did back then were quite good, and fairly new for British TV. I'm thinking specifically of *The Incredibly Strange Film Show* and one or two of the one-off documentaries, like that Elvis impersonators special. I was a little surprised that none of these shows – well-made, original programmes like nothing else being made at the time – even received any nominations for any awards. But since my re-birth, if you will, I've received a number of Sony awards for my radio work, I've got four BAFTAs on my shelf now, and a couple of Comedy Awards. So thanks for the warning, Tarby. And thanks for the snide remark, stranger in the bar. And thanks for giving me another chance, TV execs and viewers, because I like being famous, but only because I like what I'm doing and want it to stay that way.

MY LIFE AS A WOMBLE AND OTHER PART-TIME DISASTERS

Who isn't just a little nostalgic for their youth? Children, obviously. Perhaps also people who had a horrible childhood, but even then there are probably some aspects of their past they remember fondly. And bizarrely, we enjoy remembering bad times and things we've endured and suffered with almost as much pleasure as the good times. 'Where would we be without our terrible childhoods?' someone clever once said, and it struck a chord with me. That's not to say I suffered much as a child. Compared to 'A Boy Called It' I had a non-stop party. But I felt deprived at times and persuaded myself I had it tough, and I can still enjoy pretending things were hard, which will have to do for this book.

The truth is that I didn't have many of the toys I wanted, and I wanted them badly, being a silly selfish boy of the old school. I was also gawky and geeky looking, back before being a geek was almost cool. Yes, I was a weird-looking boy, physically unattractive to most people, including, I am sure, members of my own family. So I felt hard done by. They were kind enough to try to hide it from me, but occasionally I'd catch a furtive glance or sense a shudder as I walked past, and I knew I was the cause.

Frankly, it's a bit of a pisser not having more to complain about. I feel quite resentful towards my parents now for giving me such a happy upbringing. Didn't they realize they were depriving their children of the chance to make a fortune later in life with tales of being beaten, locked in cupboards or forced to dance for businessmen? I never even worried that I might get abducted, not once.

That made for lovely long summer days out riding my bike with my friends – all right, friend; I never had more then one good pal at a time – but if you grow up safe in the knowledge that even paedophiles aren't interested in you, how are you ever going to feel wanted? I strongly suspected that the rest of my family, my conventionally attractive brothers and sister, were told not to accept any sweets or invitations to view puppies by people in unfamiliar cars, but not me. They knew I was safe. 'We've warned them all not to talk to strangers, except the weird, ugly one in the middle. Nature's already taken care of that for us.'

The things I miss about my childhood are, I'm sure, much the same things you miss. Confectionery you can't get any more, certain smells, sights and even places that don't exist now. Like those odd purposeless shops you used to find on every high street selling stuff you couldn't imagine anyone making a living from, and which were almost always closed. They always seemed to have very specific but seemingly unrelated stuff on display. It was as if some clever entrepreneur had identified a previously uncatered-to niche market and leapt right in, choosing to test the water by only opening the shop for seven hours a week.

There was an especially intriguing one that I used to pass on my way to school. It was ostensibly a wool shop, and in one window were loads and loads of balls of wool, knitting needles, knitting patterns and spools of thread. In another – and this was what caught my eye – they had a fairly comprehensive display of old cigarette cards, mostly depicting famous sporting heroes from the thirties, forties and fifties. It's still a mystery to me why anyone would think that a knitting enthusiast, popping out for a ball of wool and some needles, might also feel compelled to buy a 1950s Capstan cigarettes picture of Fred Perry at the same time.

Another thing I really miss about those days is the boredom. I'm a great fan of boredom. With only two TV channels you ever wanted to watch, hardly any radio worth listening to, no internet or mobile phones or DVDs or video games, there were huge chunks of the day when you just had to amuse yourself. That's something that our kids will never experience, and although it might seem like we're doing them a favour by offering round-the-clock cartoons and YouTube and Grand Theft Auto, we're actually raising a generation of timid, pale-faced scaredy-cats, with excellent computer-game scores.

Seeing as my lazy parents weren't prepared to take on several extra jobs just to buy me toys, I had to do so myself. On Saturdays I had a number of different part-time jobs to earn some pocket money – another thing that my children probably won't ever do in the same way. It's a shame, but I suspect the days when you'd let a nine-year-old go off to drive around with a man in a van all day doing deliveries have long since passed.

The first job that I ever had I inherited from my older brother, Simon, who had in turn inherited it from his older brother, Paul. It was a milk round, working with an old milkman called George. He looked as if he was in his late sixties when I started working for him. I was about nine and he kept going for at least another ten years after that, so either he looked bloody awful for his age or they had a more relaxed attitude towards retirement back then. I imagine he could have kept going for another fifty years, as he was as fit as a flea.

A really tough, wiry old chap with leathery skin from being outside every day, he was lovely: cheerful, friendly and never horrible to me, though he was quite strict about making sure you did the job properly. It wasn't that hard a job, it has to be said, putting four pints of red-top outside someone's front door and once in a while, if they'd asked for it, a loaf of bread as well – this was back in the days before milkmen diversified much – but he took pride in his work. That was it, really: milk, bread and those pints of strange, very watery orange juice we used to have, stored in the same shaped bottles as the milk.

The round was pretty uneventful. All it involved was getting up very early, going to the milk depot, hopping on the back of one of those electric floats and driving around for three or four hours, dropping off bottles of milk, collecting the empties and stashing them in the back. You invariably went home stinking of the stuff. You'd have it all over your fingers from sticking them in the bottles to pick them up, and from there it got on your clothes and even in your hair.

In the summer it was a very pleasant way to spend a morning, apart from smelling like an old yoghurt by the time you'd finished. But in the winter it was rather less so. In cold weather I got so freezing during the round that my mum would lend me a pair of her tights to put on under my jeans, which I acknowledge marks me out as something of a soft kid. But the warmth those tights provided was more or less negated by my anxiety that someone might discover I was wearing ladies' underwear. I would imagine any number of scenarios that involved me getting knocked down, or stung by a really big bee, or knocked on the head by a falling milk crate, all of which wound up with me being admitted to hospital, where they inevitably pulled down my trousers and started to laugh at the sight of my tights. But they were a godsend on a frosty morning.

The best part of the round came about halfway through, when we used to stop at a little café on Leytonstone High Road and George would buy me a cup of tea and a slice of toast. I used to really look forward to that treat. I've never been over-fond of working, or even standing up for any length of time, so any opportunity to stop for a sit-down was to be welcomed, especially if a snack was part of the deal. The toast they served at this place – I think it was called the Central Café – was made from lovely thin white bread, heavily buttered, and George would dip his in his tea, which fascinated me. Often the butter slid off and would be left floating on the surface in little greasy globules. I thought it must make the tea taste horrible but it didn't seem to bother him, so I tried it myself, and got hooked. I still do it today, if I'm not sitting with someone too easily disgusted by a grown man sucking melted butter off soggy toast.

Only one really exciting thing happened while I was delivering milk for George. We had a customer who lived on the other side of Wanstead Flats, just down the road from my best friend at the time, a boy called Stephen Turnell. Stephen and I were intrigued by this young guy, who was, we presumed, a hippy – we were a bit vague on the defining traits of a hippy as Leytonstone wasn't exactly awash with them. Anyway, he seemed pretty wild and on his bedroom wall he had that poster of a soldier falling forward after being shot, under the caption 'Why?' To a boy just about to turn ten that was the coolest poster in the whole world. The only posters I'd ever seen on people's walls before that were either of pretty awful pop stars or attached to calendars, often featuring flowers or animals, and none of those asked questions about the futility of war.

We never went into his bedroom, by the way, but you could see it through the window from the street, where we'd sometimes hang around in the hope of getting a glimpse of what he was up to. After a short period of surveillance, mainly carried out by the surprisingly successful yet tiring jumping-up-and-down method, we decided he was friendly and had a keen interest in counter culture – and because we could glimpse a tiny part of another poster, showing what looked like a naked breast, we decided to knock on his door and ask him if we could buy a men's magazine off him.

Where did this idea come from, the notion that it was acceptable to knock on the door of a complete stranger, even if he did appear to be a hippy with a nudey poster on his wall, and ask him to sell us porn? It was born of hope and optimism, I suppose. But as it turned out, we were correct in our psychological profiling, however crude the methodology. After chuckling at the sight of two desperate, weird-looking schoolboys offering up a hard-earned shilling for the chance to see what ladies normally kept covered, he told us to wait a minute. He went back inside his house. To call the police? Or worse, our mums? No, he returned with an old magazine, which he gave us, free of charge, with the words 'Here you go, you can have this. I've finished with it.' Oh happy day.

Stephen and I spent the whole summer poring over this treasure. In truth it wasn't a proper porn mag: it was a kind of adult-film-industry what's-on-at-the-movies guide. But there were colour photographs of ladies with their shirts off advertising their forthcoming appearances in those odd British sex comedies peculiar to the 1970s, films like *The Tale of Eskimo Nell*. I can't remember ever seeing any of those productions myself, or hearing about anyone else ever seeing any of them, come to think of it.

There was another famous one called *Inside Mary Millington*, a title which mystified me at the time. I thought it must be like *Fantastic Voyage*, in which Donald Pleasence and a group of fellow scientists get shrunk and injected into someone's body in a tiny submarine. I'm quite sure it wasn't, of course. But getting that magazine was just about the best thing that could happen to a couple of boys of that age and it was the highlight of my time working for George, so thank you, nameless hippy, whoever you were.

I had a number of other jobs after my spell with George. For three or four years I worked as a kind of shop assistant/ delivery boy for a local store called Morgan's Food Fair on

Grove Green Road. Mr Morgan signed me up for the princely sum of 17½p per hour, which seemed fair enough at the time. It was only when I realized that I was getting a mere fraction of what all my friends were earning in their after-school jobs that I complained to Mr Morgan, who was the epitome of a self-taught, skinflint small businessman. After about six months of my pleading he upped my money, first to 20p per hour and then eventually, after about a year of hard labour, to 22½p. For that generous sum I was, on some evenings, running the shop virtually single-handedly.

After a while I realized there was the potential to supplement my earnings to a modest extent by nicking the odd bar of chocolate, but my heart was never really in it, unlike some of my workmates, who seemed to really enjoy the thieving and used to go home with just about every pocket and available fold of their clothing bulging with something they could either eat or sell. Presumably that's why he paid so badly – all his profits were being eaten by thieving part-timers.

My few efforts to thieve were hardly the work of a criminal mastermind. I once walked home with two bars of cooking chocolate hidden in a way that rendered them more or less inedible. Not that they were all that edible to start with because, as I soon learnt, the cooking chocolate of the early seventies wasn't great for anything but cooking, being made essentially of lard and cardboard. I took it because it was the easiest kind to get at. The regular chocolate was by the till, from which Mr Morgan never strayed too far, quite justifiably wishing to keep a beady eye on me and the other pilferers he found himself lumped with. The cooking chocolate, on the other hand, was out of sight at the back of the shop with the flour and icing sugar. I chose the milk chocolate, thinking, Well, it can't taste that different from Cadbury's, and put a nice-sized bar down each of my socks, planning to whip them straight out again as soon as I'd left the shop and got round the corner. But that particular night, one of the older ladies who worked on the till and also kept an eye on us boys said to me, 'Hold on. I'm going in a minute, too – will you walk home with me? I've got to bring the night's takings with me.' Of course I had to gallantly agree. Apart from anything else, she was going my way. Not that I'd have been a great help if anyone had decided to bop her on the head.

So there I am, in my thick glasses, and probably wearing my favourite trousers of the period, ridiculously flared bright-orange loons, with a bar of cooking chocolate stuffed down each of my scruffy, slightly smelly socks, strolling up Leytonstone High Road with this lady, who seemed absolutely ancient at the time, but was probably no more than about forty-five. It was a warm summer evening and I felt as if I had two small hot-water bottles strapped to my ankles. By the time we'd reached her house, said goodnight and I was finally able to liberate the chocolate, it was virtually dripping out of the wrapping. I gave up thieving from the shop after that. I just wasn't cut out for it – even when I did manage to get some contraband home without most of it melting into my socks or pants, the guilt I felt meant I never really enjoyed eating it.

Thieving featured a little more blatantly in my next job, when I worked for a brief spell at a Sunblest bread factory across Wanstead Flats. Often aromas from the factory would waft into our house, which was lovely when they happened to be baking bread but not so lovely on the days when they made the dough, which smelled a bit yeasty and less than pleasant. The man from Sunblest poached me from Morgan's. He was looking for a 'reliable boy', as they called them, and he asked me how much I was getting paid there. I told him 22½p an hour and after he had stopped laughing he offered me several times that to come and work for him. At Sunblest I would earn as much for a Saturday morning's work (admittedly it was a long morning, from five a.m. to midday) as I made in three nights after school and all day Saturday at Morgan's, so I didn't have to think about it too hard.

But I didn't like the job at all. I hated getting up that early. I hated leaving the house in the winter when it was still dark outside. I hated climbing into the van full of bread. And I also hated it that some of the drivers used to try to cheat people. A lot of these bread guys were young, lairy types out to make a quick buck, and when they could get away with it they'd short-change customers by supplying fewer loaves than they were charging for. Once the bread had been tightly packed in its containers, with four or five loaves flat along the bottom, another four or five wedged in vertically next to them and the rest on top, you could remove a loaf, maybe two if you were feeling particularly courageous, from the middle of each layer and the rest would hold their shape. And so if the person receiving the delivery at the shop or, God help us, at the home for the blind – which they did actually deliver to – didn't check thoroughly that the complete order was there, you could charge them for, say, forty loaves when you'd given them only thirty-six and then sell the other four elsewhere in the course of the day. Hardly grand theft, but not at all nice. I hated being party to it, which is why I stopped working for them after a couple of months.

Some of them weren't so bad, though, and I remember one especially who was a nice enough bloke. We would often stop at his house midway through the morning for a cup of tea and he and his wife would nip upstairs, telling me they'd be back down in five minutes. I'd be waiting there twenty minutes before they reappeared. With the wisdom of age, I now realize that Sunblest Man was giving his wife a pleasant Saturday-morning seeing-to, which was a perfectly legitimate way to spend his break. And she was, I seem to remember, a very pretty, typically seventies dolly bird – the best kind, as even I knew. Seventies dolly birds were invariably blonde, had pale lipstick and blue eyeshadow, wore short skirts or hot pants and used a lot of hairspray. They were also always up for it. I know all this for a fact after extensive study of the films of the period.

I was sitting in his living room one day, bored stiff as usual, when I felt something digging into me. I had a rummage down the back of the couch and pulled out something that looked like a long thick plastic pencil and that shook rather alarmingly when you pushed a button on the side. I couldn't guess what it was, so played with it for a bit, and realized it tickled if you put the end in your ear. When Mr Sunblest came down from his bedroom jaunt I stuffed it back where it had come from. I didn't work out what it was for about another six years, but still blushed when it finally dawned on me.

I had various other part-time jobs, all of which had the usual pro – money to buy comics with – and the same old con – having to work. My brief stint working as an assistant in the local greengrocer's had an added bonus in that one of the regular Saturday-morning customers was a young mum who looked a bit like Sally Thomsett, the saucy, sexy, stupid one in *Man about the House*. I had a terrific crush on her, and coincidentally found out years later that my wife, then a little girl, had had an equally huge though perhaps less specifically sexual crush on the man who was about the house, Richard O'Sullivan. If we weren't all getting on a bit by then this would have been the ideal combo for a swinging weekend.

Anyway, every Saturday I waited with growing excitement until this Thomsett lookalike came along, wheeling her hopefully fatherless baby in a pram and smiling at me with those prominent front teeth of hers. I would secretly select the larger potatoes in the pile specially for her, hoping she would notice my thoughtfulness while peeling them and realize that the fourteen-year-old who was so adept at adding up and knew his way around the boiled beetroots so well might just be the perfect man for her.

The worst part-time job I ever had was probably my last. Every summer a travelling funfair would pitch up on the other side of the Flats, offering the thrill of the Wurlitzer, the ghost train and the helter-skelter. For the more timid there was the chance to fish ducks from a small pond, or hit a metal plate that would send a rubber frog sailing towards but never properly on to a target that would guarantee a prize. All the usual games of 'skill' that were nothing more than borderline con jobs were there – try to throw a ball into a milk bottle, or rings over prizes resting on awkward-shaped cubes; attempt to get anywhere near a target with darts that never flew straight or air-rifles that wouldn't shoot true.

Lamest and laziest of the lot were the stalls that offered you three sealed tickets for 50p. You tore the perforated edge and if you had the lucky number then you would win a fabulous prize, the largest and most tempting of which were hanging as an irresistible enticement around the edge of the stall. If you didn't get lucky, as was always the case, then you still got something, just not something anyone ever wanted. People soon wise up to this sort of scam and would rush past these stalls, trying not to make eye contact with the poor sap wandering around with a basket filled with useless tickets – none of which, I'm convinced, actually had a prize-giving number – trying to drum up trade with pitiful, barely legal come-ons like 'Everyone a winner', 'The luckiest tickets at the fair' or the just plain desperate 'Three for 50p, eight for a pound.' As though having eight chances to win nothing was somehow more fun than three. So to sell the tickets the stallholders often resorted to crude show-manship, which happened to be the case the one and only time I signed on as a paid helper.

The guy who ran the stall was a deeply unpleasant chap who had received exactly the face he deserved. Imagine a mouldy peach with terrible acne and you're halfway there. His great scheme to lure in passing trade was to have whichever local idiot he could coerce into the job to try to shift his worthless tickets while dressed as a Womble. Or rather, a cheap approxi-mation of a Womble. He had a suit that was made of some sort of synthetic fur, a sort of bedraggled, almost dreadlocked, urine-coloured shag pile. It came with a mask made of the same stuff that covered your entire head. The inside was not only scratchy and smelly – a heady melange of sweat, bad breath and fear – but it was also damp. The crudeness of this wretched knock-off was such that the face had none of the friendly, unthreatening warmth of an actual Womble, but instead made the wearer resemble a gigantic, infected and probably contagious rat. Wearing a big floppy red hat.

The indignity of wearing this terrifying suit was bad enough, but after having reduced several small children to tears with my muffled cry of 'Everyone a winner', I decided to bail out early. The diseased stallholder – I'm betting syphilis – was furious, and not only refused to pay me but made me turn out my pockets to prove I hadn't dipped into what he claimed was normally a guaranteed purse of about seventy-five quid by the end of the evening. After an hour I had taken around £1.50 and given out three of the consolation prizes, which were vinyl singles with the middle missing, and were all the same – a song no one had heard of by a band that never had a hit.

I walked home feeling both crushed by having worked for such a horrible bloke for nothing, and absolutely elated to be free of my scratchy Womble-rat suit hell.

Nothing in those part-time jobs, apart from perhaps the slender brush with show business that the Womble outfit provided, gave me any clue as to what I would one day wind up doing for a living. But I don't think it's an accident that I am here. Not because I have some great gift, or am somehow super-talented – it's got as much to do with luck and perseverance as talent. I have worked single-mindedly to get where I am because it fulfils a boyhood ambition, the one genuine, lasting ambition

I had that wasn't just a whim or a fad – like being an astronaut or a mad scientist, both of which I held on to as career options for far longer than was advisable.

I finally gave up on the mad-scientist idea at about the age of twelve, when it became apparent that I was pretty useless at all sciences and that even the easy part of the job – being mad – was probably never going to be comfortably achieved. I liked normal stuff too much, and had once seen an episode of the TV series *Colditz* in which a soldier fakes insanity to escape, but then wees himself at the end. This was the programme-makers' shorthand for the fact that he had really gone mad, and so his plan had backfired. In the seventies seeing a man wee himself on TV was a rare and memorable occurrence, and it haunts me even now.

I'm sure I have seen many men wee themselves on TV since then, and several in real life. I have even weed myself occasionally, but of course as you get older that sort of thing occurs more frequently – when running for a bus or sneezing, for example. Not a full bladder-load, of course. Just a trickle. Maybe that's the key. In *Colditz* he started with the wee, and then, although he must have worked out what was happening, he didn't stop himself, even after the commandant shouted at him to stop, in German. 'Stoppen zi weeing!' he barked, I think. Whereas if I sneeze, or find myself bouncing a little too energetically on a trampoline with or without the kids present, and a little wee escapes, I turn the tap off pretty quickly.

The one exception was when I was in bed once and really, really needed to go but kept putting it off, half asleep as I was. Then I found myself getting up and walking to the loo and letting go, only to wake up to the embarrassing realization that I had only *dreamt* I'd walked to the loo, and was in fact lying on my side on a soaking mattress. Fortunately I had already been married to Jane for over fifteen years at this point, and she has stuck with me through far worse displays of oafishness than that, so we were solid. But the dream wee and my surprise at having done it is the exception that proves that I am not mad – at least not in the clinically recognized *Colditz* sense, and so tragically could not be a proper mad scientist, even today.

As for the astronaut lark, that was a common dream for most boys who remember watching the moon landing. I saw it on a little black and white telly with my dad. I don't remember my brothers or sister being around, so either I have blanked them from the memory or they weren't interested in watching man walk on the moon for probably the first time. I say 'probably' because I like to keep my options open on situations which aren't absolutely definitive, and although I grudgingly accept it's unlikely that men visited the moon before the *Apollo* landing, I have read enough Jules Verne and H. G. Wells to really *want* a Victorian gentleman in a spaceship made of copper and oak and hand-blown glass to have beaten us to it. But this hope that I might one day be one of those chosen few, those brave souls who wrestle free from gravity's selfish embrace so they can jump around in Space and say profound things to the millions watching on boring old Earth, stayed with me for ages. Right through school, even when the combination of super-poor eyesight and poor exam results in maths and physics told me otherwise.

Every year from about the age of fourteen onwards we were visited at school by a careers adviser. And every year we all sat around, grimly trying to come up with a few suggestions that might sound plausible to him without crushing our young souls the moment we spoke them out loud. I would normally offer one or more of the following: comic-book artist, monster hunter, pilot (which was only slipped in to pave the way for the next bombshell), astronaut, and one year I rounded the wish list off with boxer. This was after I saw the first *Rocky* film, in 1976, so I must have been either fifteen or sixteen. So taken was I with the movie, and the realization that I possessed all the underdog qualities needed to become a world champion from a standing start, that I went to a boxing class at the local youth club. Just the one visit. I never so much as mentioned the probability of my being an undiscovered world champion again.

The career adviser ignored the comic-book idea altogether, and was also polite enough not to mention the boxing. Monster hunting was out because you needed a good grade in at least one other language, so we normally chatted about my desire to fly. It was, of course, nonsense, based on my love of science-fiction books and movies, but he was always reasonably kind in pointing out that I lacked even the most basic requirements to start thinking seriously about flying as a career – however, the local dairy was always looking for milkmen and a new plastics factory had opened near by. I told him I'd think very seriously about both, and then I'd wander off having hopeless daydreams about using my job at the plastics factory to make a new propulsion unit for the milk floats so that I could still be in Outer Space before I was twenty.

So those ambitions came to nothing, really. But the one ambition I did stick with – a sort of anti-ambition, really – did pan out, which was the simple desire that I never wanted to work for a living. Not that I mind work as such. But my brothers and I used to walk to school, and most mornings we walked along with a neighbour who was a friend, and occasionally his dad would walk with us. He was a lovely man, with a big Edwardian-style moustache and a remarkably chipper attitude, considering that his wife was a little bit mental and his sons – he had four – were all terrible little fuckers. The police were often round at their house, asking to talk to them about misdemeanors ranging from credit-card fraud to an incident involving the youngest boy, who had taken to whacking passing old ladies around the shins with his conkers while shouting, 'Fuck off, old lady!' Why? No one knew. The older brothers were almost certainly behind it, but what any of them gained from this was never clear.

Anyway, this old chap seemed to breeze through life oblivious to the terrible legacy he had created. He was never down, always cheerful, and was rather nice to walk along with. He would leave us halfway to get his train, and we would carry on to school alone. One morning he seemed a little less abnormally cheerful than usual, and he told us it was his last day at work. He still occupied a rather lowly position as a junior draughtsman at the office he had been with for over thirty years, and it was his last day. We all thought that might be a cause to celebrate, but it weighed on him. He was given a watch, as it turned out, and was told he could come home early, and thanks for the thirty years, and don't forget your coat. He died about two years later, unhappy and unwanted and scratching around to make ends meet, while his sons continued to exasperate the neighbours with their antics.

It might seem as if I'm exaggerating, but the effect this had on me was profoundly depressing and, you guessed it, life-changing. For the first time in my life, even immersing myself in the adventures of *The Amazing Spiderman* and *The Fantastic Four* couldn't cheer me up, so I made myself a promise. A promise I really meant, and that didn't involve me one day wearing a costume or owning a harem or landing on Mars. I promised myself that I would only do what I really wanted to do with my life, and that I'd leave if things got too boring, but not before I'd earned more than enough to do whatever the hell I wanted when I quit. And even though it all worked out for me just so, I dearly wish I could somehow go back and share my good fortune with that sweet old man who used to walk with us to school.

One day I will eat myself to death. This I promise you

Hard as it is to believe, I am now a man of advanced years. Inside, of course, I still feel like a spunky, occasionally insecure fifteen-year-old, hoping to get invited to that cool party that I am convinced is happening somewhere near by and everyone else is going to. At this party everyone looks fabulous and they all know the hippest new bands and the best new movies, and at the end of the party they will all have sex with each other, but, remarkably, won't feel at all cheap or embarrassed afterwards. Chances are I have been invited to such parties many times without quite realizing it, but even when I have had a suspicion that it might all be going to happen I have usually decided to stay at home instead. This is without doubt the sensible and more enjoyable route. If I were to go to that mythical party, I'd probably wake up with an STD and my wallet missing and have to endure an excruciating kiss-and-tell in the *News of the World* or the *Mail on Sunday*.

Why do you think people do that, the whole kiss-and-tell thing? Money's obviously a factor, but it's still odd, isn't it? Presumably they want to have a little moment of fame, some attention. Strange way to get it, though, letting everyone in on the fact that you'll allow a horny stranger access to your personal nooks and crannies just because they've been on TV or had a hit record. Maybe there's also an element of revenge – if someone feels used then they may well want to get their own back, and revealing that their famous bed-fellow has an overly hairy back or snores after sex probably seems eminently justifiable.

Aftercare is the answer, I think. A couple of phone calls are probably all it takes for the sexual donor to feel respected enough not to turn you over to the tabloids. Although then you'd have to keep talking to them for ever, and if it was just a quick leg-over after a corporate in the Midlands, it seems a steep price to pay. But I always feel very sorry for both the people doing the telling and the individuals being told on, not to mention a little queasy thinking about the journalists poking and prodding away to get hold of the more salacious titbits for their Sunday-morning audience. It's not nice, is it?

I'm lucky enough not to be talking from personal experience here, but I have had one particularly memorable exchange with the papers. Someone had been carrying out a string of sexual attacks on women in London, and the one thing all the victims were agreed on was that he had a distinctive London accent and could not pronounce the letter R very well. One of the tabloids decided it might be a good idea to brand him the 'Wossy Wapist'. Just calling him a 'wapist' makes light of the whole thing – it's like saying Elmer Fudd has been on a wampage. But on a more selfish note, the last thing I wanted was my name, however humorously they spelt it, linked with a rapist. I've had enough experience over the years to know that people don't always read past the headlines, so I'm pretty certain that quite a few people would have assumed that I was the one carrying out these attacks, and no amount of protesting or printed apologies would have changed their minds. Thankfully, someone who worked at the paper warned my agent and he managed to step in and stop them.

Aside from the press implying you rape people, the big downside to being on TV is that people get to see as well as hear you. On radio you can wear more or less what you like, and you can do whatever you want with your hair and eat as much as you fancy and it doesn't really trouble anyone. But if you work on TV then you have to make at least a token effort to keep yourself presentable. This becomes harder as you get older, and not just because you start looking worse and bits start drooping or falling off or going gradually grey. It's also because – and I don't know if this is the same for women – men grow less and less bothered about their appearance and grow increasingly grumpy as they get older, and therefore don't want to have a bunch of people spraying make-up on their face and straightening their hair and adjusting the waistband of their trousers.

Being on TV is a bit like being stuck in a state of arrested childhood, but instead of your mum wiping your face with a spit-soaked tissue and brushing your hair flat there's a small dedicated team of professional fussers to do it. It's probably just Nature's way of making sure that once you've started earning enough in showbiz to be able to buy as many cheeseburgers or hotdogs or Mars bars as you could possibly stuff down your throat in one glorious, gluttonous sitting, you don't actually do that. Although I'm strangely proud to report that, on occasion, I have managed to avoid thinking about the consequences and eaten as much as I possibly can. Honestly, it's a miracle that I can still get about unaided, seeing as I have at various times eaten several large packets of biscuits in one sitting, then gone to the cupboard searching for marzipan or chocolate or cheese or something to finish with.

I remember eating at least two Mars bars *after* a full Indian meal, including starter, and due to the slightly odd shape of my lower torso looked pregnant for most of the afternoon. Despite the sarky comments I got from people I worked with, as a dessert it was great and I recommend you try it. They should offer it in the restaurants to save you nipping into the newsagent's on the way home. Imagine two Mars bars, slightly heated up, with vanilla ice cream. Sweet baby Ganesh, I'm drooling on my keyboard.

I've also been known to consume a whole loaf – family size, not one of those stupid baby loaves that no self-respecting adult would want to be seen buying – toasting it and buttering each slice lovingly, maybe adding a smear of Marmite, and eating it standing up in front of the toaster while waiting for the next two slices to be done. I'm sure this is why most kitchens have the toaster next to the kettle – so you can keep a fresh supply of tea coming while you gorge yourself.

Bizarrely, this gorging tends to happen more often when I am on a diet than when I am cruising along not dwelling on calorific intake, or trying not to eat carbs after four p.m., or not mixing green food with red food unless there's also white food on the plate – or indeed wondering how many calories I've just burnt by walking to and from the toilet rather than having someone carry me there. Which doesn't happen anywhere near as often as you might think – or I might like. If you were rich and lazy enough to employ someone to carry you to the loo, would you, do you think, have the strength of character to stop there, or would you eventually insist that, for a small cash bonus, they wiped for you as well? Horrible thought, I know, and I apologize. But I bet it has crossed Bill Gates's mind.

As Spiderman says, with great power must also come great responsibility. Equally, with great gluttony must come the occasional diet if you still want to appear recognizably human. Over the years, I have tried any number of those slightly potty new diets that come along, get several pages in all the upmarket Sunday papers, then a year later are being touted as the next big thing by all the tabloids.

I rather like that – it upsets the normal order, in that the thin edge of society on the top get used as the testing rabbits for once, and only when a diet's been declared to work and not actually caused anyone to drop dead do the more sensible and suspicious and perhaps slightly less vain lower classes jump on board. I tried food combining for a while – I think the main rule was not to mix proteins with carbohydrates, so you could have weird things like avocado sandwiches. I'd have two in one sitting – delicious, but I never lost weight.

Jane and I, in an attempt to achieve svelteness in rhythm with each other, have from time to time co-dieted. We have embarked on the journey of weight-loss together, hand in pudgy hand.

This is not necessarily the smartest thing for a couple to do if they want to maintain a happy household. For a start there's the competitive element. On the one hand, it's quite nice to have someone to compare your progress with, someone with whom you can celebrate or commiserate the fact that, despite eating only bacon and cheese and drinking only water for the last twenty-four hours on the Atkins diet, you have managed to put on two pounds. However, co-dieting is only a good idea if I win, and lose considerably more weight than Jane. This is not quite as mean-spirited as it may sound — it's not just down to the simple joy of winning, but also because I have never looked at my wife and wanted her to look any different than the way she does at that moment. I have perhaps too publicly gone on record as being a lover of the fuller-figured lady. You can't beat a girl with plenty of junk in the trunk as far as I'm concerned, so the female predilection for dieting has always seemed a little bit of a shame to me.

One diet that Jane discovered and we both tried went under the not-so-catchy title of 'Neanderthin'. You might have guessed, although it's a long shot, that Neanderthin claimed we could get a lean and healthy look by eating like Neanderthal man and woman would have done. In other words, essentially we were allowed only food that you can catch or that might fall from the trees. Old apples, small rabbits, that sort of thing. But after a couple of days on berries, nuts and some chicken which I persuaded myself had been an old one that had died of natural causes, we started in on the Nachos and dips again. I suspect if we had taken the Neanderthin theory fully on board then it may have worked, especially if we had gone shopping wearing only animal skins. Nothing helps keep you on a diet more than having your love-handles out on display. That's why it's always easier to diet in the summer – in winter you can just tuck your extra folds away and forget about them.

Another weight-loss adventure that Jane and I embarked on together doesn't show either of us in a particularly good light. It was after we had dabbled with the Atkins diet several times and both found that it works to begin with, in that you do lose weight. But you feel sort of greasy, and you begin to suspect that you probably smell quite meaty, a suspicion not helped by the fact that dogs seem to get more excited when you walk into the room, no doubt seeing you with some sort of advanced dog-vision as a fleshy, walking bag of sausages and bacon rind that might one day split open and spill on the floor, creating dog heaven on earth.

You really do get to eat a lot of meat and cheese on the Atkins diet, and consequently the things you miss most are all the things you're not supposed to have: bread, crisps and sweeties. You can only eat so many chunks of ham wrapped in cheese with cream on top and a teeny-weeny bit of salad on the side, washed down with creamy coffee, before you start to feel both nauseous and bored. But Jane found a brilliant-sounding diet online that seemed to offer the benefits of the Atkins diet with a delightful get-out-of-jail clause. You had to stick to very strict Atkins rules all day, but for one hour, after dinner, you could eat what you liked. Anything. We read it at least three or four times to be certain. Any bloody thing you liked for a whole hour, after a day of rather lovely cheese and meat indulgence. Now, with the benefit of hindsight – always a wonderful thing after the event – I realize that they probably meant you can eat anything within reason as a little reward for being so good the rest of the day. Maybe half a KitKat, or a couple of digestives. Not, as Jane and I chose to interpret it, that you can eat as much as humanly possible in those golden sixty minutes, especially all those foods and treats that are clearly going to make you swell up like Augustus Gloop. A comparison that will become all the more relevant when I tell you what happened at the end of our short experiment with this remarkable eating plan.

We were on holiday when we tried it out, and all day we'd be kind of good, only eating loads of cheese and double cream and mountains of meat and the occasional tiny bit of salad or a green bean, and drinking only water or diet drinks or black coffee or coffee with that double cream in it again. Then after our evening meal, when the golden hour of eating anything started, we would swoop back to the buffet and devour any and everything left. Like sugar-crazed, wobbly pink locusts, we'd comb the table for bread-based treats. One evening I went back for – and I'm not exaggerating – three extra portions of tiramisu. I say portions, but each helping that I ladled out to myself would have satisfied four normal people. That's like polishing off your meal with twelve desserts. Is it shameful to say that I'm oddly proud of that accomplishment? Further to this gut-busting adventure in gluttony, we had taken the trouble, before dinner, to stock up on a tooth-rotting selection of old-school confectionery from the holiday village shop. Sherbet dib-dabs, flavoured liquorice, Twizzles, sugar mice, those foam shrimps that I suspect have a shelf life of decades, and my personal fave, the foam banana. Christ, I love those little spongy fellas. In fact, if I ever wind up on Death Row, I promise you that, no matter what the main course is, my last dessert on the planet will include foam bananas. Having stocked up on just about every calorie-laden, totally-bad-for-you sweet we could find, and with the clock ticking on this wonderful one-hour, all-you-can-eat window, we relocated to the square and ate and ate until we could eat no more. I'll be honest with you, that diet was quite hard work, and only the amateur scientist in me made me carry on, even when after day three I felt I could have survived for the rest of the holiday on only water.

Did we lose weight? What do you think? But we kidded ourselves it might be working, and as there were no scales in the somewhat basic chalet-style rooms in the resort, the traditional method of checking your progress was impossible. There was no point asking my wife because she is a well-meaning liar when it comes to this sort of thing. However, by the end of the week I strongly suspected that something was up. The room Jane and I had was next door to the room that our children were in, and to get from one to the other either you had to go into the hallway and knock on the door or, as we discovered early on, you could squeeze through the gap in the partition on the balcony. It was hot, so normally the doors on to the balcony were open, and so we nipped in and out of each other's rooms via this shortcut.

The first few days, no problem. But after about three evenings of golden-hour gorging, when the children called me to come and look at something, or fix something, or stop someone arguing about something, I could barely squeeze through the previously quite roomy gap on the balcony.

The perhaps predictable ending to this sorry tale is that on the final morning I actually got wedged there. Stuck, wearing only white underpants, for all who passed by below to see. A fat man, possibly a porky, under-dressed burglar, who knew? Wedged in between holiday rooms while the hot sun beat down on his lobster-coloured paunch. With Jane pulling my sweaty thigh and the children pushing my shoulders we finally managed to get me back on to one side, horribly grazed from the light pebble-dashing on the partition and robbed of any dignity I might once have been able to count on in front of the kids. The fact that they had first searched for the camera and taken some pictures of me in my trapped state only added marginally to the embarrassment. And upon arriving home, I was further delighted to discover I'd put on just under ten pounds while on my 'diet'.

Holidays aren't the best time to lose weight, obviously. Especially not Christmas holidays, and especially not Christmas holidays on a cruise ship. Have you ever been on a cruise? I've done it now and hope I never need to again. There's nothing to do but eat. Eat and watch films you've already seen, or look at the sea, which doesn't change much, or talk to people with whom you have nothing in common apart from the fact you are stuck on a bloody giant boat together, bored out of your minds.

Jane and I went on a Disney cruise with the kids once, mainly because they had nagged us into it, but also because we're huge fans of the whole Disney experience for families, and figured if anyone could get the cruise formula right it would be them. Our youngest, Honey, was about three at the time, which would make Harvey about six and our eldest, Betty, about nine. The kids' clubs were of course tailored for different age groups, so we had three different places to deposit them. And of course, like all cruise ships, the Disney boats are *huge*. You'd no sooner dropped one child off at the first club down the far end of this huge boat, walked back with number two to drop him off at his club and then carried on with the youngest to put her in the crèche, than you had to walk all the fucking way back and get number one out of the first club because the hour would be up, and then get number two from the second club, and then come and retrieve the little one, who inevitably needed to have her nappy changed. It was about as un-relaxing a holiday as it is possible to have.

Apart from dropping children off at and picking them up from activities, the only other pursuits on board appeared to be ping-pong and eating. So we played a little table tennis, but that keeps you occupied for no more than an hour, tops. The rest of the time I ate. Huge buffets are laid out at meal times, and for the rest of the day you can buzz the kitchen from your room and have them send cookies and ice cream down. I enjoyed this service more than most, and by the third day I was on first-name terms with the waiter. By day four he knew exactly how huge my appetite for cookies was, and by the end of the week he would just bring a couple of packets with him every time he knew he would be passing.

Pretty soon it looked like we might be heading for a repeat scenario from the previous holiday, but this time I would be wedged in the cabin door rather than just a partition. So Jane suggested that rather than only eat, I might enjoy one of the many spa treatments on offer. This was a radical suggestion, because I'm not one for treatments. For example, I don't favour massage as an experience. I don't like people poking or prodding me – I really don't see the appeal of having strangers touch and rub you. It feels a little like you're being prepared for the oven, and they always rub too hard or not hard enough and I get embarrassed having to tell them what to do, and frankly I'd rather just have a nap.

So I didn't want a massage. The only thing that sounded vaguely tempting was something called a body wrap, which was meant to make you feel rejuvenated, refreshed and – oh happy coincidence! – lose about two inches around your waist. So I plumped for that, and although part of me suspected it may well be embarrassing, I consoled myself with the certain fact that seeing as we were sailing towards a small Caribbean island at the time, there was no way I was going to be recognized and made to feel all self-conscious about stripping off.

I reported to the small changing room at the set time and got naked, before climbing into the small white paper pants that had been thoughtfully provided. They ripped as I pulled them on, so I had to hold them in place with one hand while I waited. It was also a little nippy in there, and the seat was shiny plastic, which initially was too cold, then became hot and sticky and caused my arse to sweat an alarming amount. If there is a scenario in which an overweight male in his early forties can be made to feel less happy about his situation and appearance, I can't think of one. But when the young lady who was to give me the wrap came in and turned out to be a girl from Manchester whose mum was apparently a huge fan of mine, I accepted that no matter how bad things are, they can usually still get worse.

The young Mancunian sized me up, then began wrapping me

in this sort of hot seaweedy bandage before asking me to lie down for half an hour. The weather wasn't great that day and the sea was quite choppy, so we were lurching about a bit, and I recall thinking that this was just about the most unpleasant experience you could ever have on a boat.

Thirty minutes later I was unwrapped, allowed to stand up in my torn paper pants, now looking not just blobby but bright red and with a hint of a stripe. I could tell from the disappointed look in the girl's eyes that not only had the miracle seaweed wrap failed to work its magic, but also that her mum was going to be told every awful detail. Thankfully the fridge in my cabin had been restocked in my absence, and I found the seaweed had stimulated my appetite enough to go for a new personal best of three packs of cookies and four scoops of ice cream.

USE IT OR LOSE IT.
THE ART OF SEXING

At this point I'd like to advise my children, my parents and anyone else who doesn't want to delve too deeply into my hugely enjoyable, if at times fruitless adventures in the realm of Venus to skip ahead. For those with the stomach and enough morbid curiosity to press on, I can promise that you will, by this chapter's end, know more than you'd probably care to about sex and me. That's not to say I don't intend to cover a lot of other topics. But even though what follows is a bagatelle of pubescent and pre-pubescent memories, sex inevitably rises to the top.

Perhaps it's because I have always been inordinately fond of sex. Some may say a little too fond, because it is a subject that crops up with remarkable regularity in my conversations both when I'm working – which more often than not means talking for a living – and when I'm just living and happen to be talking, in my regular day-to-day encounters with people. That's not to say that if I open the door and the postman's there I start the conversation with a cheery 'Did you get any last night?' No, that would probably be the second or third thing I'd say – normally I build up to it, I give them a little conversational foreplay first. But it is a subject which fascinates me. I'll be honest with you – sex is probably my favourite physical activity.

In recent years I've developed a love of tennis and I'm also quite fond of skiing, although I've only been twice and I didn't show any particular aptitude for it. Skiing loses out to sex because you occasionally get a bit cold and frostbitten, and unless you're interested in going al fresco that's not going to happen with sex. And although I love tennis dearly, and like to think I've grown reasonably competent at it, on occasion I do have a tendency to knock the ball into the net when serving, which is frustrating. I can say with all honesty that I've never endured the sexual equivalent of a double fault. Tennis and skiing both lose out, too, because neither of those fun, calorie-burning pursuits guarantees that you'll see at least part of a lady naked.

I suppose it should go without saying – but that never normally stops me so I'll happily confide – that over the years I have had many fun and interesting sexual encounters with my beloved partner Jane. She has patiently put up with my requests for sex in just about every room in the house, on every item of furniture, wearing every possible combination of hats, socks, shoes, gloves, belts, Christmas tinsel and so on. It's a peculiar thing that, dressing up for sex. You just have to walk down any high street now and you'll see at least one shop that sells novelty nurses' outfits or sexy witch basques or tarty versions of police uniform, with optional handcuffs, all designed solely for bedroom use. I wonder if deliveries have ever got mixed up. I'd love to see the expressions on the faces of a bunch of newly recruited traffic wardens when they're sent off to get changed for the first time into the official outfit of intimidation and oppression – which these days seems to be a scratchy jumper and unflattering trousers – only to find they've been given a skimpy PVC version with vibrating truncheon.

It's odd that the dressing-up-in-bed thing is done so much more by women for men than vice versa. I did once or twice drag on a frilly shirt, but I suspect that women's brains are hardwired a little more interestingly than men's. We respond with Pavlovian immediacy to a stocking like drooling idiots, even if it doesn't have a leg inside it at the time. Women, on the other hand, don't seem to find socks held up by garters any-where near as enticing.

I liked sex long before I tried it. Even when I was a small child it seemed to me that girls always looked and smelt so nice that getting as close as possible to them was a good idea and should be attempted whenever possible. I would quite cheerfully have engaged in appropriate pursuits in order to enjoy such intimacy, but what? I didn't yet play any sport, I felt and looked foolish when semi-naked, so swimming and sunbathing were out, and I didn't meet a girl who liked comic books as much as I did until I was in my mid-twenties. The fact that she later became my wife and that we have now been married for over twenty years is obviously proof that a love of comic books provides an unshakeable bedrock for a long-term relationship. Or maybe just that she loves me enough to put up with my constant harping on about whether Batman might beat Captain America in a fight, or whether the Hulk could ever get angry enough to knock out Superman with one punch. But either way, it was never going to be my looks that would get me close to girls. A malnourished giant in too-short trousers wearing thick-lensed glasses and sporting a tufty head of greasy hair just didn't cut it. You rarely see that kind of thing any more. Social Services must swoop in quickly and nip situations like that in the bud. But that was what I looked like, and I'm sure it goes a long way towards explaining why I didn't get any action until fairly late in life.

Now I liked the idea of girls enough to want to be with them regardless of sex. I hoped that would happen eventually, but it would have been lovely just to hang out with some real live girls. I simply didn't have the first idea as to how that might be accomplished, or indeed what girls might get out of it. Back in east London in the sixties, boys and girls weren't encouraged to spend any more time together than was absolutely necessary. Apart from a happy few years at infants and then at junior school, I spent most of my childhood in single-sex education. What a miserable and hateful system that is. I imagine the thinking behind it is that boys and girls, as they head into and through puberty, find one another distracting. So, in the interests of their education, they are best kept apart. Obviously that's a stupidly flawed theory, because the less time you spend with the other lot, the more time, inevitably, you spend thinking about them, pining for them, fantasizing about them, ultimately learning nothing whatsoever of any use about them. But that's the way it was for me between the ages of eleven and eighteen, from the day I loped lankily off to secondary school in my too-short brown herringbone flares and thick glasses, which allowed me to focus only briefly on the young ladies heading off in the opposite direction to their own schools, or work, or housewifely chores, right up until the time when I was old enough to vote and, horribly ill-prepared, made my first fumbling gropes towards a grown-up relationship.

But before we embark on those teenage years of adventure and consistent disappointment, let me share with you the treasure trove of information I managed to gather in my early schooldays about girls and sex and about what boys needed to do to get it.

I knew from the start that girls were not like boys. I suppose I knew that because, quite sensibly, we were dressed differently by our parents. Girls were also prettier than boys, smelt nicer than boys and had things in their hair that made them look prettier still. Prettier even than pretty boys, of which I was not one. I had a crush on two girls from almost my very first day at school. One was a blonde called Maxine Stevens and the other was – oh cruel fate! – her best friend, Kay Gillingham. Kay was brunette. Both were nice enough to me and probably had no idea that I harboured secret fantasies about rescuing them from cartoon monsters or gangs of other boys who were teasing them; fantasies that ended, without exception, with Maxine and Kay being incredibly grateful and hugging me, and everyone else cheering me for being so brave and handsome. As far as I can recall, this never actually happened in real life, although I think I once nearly got to kiss Kay, many years later, when I met her in a local pub with a friend who was even more spectacularly inept around girls than I was. So Maxine and Kay remained, sadly, the unattainable goddesses against whom I judged all other girls until I was at least twelve.

The first time I got to participate in anything of a vaguely sexual nature was when I was about seven. The girl's name was Joyce and although I can clearly remember her second name – something wonderfully exotic and filled with promise – I shall withhold it in a belated attempt to appear a gentleman. Her parents had come from somewhere in Africa – I can't remember ever asking her for details – but she, like me, had been born in London.

The arrangement was that Joyce would permit me and my friend Stephen to have a look up her skirt and past her knickers – Joyce had obligingly offered to hold them to one side for the occasion – under the desk, providing we returned the favour. It was more a matter of curiosity than sexual desire, but whatever our motivation, when the deal was struck our hearts started to pound.

Stephen went first. After a bit of embarrassed fumbling around he 'dropped' his pencil from his desk and shimmied down to retrieve it. He was blushing furiously when he began his descent so it was hard to tell how much redder the experience made him, but when he re-emerged, proudly grasping his pencil and looking like he finally understood the meaning of it all, his face was like a baboon's arse. Redder, in fact. Like a baboon's arse after a thorough spanking and a spell in the sun during which time the baboon has unwisely forgotten to put sunblock on his exposed buttocks.

My turn next. I dropped my pencil, glanced up to make sure

that Mrs Bendall, our form teacher, wasn't paying us any undue attention, and down I dived.

Let me pause for a moment and tell you about Mrs Bendall. She was a very large, rather square, matronly Welsh lady. For several years I was convinced that she was actually Ronnie Barker in drag, and the fact that she also took us for country dancing reinforced that notion. There was one episode of *The Two Ronnies* which ended with big Ron and little Ron dragged up and dancing around ringing bells, which more or less confirmed I was correct. I met Ronnie Barker twice before he died, but on both occasions I was so excited to be in the presence of one of my childhood heroes that I completely forgot to ask if there was a connection.

I'm still at a loss to understand what country dancing was all about. The only purpose it can possibly have served was to get young children running around a bit and filling their lungs before the tyranny of PE took over at secondary school. I don't imagine kids today have to endure anything remotely as pointless, but perhaps if there was more country dancing and less of whatever they force them to do today we'd have a nicer, less scary generation on the way up.

The basics were these – we'd form a large circle, hold hands and skip around in time to the music, periodically skipping towards the centre of the circle and then skipping back out again. I don't remember Mrs Bendall ever trying to teach us any steps or moves that might reasonably be construed as dancing, but occasionally she would give me a Spangle afterwards so I like to think I was rather good at whatever it was we were doing. She was a lovely, kind lady, Mrs Bendall, and if it hadn't been for her thick, glossy facial hair I might well have developed a crush on her. Come to think of it, she probably looked more like Robert Maxwell with a moustache than Ronnie Barker.

Anyway, right now she wasn't looking, so I half slipped, half fell off my stool and found myself looking at Joyce's smooth, black legs. I saw her hands appear, and she hoicked up the hem of her school skirt. Her clean white knickers dazzled me. I felt ashamed and excited and petrified all at the same time – a marvellous cocktail at any age – then she pulled them to one side, and I saw . . .

Nothing.

In addition to her hand being partly in the way, her skin was so dark and the contrast with the white of her knickers so pronounced that I couldn't make out one solitary detail. As Watson might have put it to Sherlock Holmes, the game was hardly worth the candle. I stayed under the desk for what seemed like a decent enough time, peering feverishly at the shadowy recesses of her loins, before coming up for air, smiling, blinking and trying my best to look as if I'd just had a real eyeful of something very special indeed. Then it was Joyce's turn. She ducked down as Stephen and I dangled our tiny and unimpressive little tinkles before her. After what felt like bloody ages, with the cold air beginning to worry my small, pink extremity, she reappeared looking a little unwell.

None of us ever spoke of it again, and I apologize if it seems ungentlemanly to give the episode an airing now, so many years after it took place, but for Christ's sake, I've got a book to fill.

I didn't see naked female flesh again, apart from in magazines, until I was eighteen or nineteen, when I finally lost my virginity to a very nice girl with whom I am still in touch today from time to time. I have no idea where Stephen wound up, or where Joyce might be, but I hope she is alive and well and still wears beautifully clean white drawers.

After that my school years were sexually uneventful, at any rate in terms of actual contact with real live humans. I saw my first breasts – or at least the first breasts that weren't attached to my mum, before I left junior school. Someone – it might have been a boy in the next year up – had found a magazine his dad had hidden in a drawer in his bedroom, beneath his underpants, or possibly his socks. Why is it that the sock drawer is the traditional secret compartment in adult lives? I too found a copy of a mildly erotic book hidden, or at least buried, in my mum's tights drawer when I was little. I wasn't actually snooping, it was a legitimate search for a pair of tights to wear under my jeans for my milk round, and as a result I discovered this book. It was called *My Secret Garden*, not to be mistaken with *The Secret Garden*, a popular Edwardian kids' story. Although the book I stumbled upon was hardly hardcore, it was a little risqué. It was made up of what I'm sure were fake case histories of women recounting their sexual awakenings. One described working in a factory and how, when bored, she would squeeze her thighs together around the pole that ran from her conveyor belt to the floor. It vibrated, so was obviously pretty useful as a means of alleviating the inevitable tedium of working on a production line. Another had a fantasy about being caught by bears in a wood. I found the whole thing very confusing and more than a little disappointing. It was returned to the tights drawer only half read.

But the discovery of legitimate porn by my friend was a different matter. My first reaction was shock and awe at the sheer daring of this kid. To have the courage to delve into the forbidden drawers in your parents' room! In my eyes he was Raffles and Robin Hood rolled into one – a brilliantly audacious burglar who was prepared to share his incredible haul with us.

The complete magazine was considered too bulky to smuggle into school and too likely to be missed, but he had ripped out a page from near the front that he hoped would go unnoticed. It had a disappointingly large amount of text, but one of the news items was illustrated with a photograph. The story was about a showgirl currently wowing the crowds in Las Vegas, and the photograph showed her onstage, baring her teeth in a rather angry fashion and aiming her fabulous chest at the camera.

The alarming thing was that her breasts had been painted to resemble melons. They were bright green. Bright green with a faint stripe on them to represent the markings you get on certain varieties of melon but never, thank the Lord, on breasts. It gave us a little bit of a thrill, but, to be honest, it was more of a mystifying encounter than an erotic one. It left too many questions unanswered. We were smart and worldly enough, even at eight, to realize that those boobies had been pimped, to use the modern vernacular. But why? Weren't they an exciting enough sight as Nature intended? And if the melon paint-job and go-faster stripes had been added to arouse men, then what could we expect to happen to our minds over the next ten years that would make us seek out melon-breasted ladies in preference to the real thing?

With only this small piece of research material to guide us, we speculated and pondered the matter for many days, weeks, months even, until the big brother of another boy let us take a quick flick through a copy of *Men Only* he claimed to have bought himself, like an actual horny adult, from a newsagent. We soon found out that he had stolen it from a local second-hand bookshop. Still, a five-page spread featuring the charms of *Men Only* regular Fiona Richmond was enough to reassure us that a) women's breasts did not have to be huge or painted like melons to be arousing and b) just because a lady took all her clothes off for you, it didn't mean you would necessarily fancy her.

Fiona was a bit masculine-looking in the face department for me. She was very strong-chinned, but more than made up for it by being incredibly obliging when it came to showing off the rest. However, I always knew that her chiselled jaw would have prevented true love ever blossoming between us – sorry, Fiona. It wasn't until many years later, when I managed to get hold of a copy of *Knave*, in which a round-faced beauty who looked a little like Susan Penhaligon from *A Bouquet of Barbed Wire* posed provocatively wearing only a cloche hat and brown leather boots, that I first fell in love with someone I knew I'd never meet. Part of me would still like the chance to at least buy her a cup of tea and thank her for being there for me during those difficult teenage years. Although she would of course be about sixty now, so might not want to be reminded that she had once been made available for teenage boys to project both their romantic fantasies and their bodily fluids all over.

Men's magazines, as they were and continue to be euphemistically referred to, were great if you wanted to look at pictures of pretty women naked, and they occasionally had interesting articles about thorny issues such as whether or not a real man would carry a handbag. John Peel was interviewed in that edition of *Knave*, and although he claimed it was OK because he needed one to carry his record albums around in, the general message was that you'd look a bit gay if you used one for anything else. But they were bloody useless when it came to supplying any information on the vital subject of what girls were actually like, and how you might meet or talk to them. Not that the women in those mags were anything like real girls, who rarely seem to enjoy lying around for hours wearing nothing but boots and a half-awake expression.

Luckily, my mum had an ancient copy of *Cosmopolitan* on her dressing table – obviously not considered so racy it needed to seek refuge under the tights – which lived there for about five years. It's not that she was a slow reader, just that people didn't seem to buy magazines with anything like the regularity they do today, and I think she was just taking her time with it. Money was probably a factor as well. Anyway, although *Cosmopolitan* didn't contain anything on how to talk to girls, it did have lots of articles designed to help women get men interested in them. These gave me a little bit of an insight into the possibility that girls might be just as keen on and just as ill-informed about the opposite sex as I was, which was a relief.

Elsewhere in the mag was what I considered at the time to be a very useful feature. It was called something like 'How to Improve Your Lover – Sex Tips that Will Turn him from a Dud to a Stud'. That dud/stud thing made a particular impression. Yes, I was a dud. Yes, I wanted to be a stud. Teach me, oh wise

Cosmo women! Most of it I only dimly recall – stuff about taking your time and not grabbing straight away for the ta-tas or the la-la. But there was this one pointer to help a man become an absolute whizz at oral sex. This was an indispensable piece of information. First of all because until I read it I'd had no idea that oral sex existed, at least when it came to men doing it to women. And secondly because I knew that if I followed the exercise as described, I would no longer be a dud, but a fully qualified, super-confident, damned-near-irresistible stud. This is what it said:

Get him to practise with his tongue on the centre of a peeled orange.

That was it. Peel an orange and stick your tongue into the hole at the top. Now, I do not wish to cast aspersions on any of the varied but never less than delightful female genital accoutrements I've encountered up close thus far in my life, but not one of them resembled, in either taste, texture or size, the small citrusy hole at the top of an orange. Neither has any of them ever presented me with a thick layer of chewy pith to get through, filled my mouth with pips or squirted me in the eye, I'm relieved to say.

But I can honestly say that the many hours I spent tonguing Spanish oranges and putting up with strange looks and the odd sarky comment from my friends at the time – who must have thought I was really very peculiar indeed – have in no way improved my ability when visiting the downstairs front department. Talk about irresponsible journalism. Why would they do that to a young man? Why write an article filled with such patent nonsense when it could easily fall into the hands of an impressionable youngster and gain him a reputation as a weirdo among his small circle of equally nerdy and unworldly friends? On the plus side, I've never had scurvy.

So desperate was I for a sexual experience that involved something more than my imagination and my right hand (or a satsuma) that I tried on one occasion – and please God, if you are in any way related to me and haven't yet skipped ahead, do so now or promise never to mention this to my face – to get up close and personal with the family vacuum cleaner. The details are hazy now: no doubt my brain has deliberately tried to delete as much of this event as possible in the interests of self-preservation. But from what I can recall the house was empty, more or less, and the Hoover had been left in the bedroom I shared with my four brothers. I don't think there was anything about the Hoover in particular that attracted me – this was long before they put cute, smiley faces on them, and it was just a smelly old plastic vacuum cleaner.

I suspect that this practice, at least as a one-off, is nowhere near as rare as you might think. A few years back that fabulously talented yet sexually insatiable powerhouse that is Russell Brand admitted to having done the same thing. I didn't come out about my own experiences at the time because I didn't want to spoil his moment in the limelight. What's the point of making a big embarrassing confession in public if all your mates just chip in that they've done that as well? I must have already been masturbating – one eye shut and the other squinting fearfully at the door that had no lock on it – when I spied this sucking temptress sitting in the corner. I knew the basic principle of vacuuming, and thought that the long aluminium tube bit might just work in tandem with the wrist movements I had grown so adept at, so I reached for the nozzle, turned her on (note that the Hoover has instantly become a lovely lady desperate for some callow boy to make sweet love to her) and gingerly inserted myself into the tube. You've probably already guessed that not only did it feel nothing like actual intercourse – not that I was going to find that out for many years – but also it was deeply unpleasant.

I suspect the main cause of my terrible discomfort was the level of suction involved. I wasn't to know it yet, but the suction power of a Hoover is far, far greater than what is called for in these circumstances. To make matters worse, I imagine my mum and dad had gone for the economy version which, while doubtless efficient at sucking up all sorts of crap from our cheap carpets, had unaccountably not been supplied with that all-important blowjob setting.

And not only did it hurt like hell, but the sound it made changed from the familiar white noise of a normally functioning vacuum cleaner to a kind of strained, unpleasant whining, a sound I was positive would alert anyone within earshot that somebody had been stupid enough to put their cock into the nozzle. I tried to pull out but that was even more painful, and the volume went up several decibels. The Hoover now sounded like a fat drunk robot calling for help as a boy abused it. I imagine. While we're on the subject, how long before someone invents a robot that provides this sort of service? Surely we have the technology by now, and anyone who's watched late-night television knows there are more than enough lonely weirdos out there who'd buy it. Maybe I'll suggest it to Duncan Bannatyne next time we meet. That's an episode of *Dragon's Den* I'd like to see.

Mercifully, though, nobody came to investigate and by manoeuvring myself very carefully, I managed to reach the Off switch and put an end to the torture. And apart from having a bright-red, angry-looking ridge around the end of my penis which didn't fade for about two weeks, I emerged from the experience undamaged and slightly wiser. If I was ever again tempted to bring myself off with a vacuum cleaner, I vowed, I would find one with a more accommodating nozzle and at least two or three different speeds. Are you listening, Dyson?

Although, as I said, I don't think this kind of experimentation is as rare as we might like to think, confessing to it probably is. If you could be bothered to check, I bet that some time in the late seventies or early eighties the *British Medical Journal* published an article on penile injuries caused by vacuum cleaners. And that's just the tip of the iceberg. Someone I once knew who worked as a porter at the local hospital delighted in sharing with us mind-boggling tales from Accident and Emergency involving people's privates. Over the years he swore blind that he had personally seen patients wheeled in with the following rammed up their bums: milk bottles; light bulbs; Barbie dolls; an electric toothbrush; candles (up to nine regular-sized table candles in one go, he insisted); and, in the oddest case, a training shoe.

While most of these injuries were self-inflicted, we did wonder whether the training-shoe victim might have been unlucky enough to have angered someone, while naked, who happened to be tragically incompetent when tying up laces securely but had *great* aim.

Of course, most of the 'information' we enthusiastically passed around as kids was complete nonsense. It took me at least ten years to unlearn the 'fact' that most women don't like having it off and regard sex as a deeply unpleasant chore to be endured only if they want to make babies or need shelves putting up. Apart from nurses, obviously. Nurses, it was believed, liked nothing more, after a back-breaking eighteen hours washing elderly patients' bedsores and stitching up drunks, than to accommodate every spotty teenager who happened to offer them a cider at a party.

So convinced were we that nurses were just about our only hope of getting any action that we would eagerly seek out gatherings where we thought a nurse or two might pitch up. This fallacy was one of the few glimmers of hope I had to hold on to, and it was lovely while it lasted. Don't get me wrong: I'm not suggesting nurses don't like sex – I'm sure they have a healthy and sane approach to it – but they proved to be far from the desperate, permanently game nymphos that all young men living in Leytonstone in the seventies declared them to be.

Thankfully, I was what we describe rather charmingly as a 'late developer'. That's not to say that the normal hormonal changes didn't kick in when they were supposed to. I vaguely recall a brief period of anxiety during which I noticed that some of the other boys at school were beginning to get a little smellier and a little hairier than they had been previously, but before I had time to dwell on it I, too, had sprouted pubes and become aware of the musky aroma emanating from my armpits and feet that delightfully heralds the approach of manhood. A key sign that we no longer considered ourselves boys, but rather strong, forceful, lusty young men, emerged some time during the school summer holiday of 1973. There was nothing amiss in July, when I said goodbye to the usual assortment of sporty types, bullies and oddballs that made up most of the year − I only had about two actual friends I would see and keep in touch with over the summer − but when we all gathered for the first day of the new term the difference hit you immediately. The smell.

It was as if someone had sent us all a memo that we had decided we must follow without question. Here's what it might have said:

```
Dear Pubescent Teen,

The time has come. You are ready to embark on the
biggest adventure of your life. You will soon snog
someone and might also be able to put at least one
of your hands inside their clothes and root around
for a bit. You probably won't enjoy either of these
activities at first because, quite frankly, you will
be terrified that you are doing it all wrong. And,
almost without doubt, you will be doing it all
wrong, but the girl on the receiving end probably
won't realize that, so don't panic. If you really
mess up, just pretend you were never trying to find
a nipple under her vest, and that button on her
shirt you so lovingly caressed for forty minutes
on her front doorstep was in fact what you had
been looking for all night. You love buttons! What
could be more fun than rubbing a button while
kissing a girl, worrying that you're moving your
tongue around too much in her mouth and wondering
```

whether she can taste the Toast Topper you had for
tea before coming out on this night of wild
debauchery?
   But to reach these lofty heights of sensation you
need one thing. And you need lots of it. AFTERSHAVE.
The adverts have been telling you this for ages, but
you must wait no longer. Follow the advice of Henry
Cooper and splash, yes, really splash it on all
over. Be like the bloke in the Denim commercial and
marinade your chest in it. Get practising your self-
defence because, as was revealed in the short
documentary masquerading as an ad for Hai Karate,
you will literally need to fight women off. But only
if you absolutely soak your skin and clothes in
cheap, pungent, spicy and sweet mass-produced
perfume for boys. Go to it!

Yours helpfully,

The God of Sex

Yes, we had all got that memo and we had acted upon it to
the letter. Even now, as I write, I can feel my eyes beginning to
water and my throat constricting at the memory of that first day
back at school in September. Thirty-six of us crammed into an
unventilated classroom all morning with a toxic cloud the
colour of a day-old bruise hanging over our heads. One boy
passed out during the mid-morning break, but it was unclear
whether that was due to the build-up of Old Spice in his lungs
or the fact that Michael Ponsford, the unfortunately named class
hard nut, had kicked him in the nuts during a game of Barge.

   I think this was peculiar to our school, but it was a craze that
grabbed hold and didn't loosen its grip for about two years. The
rules were simple. If you were lucky enough to spot another boy
of roughly your size standing up, you would run up behind him
and leap into his back, shoulder first. When you managed to

catch someone full force who hadn't seen you coming, the effect could be quite spectacular. They would go flying through the air, sometimes six or eight feet. Fortunately, boys are fairly resilient creatures and no one got seriously injured. It also served to hone our reflexes somewhat. One kid, a friend of mine called Patrick Robinson, was like a bloody cat. You could hit him full on from behind and he'd roll with it before springing gracefully back on to his feet like a panther. He was the king of Barge, for sure.

This trial by aftershave was probably the biggest health hazard faced by teachers in all-boy schools back in the seventies. It was at its most dangerous following the Christmas break, when the male youth of east London would reluctantly drag themselves back to their classes, after a couple of weeks of Christmas telly and Quality Street, doused in whatever potentially lethal fragrance they had been given by their aunts or uncles or particularly unimaginative parents. Thank Christ nobody was allowed to smoke during assembly. The fug of chemicals that permeated the air as we mumbled our way through the hymns every morning, avoided only by those lucky enough to be Jewish or Sikh, would have turned the hall into a giant incinerator.

Smoking was pretty much tolerated elsewhere, at least among the sixth-formers. It seems amazing in this health-conscious, nanny-state age that teachers turned a blind eye to kids smoking in the playground and even, in a couple of cases, in the classroom, provided that they stayed near the back and didn't cough too much. Seriously, it was so commonplace that I'm surprised smoking wasn't a course option alongside social studies and drama. It would probably have been more useful to most of the kids there.

I never had a proper girlfriend until after I left school. And seeing as I failed all of what were then called O levels the first time I took them, I was still there when I was eighteen. But, you know, I really didn't miss having one too much. My passion, my love, my only genuine interest before I reached voting age was comic books. Specifically, American comic books. Even more specifically, Marvel comic books, written by Stan 'the Man' Lee and drawn by those two giants of the industry, Jack 'King' Kirby and 'Sturdy' Steve Ditko.

I have my brother Paul to thank for this obsession as it was he who first introduced me to comics. I'm trying hard now not to rattle on about my passion for these four-colour adventure stories, because I know if I digress into a long rant about why Steve Ditko was the greatest Spiderman artist and just how cruelly the comic-book industry treated the genius Jack Kirby, or a detailed analysis of the Agents of Thunder or Herbie, the Fat Fury, we'll be stuck on the subject for some time. Such rambles can last for several days, to the evident discomfort of my audience, usually people who work for me and who therefore feel obliged at least to pretend to listen with something approaching interest. I've noticed that their eyes tend to glaze over and their chins droop towards their chests, like those young IT workers you see on the last tube home dozing off after seven or eight pints of cider. So I've had to learn to stop myself before I send them into a coma.

Suffice it to say, for the moment, anyway, that I kept my comic collection, such as it was then, in two old wooden drawers under the bunk beds I shared with Paul. I had the top bunk, he had the bottom. Traditionally, it seems, the top bunk is the prized position, and I don't remember how or why it was decided that I should have it – it was just the way it was. As I mentioned, we shared the room with my three other brothers, and although it was a relatively cramped space for five boys, we all got along surprisingly well. I guess this was because of the great job my parents made of raising us all to be level-headed and respectful of others. Or maybe it was because we all had very different interests. Of the five of us, I was the least bothered about sport, finding no joy whatsoever in either playing or watching anything that involved fit people wearing shorts chasing after balls or jumping over or throwing things. As a result I spent as much time as possible indoors, and managed to compensate for the awful wasteland that was daytime, early-evening and weekend telly by gorging myself on comic books.

When, as was often the case, I had no new ones to read, I would invent my own characters and occupy myself for hours trying to draw professional-looking comic books of my own. I came up with the Mutant Army, a thinly veiled knock-off of the X-Men, but could never get them to look right. Partly this was due to a simple lack of skill, but I think it was also because I didn't realize how much time the artists devoted to each panel, laying out the drawing and roughing out sketches before committing to the artwork proper. To me, it somehow felt like cheating if I took longer to draw it than to read it.

This rather slipshod and impatient approach to creativity has dogged me throughout my career, and I'm sure it's no coincidence that I've always preferred making the kind of TV shows you just do more or less live, before moving on to the next one, rather than more considered, lovingly crafted work that requires far greater application and concentration. The exception would be the documentaries I have worked on over the years, where I'll happily spend hours and hours trying to get little details right, and normally find the fact that you have to finish them and hand them over to be broadcast deeply frustrating. Give me more time! We can make it even better!

Whatever the case, comic books kept me excited and filled my days. My first thoughts on waking and my last before going to bed were always of the Fantastic Four, the New Gods, Spiderman, Mr Miracle or even the brilliant Kamandi, the Last Boy on Earth. In fact, one of the greatest dreams I ever had was one in which I was summoned down to Hell by the Son of Satan, admittedly one of Marvel's lesser characters, and the Ghost Rider helped break me free.

You're glazing over a bit, aren't you? Sorry. Anyhow, this obsession with comics – and it really was an obsession – only began to take a back seat when girls became too attractive a proposition for me to ignore them any longer. It's weird the way boys develop – or at least it's weird the way this boy developed. It wasn't that I didn't like girls or like the idea of getting friendly with at least one of them, even if I was motivated merely by a desire to smell their clean, long hair and lovingly lick their small, pink ears. But I couldn't envisage any way of getting close enough to one to start a conversation, let alone begin to imagine what I might say to her if, by some miracle, I ever did. I sensed that it would be tricky to try to break the ice with an opening gambit about the comics created by Jack Kirby after he left Marvel and went to DC Comics in the early seventies (a golden age, but for God's sake don't get me started), but I was far too petrified even to make a stab at it.

So scared was I that when I caught sight of a particular girl for whom I nurtured an unhealthily strong affection – I'd never spoken to her, of course, but I saw her on the way to school every day – I would sometimes forget to walk. Given that I was at least fifteen, maybe sixteen years old, I am only too aware of how ridiculous this must sound. But as soon as this sultry little thing, whose name I never discovered, appeared on the horizon, wearing, of course, the traditional 1970s school uniform, complete with white socks, and no doubt nursing her first Benson & Hedges of the day, my legs would go all wibbly. Once or twice I feigned a loose shoelace in order to kneel down and steady myself by pretending to tie it until she'd gone, but it wasn't long before it dawned on me that she would get suspicious, or worse, imagine I was some kind of mummy's boy who had never learnt how to do up his shoes properly and, rather than put in the work or ask an adult, was happy to struggle to school each morning stopping every hundred yards or so to wrap the laces into some sort of useless bunch that would soon flop apart again.

I then stumbled on what seemed like the brilliant concept of banishing all thoughts of her from my head by concentrating on a popular rhythmic pop tune of the day and walking in time to the beat. This worked, more or less, although I'm sure I must have seemed oddly jaunty as I bopped past her silently humming 'Chirpy Chirpy Cheep Cheep', or some other hit from the recent past that had a consistent, easy-to-remember beat. Showaddywaddy and Mud were both good bands for that as well, as was, 'Billy Don't Be A Hero' by Paper Lace. But don't even think about trying it to 'Bohemian Rhapsody'. You'd trip up like a baby giraffe.

My first actual brushes with real live girls were predictably unsuccessful. I can remember the exact date, time and place of my first proper grown-up kiss, although unfortunately I can't tell you anything much about the young woman lucky enough to have been on the receiving end. It would have been approximately twelve forty-five on the morning of 1 January 1978 and I would have been seventeen. I know the date because not only was it New Year's Eve, but it was also both my dad's and my eldest brother's birthday. We always had a bit of a party to celebrate that – nothing huge, but as we all grew older it was noisy enough to keep the neighbours awake – and this was the first year I decided to flex my wings and do my own thing on New Year's Eve. By now punk rock was in full swing and I was as punky as a timid seventeen-year-old with terrible eyesight could be. I can't remember what I was wearing, either, sadly, but it would have been a home-crafted concoction of some sort, in keeping with punk's anti-consumerism message and my own modest resources.

Anyhow, I remember the date and the time and the place because this was the first year I felt confident enough to break away from the family shindig. Up until about fifteen or sixteen it seems unthinkable that you won't spend every Christmas, New Year and birthday together as a family. But the siren calls of both the other sex and the arty New Wave band Ultravox playing live at the Marquee in Wardour Street proved to be hard to resist. The gig was, I imagine, great. We were so keen on drinking as much lager as possible from those horrible plastic cups and throwing ourselves around that it was always a bit difficult to remember any of the actual music. But it felt extra exciting to be out on New Year's Eve, and away from my family. I felt cool, rebellious and very sophisticated. So much so that after throwing up on the pavement outside I challenged my friend Steve Taylor to a competition.

Traffic was gridlocked in Soho, and we decided to see who could run over the roofs of the most stationary vehicles before an angry driver managed to grab you and pull you down. We detoured via Trafalgar Square, but most of the midnight revellers had drifted away and only the litter was left, showing what a great party we had just missed. It was all a bit depressing, so we opted for the last tube train home.

Walking down to the platform, drunk and singing and falling over, we saw two beautiful, perfect young women. Alcohol does that to you, thankfully. I can only assume that in reality they were pretty monstrous, because neither of us was much to look at, so for them to be as obliging as they were must mean they were also on the fringe of desirability and hideously drunk. I don't think we even spoke. A sort of alcoholic telepathy allowed us to communicate that we both wanted to go home having had a little contact with a real live human, so we lunged for the girls and started to kiss.

So far, so perfect. I know it's hardly Jane Austen, but we were all consenting and none of us had passed out. The kissing was tentative to start with, and then I decided to throw caution to the wind that always blows down the tube tunnel, and try for a little tongue action. I didn't really want to, but I knew it was the next step up in kissing after the basic mouth-to-mouth technique, so felt I had to try it. I should have checked first, I now realize, because the obliging young lady on the receiving end was not only drunk but also eating fish and chips. As my tongue snaked in it encountered not another person's sluggy appendage but instead a mushy pellet of partially chewed cod, generously seasoned with salt and vinegar. Of course it didn't put me off – I suppose I was so excited to be finally doing what we were doing that nothing could have spoiled the moment. I did think it a bit off when she popped another chip in when we came up for air, but then again she had been eating before we started and you wouldn't want your takeaway to get cold just because you'd been grabbed by a punk.

Recently, while watching *Springwatch* with the excellent Bill Oddie, I noticed that the feeding methods of young birds are not dissimilar to my first grapple. The mum flies into the nest with a partially chewed worm or cricket and drops it right into the mouth of one of the waiting babies. I don't think I actually ate any of my first partner's supper, but I still find the tangy smell of salt and vinegar on batter to be highly evocative of that night.

The evening ended in a memorable way as well. We got on the train and carried on kissing in that oddly unselfconscious way that kids have of zoning out all the disapproving stares and tuts from the adults in the carriage, fumbling and frolicking in plain view with no shame. She got off before me, in more ways than one, and when I finally got back to Leytonstone I realized that I had left my key at home. It being the big family party night I hoped they would still be up, but the lights were all off. Rather than ring the bell – which was more of a horrible buzzer my dad had rigged up – and wake the whole house and the adjoining ones, I used a small penknife I carried – it was only about two inches long and was intended for craft use only – to knock the window lock open in one of our old crumbly double-sash jobs. Breaking and entering must be a lot harder for people these days, I'm sure – back then you were never really locked out of a house providing you could find a stick or something thin to open a door or window with. Anyway, I opened the window and climbed through, falling to the floor in a most disgraceful and drunken way. At that moment the lights went on and my family all started to shout and cheer. They'd seen me staggering down the road and had turned the lights out to surprise me, not really expecting me to break in rather than use the front door. It was just about the perfect end to the perfect night.

The upside to my almost total failure to get any action is that I also avoided the awkward side-effects that promiscuity offers. Very, very early on in my adult life I got, for the only time, something approaching what might be described as a sexually transmitted disease. Now you might think I'm pussy-footing around this a bit by saying it might have been a sexually transmitted disease, but I honestly have no idea where it came from because at the time – and I'm pretty confident that my memory serves me correctly – I had only slept with one person, and she was lovely and only slightly more experienced than I was. I persuaded myself instead that it had been given to me by some naughty elves – like the ones who used to work for that lazy cobbler and made all those shoes while he was asleep. Clearly they had crept under my covers and introduced some frilly decoration for aesthetic reasons only they understood.

At the tender age of about nineteen – and this would have only been about six months or a year after finally losing my virginity – I noticed (and those of a faint heart might wish to skip ahead a little bit here) a small fibrous growth on the underside of my penis. I am using the medical word for my cock here in the hope that it might make this seem a little more palatable and also might appear as if it is serving some serious purpose, as opposed to the cheap laughs I hope to get out of the situation later on.

Anyway, it didn't really trouble me until it multiplied, so that what began as one little nodule became two in the space of a week or so, and then, quite wisely, I thought I should have it checked out. So I went to our family doctor, who I believe was a Dr Patel in Leytonstone High Street, a very nice, elderly man, and as you may have guessed, an Indian. And I showed him my penis, which I suspect he'd seen before, but not since I'd grown into a full-blooded young man who was capable of using his penis in the way that men should do. In fact it was the first time, as an adult, that I'd had to take my pants down and get the old man out in front of another old man. So it was a genuine rite of passage. He studied my penis and his verdict was that on the underside, right up near the top bit, under what is called the mushroom, I believe, in doctor circles, I had a genital wart.

Now this was bad news. Nothing had prepared me for the possibility that you could get warts upon your genitals, nor had I ever had a wart on the rest of my body. There may have been a small growth on my finger once that was removed, but I can't really remember it that clearly so conceivably it happened to someone else, maybe one of my brothers. Anyway, I was alarmed and a little bit ashamed. No, there was nothing to be ashamed of, he reassured me, these things are very common and easily treatable, and he told me how. He gave me a prescription for some wart-removing liquid and then he took the trouble of drawing a rather crude illustration to show me how it should be used. Dr Patel continued by saying this was very powerful stuff and I must apply it only to the wart itself and not to the skin around it – it would kill the wart and it would drop off, but under no circumstances must I paint it anywhere but on the wart. Thank you, I said, and he advised me against sexual contact for the next few days until the wart had disappeared and he sent me on my way, out into a waiting room filled with middle-aged ladies who I swear had overheard most of the conversation, because they looked at me quite differently on my way out than they had on my way in. When they hadn't looked at me at all, in fact.

Off I went to the chemist's, taking the trouble of going to one which was quite a bit further away from my house than I would normally go to, for fear that the stigma and shame of the genital wart would linger for the rest of my life if it was known about by my local pharmacist. Little did I know that some twenty-eight years later I'd be writing about it in a book.

Now I don't want to cast aspersions on Dr Patel's medical skills, but the product he had prescribed was an over-the-counter treatment which I later saw advertised on TV for burning warts off people's fingers. Possibly my penis at that stage looked a bit like a finger, but as I'm sure you're aware it is made of a more sensitive material and serves a very different function to a finger. At least mine does. Anyway, I took the liquid home, and it was in a very small, plain, uninteresting brown bottle, which looked a little like those bottles of Rescue Remedy that you see bonkers old ladies squirting into their mouths when they're a little bit panicked, fully aware, I'm sure, that essentially it is brandy in there and that's how the rescuing is done. When I was home I took out the bottle, which came equipped with a small paintbrush on the inside of the lid, and very gingerly painted the liquid on the small wart. And it was only a small wart. It wasn't a full-blown ugly thing. You really had to look quite hard to find it, to be frank. So I painted the liquid on the area as described by Dr Patel both verbally and in his marvellous illustration. Nothing seemed to happen.

The next day I did the business of unfolding my equipment and looking closely and intently, only to see that the wart looked exactly the same. So I reapplied the liquid, left it to do its work and, as I was at university in those days, I imagine I went off to read about modern history and enjoy too many pints of lager in the pub. I came home feeling slightly sleepy and examined my equipment again, only to find once again that the said wart was still in place. Now slightly angered by the lack of progress made by the wart liquid and no doubt fuelled with a certain kind of devil-may-care brio that seven or eight pints of lager will give a young student, I decided to go hell for leather and slapped the liquid all over the entire end of my penis. Then I went off to blissful sleep, and woke up the next morning to find that, rather like a magical occurrence in a fairy tale, my cock had swollen up and now resembled a rather angry sausage with a medium-sized peach attached.

While this might have been impressive in many ways it was also hideously painful. I figured out that the liquid kills the surface layer of skin, and so for a robust little wart might need a few days to do its job. But on the normal soft skin down there it had worked like paint stripper, and overnight it had removed the entire surface covering of my beautiful, proud, flute-like cock, which had decided to take protective measures by swelling up bigger than you would have thought possible. As a consequence I was now carrying around what looked like a small length of rhubarb glued to a large, slowly festering tennis ball. I explained this to my girlfriend at the time and after I had managed to calm her down enough to stop her packing her belongings we decided that we would leave it a few days to see how things progressed. And agreed we'd probably never have sex again.

It took about a week or ten days before things really started clearing up down there and it was agony. But there was a plus side. The whole process was rather like a snake shedding its skin – a bit messy and uncomfortable when you're only halfway there, but when it's over, well! It was even more beautiful; it was like a brand-new penis. As a matter of fact, I'm surprised that the sort of people who sell Botox to elderly women and suggest that you pump the fat from your arse into your lips to make yourself look a little bit plumper and poutier haven't started selling genital-wart liquid as a way of rejuvenating your tired undercarriage, because mine was sparkling and brand new, as smooth and rosy as a newborn's cheek with ne'er a sign of a wart. So Dr Patel's methods may have been suspicious but the end results were all I could have hoped for. I did ask my publishers if they would like a photograph to accompany this piece, but they have stopped answering my calls.

All I want for Christmas is Everything

They say that as you get older your memories of recent events grow harder to hold on to or to summon up, while incidents in your childhood and early adulthood return with crystal clarity. Which, when I was young, used to scare the life out of me. I thought the older version of me would hate to be bumming around not knowing what happened yesterday or the day before, whilst wallowing in the crisp memory of what happened thirty or forty or fifty years ago. No wonder old people keep losing their keys and mobile phones – they think they left them in the 1930s.

Of course, back then I hadn't realized that there is a plus side. With the benefit of time and distance, even mundane events take on a far more interesting hue. A walk down to the shops that I made last week doesn't bear dwelling on, but if I try to recapture the sights and sounds that accompanied a similar event back in 1985 or 1972 then it's oddly thrilling. The different cars, the shops that no longer exist, the haircuts, the deformities – all those little details that I took for granted at the time are now delicious treats to be savoured at leisure. So I've come to the conclusion that memory adjustment is one of Nature's brilliant design features because, when I think about it, what happened to me last week is of no real interest to me. I love watching my children growing up, and wandering around with my dogs, taking a nap after lunch and so on, but it's all pretty mundane, to be honest. My life has settled into a happy routine. What I do one week is broadly similar to what I did the week before, and that's exactly the way I like it.

As you get older you cling more to routine and regularity and you don't like surprises quite as much as you used to. Or loud music, reality TV or too much excitement of any sort. You don't really want to go out and have a wild night that will go on for four or five, six or ten hours longer than it should. You no longer want to wake up in someone else's bed, or a skip, or spend the whole night ricocheting around town then hang about waiting for a night bus.

A perfect evening for me is to get home quite early, browse the internet and bid for something I don't really need on eBay, chat with the wife and kids, stroke the dogs, watch a bit of TV and, after dozing off in front of whatever is on, head for bed. Normally at about ten thirty. Then it's into my PJs, do a wee, brush and floss, do another wee, make sexual advances to the wife – and as you get older, it doesn't really matter whether they are accepted or not, because, frankly, just the thought that you *might* get your leg over is very nearly as satisfying as the real thing. And considerably less tiring. Nowadays, just lying next to a nice warm human and a small furry dog is a pleasant enough way to end the day. Then do another wee, and sleep, trying not to wee again until morning.

But the prospect of being able to remember the sixties and seventies clearly is growing ever more exciting to me. I'm not quite old enough for it to have kicked in fully yet, but already some distant events are beginning to shimmer into focus. It's like suddenly finding a pair of glasses designed for looking into the memory distance. Although the fact that I can still remember the recent past means that I must currently be wearing the equivalent of bifocals. Maybe that's something opticians could develop: memory glasses that help people to see back to 1965. It would make for an interesting eye test when you went in for a check-up. 'Can you see the past clearer now . . . or now? Do things seem happier with this lens . . . or ten years further back?'

That reminds me of a conversation I had with Vic Reeves and Bob Mortimer in the early nineties. They were new faces on TV back then, and my company at the time, Channel X, had been lucky enough to get involved with them. *Vic Reeves Big Night Out* was essentially a show that Vic and Bob had created and performed as a raucous live event in various pubs and clubs in south-east London. We just streamlined it and filmed it for TV. But hanging out with the two of them was not only inspirational, but also tremendous fun. One of their flights of fancy involved thinking up the single as-yet-uninvented new invention that would transform your life for the better. I can't remember what I came up with, but either Vic or Bob suggested a sort of projector hat that, when worn, could project an image of whatever memory you summoned up. The noblest use of this, we all agreed, would be to project images of all the bosoms you had been lucky enough to get a look at, so that your friends might also enjoy admiring one of Nature's greatest gifts. It would also give the owner of the hat and of the memory a chance to have a longer, more leisurely look themselves. All too often a young man rushes through these moments looking for the greater gratification that lies maybe thirty minutes ahead. But with our patented Projecto-Helmet™ you could linger as longer as you liker. If any millionaire investors are interested, I think I still have Bob's early sketch detailing the procedure. Come on, Sir Alan, we could make a fortune!

Anyway, it's nearly Christmas and at this time of year I often find myself thinking back to Christmases gone by. Those that I've celebrated with my wife and our children are still clearer for me than the ones when I was a kid. But there are a few that I do remember from when I was young. Or maybe it's the family stories of those events, retold so many times, that have lodged in my head, rather than precise recollections of what really happened. Holding on to memories on purpose is tricky, isn't it?

I can recall, with alarming clarity, half swimming, half standing in a swimming pool in the grounds of the Walt Disney World Resort with my friend, Danny Baker. We were on a family holiday together, and while the children – all tiny then, all big now – frolicked and splashed in the water we discussed just this topic – how fleeting memories are and how tricky it is to hold on to those precious moments. Danny had a theory – which works, but is flawed. If you really want to grab a moment and hold on to it, despite its best attempts to wriggle away, then you need to do something large and loud and deliberate while forcing yourself to lock the memory in. Together we counted to three and shouted 'NOW' very loudly indeed. A family near by all rushed from the pool in horror and a passing pregnant woman had to sit down as her waters broke. But certainly that memory has stayed with me. Here's the flaw in Danny's otherwise brilliant discovery. It's all well and good if you want to preserve the sort of moment that won't be utterly ruined by you screaming out loud and pinching yourself to lodge it in the brain bank. But I don't think a first kiss, or the moment your children are born or when your wife-to-be says 'I do' will in any way be enhanced by you shouting out 'NOW' at the critical point. Furthermore, of all the memories I wish I had held on to with absolute unwavering clarity, the sight of Danny Baker in a pair of trunks finishing off a can of lager while a pregnant American looks on disapprovingly doesn't even make the top thirty.

Anyway, Christmas. I've always loved Christmas. I love having a nice tree in the house, seeing the lights twinkling inside and out, the evocative smells, the cold. Having the chance to go shopping with the family. I buy presents for relatives and friends and all the people I work with, which means that, as I've become more successful and the number of shows I do has grown, my Christmas list has become rather on the long side and I'm buying presents for close on two hundred people. Admittedly, for around a hundred of them it's champagne and biscuits, which isn't too great a strain on the ingenuity, but since you hope they'll think of you when they're eating the biscuits, you want to make sure you choose good ones. If you give people a packet of Rich Tea they're likely to think, Happy Christmas, you miserable, unimaginative, lazy bastard. But a nice box from a nice place, that's a lovely gift, so much better than a book token or a pen. I always order about ten or fifteen more than I think I'll need, because inevitably I'll have forgotten a few people. One of the added benefits of this is that when everyone's finally sorted out, there are always two or three boxes of quality biscuits left over, which I give to myself as a Christmas bonus.

This is no accident. I deliberately adopted this approach after spending a little time with the uniquely talented film director and artist David Lynch, who I interviewed way back when for a series of specials for Channel 4 on unusual film-makers. The other three in the series were Aki Kaurismäki from Finland, Pedro Almodóvar from Spain, and the brilliant but quite possibly insane Alejandro Jodorowsky from all over the place but now living and reading tarot cards in Paris. I found it tremendously exciting to be interviewing them all, but Lynch in particular, as I had been a huge fan of his ever since I saw his first feature film, *Eraserhead*, back in about 1978.

Anyway, I spent a few days with Lynch in Seattle, where he was working on the TV series *Twin Peaks*, which had just begun. Many of the meetings we had took place in various coffee shops that he had frequented over the years, and he never failed to order himself a little piece of cherry pie or a doughnut when he had a coffee. How on earth he wasn't magnificently obese I still haven't figured out, but did he ever love pie. When I asked him about his pie-eating proclivity, he simply replied that you should give yourself a little gift every day. It was one of those oddly simple statements that immediately made sense. He didn't mean you necessarily had to buy yourself some pie, or even buy yourself anything. He just meant, I think, that you should find a moment or two to reward yourself and administer a little shot of happiness, whether you'd done anything to deserve it or not. I have adopted his sanity-saving approach to life, although my self-giving might be getting out of hand. What started with one little thank-you a day has ballooned and I often now give myself ten or twelve presents a day. Indulgent, I know, but trust me, it takes the sting out of middle age.

I may not celebrate Christmas in the same way my family did when I was a kid, but though they didn't have much money, both my parents always made a big effort, and I suppose that's where my love of the festive season originated, instilled by my mum, in particular. Back then Mum's idea of decorating a tree was covering it with so many baubles and so much tinsel that the tree itself disappeared. Basically it would become a large, triangular pile of synthetic glitter in the middle of the living room with a faint piney smell seeping out from underneath. If so much as a glimpse of green could be seen, if there was a pine needle sticking out or a little bit of bark showing, she considered it a failure. A lovely day, Christmas was. We always had nuts, and tangerines or clementines, which we never saw for the rest of the year.

Come to think of it, what is a clementine? How does it differ from a satsuma or a tangerine? How do any of them differ so greatly from a small orange that they deserve their own sub-category? An apple is an apple is an apple and the same pretty much goes for pears. But these seasonal mini-oranges are a little too full of themselves, if you ask me. They smell nice, though.

It's good to have treats you keep just for Christmas – it's

what makes it special. We always had Christmas dinner together, and there was always at least one big tin of chocolates. Though with about ten people swooping down on them – six kids and two grown-ups, plus a couple of rogue uncles who'd invariably turn up – they never lasted long. It was about that time that I mastered a simple act of sleight of hand that I still occasionally employ today at premieres and swanky functions. As the tin is offered you pick one, but grab at least two more and conceal them in your palm, making sure that they get transferred as quickly as possible to a pocket or, failing that, your cuff or your dressing-gown sleeve.

It takes some perfecting, though, and you need to be prepared to get caught a few times and receive either a Chinese burn or a 'dead-arm' – that delightfully well-placed sharp punch in the shoulder that causes numbness for hours, so beloved of big brothers when they catch a younger, greedier one stealing. Luckily I have never been caught out at a premiere, although Jeff Goldblum nearly caught me palming an extra mini-burger at the post-premiere party for *Jurassic Park*, and I imagine he can give a good dead-arm when the need arises.

For us kids, the presents were, of course, the biggest excitement. My parents scrimped and saved to get us lovely things, albeit often second-hand, and put a lot of thought into them. Not surprisingly, my fondest childhood memories of Christmas involve gifts. These are my top three, in ascending order.

At number three is my Styrofoam glider. I was fascinated by flying toys and my heart's desire was a remote-controlled plane. Obviously my mum and dad couldn't afford one of those – they're hugely expensive even today – so they got me this

Styrofoam glider, which must have been about three and a half feet long with a wingspan of about three or four feet. You assembled it by inserting one giant wing through a pre-cut hole in the body, bunged a few stickers on it, took it outside and threw it into the wind. Simple as that, but man was it fun.

Christmas Day that year was cold and fresh, with a piercingly blue sky, but there had been no snow since winter arrived and the pavements were dry and clean, so to me it didn't feel like Christmas. It was how I imagined the weather might be in Finland or Norway when there wasn't any snow: almost too clear, too clean, too bright. There wasn't much wind, either. All the same, I went out on to Wanstead Flats with my glider, wrapped up reasonably warmly, if not as warmly as I should have been, and spent a delirious hour or so chucking it into the sky.

Wanstead Flats was essentially just a big patch of flat grass with a bit of forest round the edge. It wasn't especially nice, being largely flat, hence its name, and a bit scuffed and scrubby, with a fair amount of dog poo and cowpats. I was never sure where the cows came from but some days you'd go out and there'd be twenty or thirty of them there. They must have belonged to someone, but there were no farms or farmland near by, and we never saw anyone deliver them or take them away. Anyway, it was a good place to ride your bike in summer, and the flatness was broken up by one tiny little hill near the back, which came in handy as something to aim for if you went for a run. From there I was lucky enough to catch an occasional breath of breeze that lifted my glider and carried it a pretty impressive distance.

I loved that glider, and it lasted, oh, a good couple of days before, inevitably, one of the flimsy Styrofoam protruding bits, a rudder or something, snapped off. I decided to stick it back on with Airfix glue – just the job, I thought, seeing as it was specifically meant for model planes. Unfortunately, having been designed for hard plastic planes, not Styrofoam gliders, it immediately melted what was left of the rear fin. I watched in dismay as what had once been a proud, jutting limb dis-integrated into a sort of amputated stump before my eyes, and that was that. I have come to realize over the years that I am not an especially talented fixer of things, and DIY is to be avoided whenever possible, but the sadness I felt as I watched the glue eat into my lovely plane was immense. I had to steal several extra chocolates from the Quality Street tin to get over it, and by then the only ones left were the hard toffees and the orange creams, so they didn't really help that much.

At number two is *the* most expensive present I ever had as a kid: a Chopper bike. We all got one, all five boys, and my little sister got a girl's version, which might have been a Chipper, or a Tomahawk, I can't remember – I'm still waiting for the 'bikes' segment of my long-term memory to come back into focus. Anyway, Choppers were for boys and if you were a girl you could have either a Chipper or a Tomahawk, so it was one of the two. We were amazed and delighted, because Choppers, with their funky Hell's Angels-style seats, their dramatically high, forked handlebars and the gearstick centred on the crossbar, with its ever-present risk of castration, were *the* latest thing. I think my parents bought them from a catalogue, to spread the cost, and spent the next twenty years or so paying for them. In fact, my father may well still be paying for my Chopper to this day. But if he is – Dad, it was well worth it, because we were just so thrilled. Being kids who didn't often have brand-new toys, it was the most fabulous thing ever.

We didn't mind at all getting second-hand stuff, but one year there was a toy whose history I was a bit more familiar with than I'd have liked. I used to play with a boy from a nice family across the road. He was a bit younger than me, but I graciously overcame my age-based sense of superiority because he had Thunderbirds Four and Two. Four was the little yellow one that went under the sea. Two was my favourite: the green one that looked like a slightly squashed gherkin and carried the other vehicles in its belly. He had carved his initials on the undercarriage so that no one ever nicked it.

Not long before Christmas it disappeared. He told me that his mum and dad had cleared out his old toys to make room before Santa brought the new ones, and they'd given it to the school fête. Fair enough, I thought, even though I was disappointed that I wouldn't be able to play with it any more. Then, when I opened my presents on Christmas morning, I unwrapped a Thunderbird Two with some tell-tale initials carved on the bottom. I was surprisingly pleased. Granted, I was a tiny bit embarrassed to know that my Christmas present was a toy I'd been playing with all year and which had clearly belonged to someone else, but I was so made up to get the Thunderbird Two that it didn't really matter. I used some of Dad's sandpaper to remove my mate's initials and it was as good as new.

But back to the top three, and at number one . . . the best present I ever got. Bizarrely, it was neither big nor pricey nor

especially fun to play with, and it certainly never attracted anything like envy or was coveted by my friends. It was a small
figure of a deep-sea diver made of soap, attached to a rope. I've
no idea why I was so fond of this thing, but it just goes to show
that when it comes to capturing a kid's imagination, the amount
of money you spend is irrelevant.

What I actually wanted that year – which would have been
1969, I think, when I was nine – was the new Major Matt Mason
man in space doll, presumably rushed out by Mattel while the
moon landing was still reasonably fresh in our memories. The
Major Matt Mason man in space was a fantastic toy, a small
spaceman in a white spacesuit with black bendy bits at the arms
and knees so that you could position him as you liked, thanks to a
kind of wire frame inside him that held him in shape. He also had
a removable space helmet. He came in a blister pack with his own
little space-track vehicle and, in some versions, with a
jet-pack which had a thin bit of string running through it and a
hook you could attach to a door or window frame. When you
pulled the string he'd climb slowly up it, or shoot up fast if you
were brave enough to yank it hard. There was also an endless
range of accessories for him – the Major Matt Mason star seeker,
the Major Matt Mason space shelter, space probe, space crawler,
fireball space cannon, supernaut power-limbs – you name it. He
was just a great toy and I really wanted the one with the jet-pack.

I did eventually get it, but not for years, and of course now,
thanks to the wonders of eBay, I have every single Major Matt
Mason toy ever made, and I dust them and love them and play
with them nearly as much as I would have done if they had been
mine back when I wanted them most.

Anyway, in 1969 I was given this little soapy man instead, which you might think would have been a crushing blow. But there was something about this soap-on-a-rope deep-sea diver in his old-fashioned helmet. I don't know whether it was that he smelt nice, or was so neatly carved, or the notion that I could have him in the bath with me, but for some reason I grew very, very attached to that fella. So attached that, of course, I didn't want him anywhere near the bath in case he wore out. I kept him safe in his little box. His helmet looked a bit like a space helmet, I suppose, and I somehow convinced myself that he was a very rare, multi-tasking and ultimately superior version of the original Major Matt Mason himself, even though he was made of soap, didn't bend and was obviously ill suited to space travel. Improbably, he remains the favourite toy of my childhood, which I hope seems rather sweet and not just mental.

The first Christmas Jane and I had together was before we were married, in the first flush of our youthful romance. I say youthful because Jane was only sixteen when we met; I was actually twenty-six, but of course acted much younger and much more stupidly than she did, so we made a pretty good match.

Once we'd moved in together, planning our first Christmas in our own place was great: it was exciting doing everything for ourselves. We went out of our way to get a nice tree and decorated it painstakingly, we ordered loads of good food, quality champagne, mince pies and so on and invited some of the family over. With everything more or less ready for the big day, we went out on Christmas Eve and came back to find everything in a terrible state. A table lay on its side, the tree was in a heap on the floor and there were smashed baubles and decorations strewn all over the room.

At first we thought we'd been burgled. It turned out, however, that one of the two beautiful white cats we had then – a Persian called Bella and a chinchilla called Bea – had wreaked this havoc. We'd noticed that Bea had taken a liking to our tinsel. Instead of the traditional furry-looking tinsel my mum always had, we'd gone with the more minimalist, modern, thin strips of silvery stuff that was hip in the late 1980s, the kind you hang and drape rather than wrap around the tree. It was too much of a temptation for Bea, and she had been pawing at the strands on the lower branches. Evidently she'd found she liked the taste and had started eating them. Having exhausted the accessible bits, she'd taken to climbing higher and higher into the tree to get more.

Piecing together the events of that night – and this is pure conjecture, because of course we weren't there – I think she must have jumped into the tree and realized, too late, that it was not half as sturdy as the proper trees rooted in the ground outside. After clinging on for a while, and probably eating a bit more tinsel, she brought the tree crashing down, knocking over the table. Amid the ruins, she more than likely decided she might as well polish off the last of the tinsel.

We managed to reinstate the tree, got hold of some more decorations and smartened the place up before Christmas Day, but unfortunately that wasn't the end of it. The tinsel wasn't as easy to digest as it had been to eat, and the poor cat obviously had it working its way through her for days, until it finally came out the other end, still glistening beautifully but now enhanced with blobs of poo attached to each long strand, which she couldn't get rid of, presumably because the other end was still halfway up her intestines. So just as we were welcoming our guests into the house she'd be running around, trailing a length of what looked like silver string from her arse with three or four small brown nuts attached. Quite festive in a way, I suppose, but not really in keeping with the stylish ambience we'd envisaged for our first Christmas as a proper couple. I'm glad we went with the thin strips of tinsel though – imagine how uncomfortable she'd have been with the fluffy stuff hanging out.

When Bea had kittens, I learnt early on, and excruciatingly painfully, that they had inherited her mischievous streak. Just thinking about it now has me wincing. Funnily enough, it was Christmas time again. The day before Christmas Eve, Jane and I had at long last moved into a new house with our first daughter, Betty, who was six months old, having been promised by the builders renovating it for us that it would be ready before she was born. Now it was finally finished, or at least, finished enough to be habitable, and we were so excited to be installed in a place that really felt like home in time for our first Christmas with our beautiful baby. With Bea having recently produced a brace of soft, snuggly white kittens, everything seemed as perfect as it could be. Until, on Christmas morning, the upstairs boiler stopped working.

The house was one of those narrow, terraced jobs laid out over four floors and the previous owners had built up into the attic. It wasn't huge, but because of the height of it, the builders thought it would be a good idea to have a boiler at the very top to heat the upper floors and the water for the bathroom, as well as one in the basement serving the kitchen and living room.

Now the upstairs one was buggered, and there was no chance of getting anyone out to fix it for several days. It wasn't the end of the world – the boiler in the basement was OK – but we still faced a chilly Christmas with no prospect of a bath, which wasn't exactly the cosy idyll we'd been looking forward to.

My pride as a new homeowner, husband, father and general provider for my little family's basic needs was at stake, and I wasn't going to let the small matter of my complete ignorance of plumbing or indeed my general uselessness around anything mechanical stand in my way. I had maybe one spanner in the house, but I was determined I was going to fix that boiler myself.

In the event, I never did get to mend the boiler, because it wasn't actually broken. It had simply overheated and been locked by its safety mechanism. All you had to do to restart it was press a small button on the side, but for some reason the plumbers had not thought it necessary to show me this handy device, the useless bastards, and there was no mention of it in the glossy pamphlet they'd left.

So, armed with my spanner and the useless pamphlet, and dressed for the job in a slightly dirty white bathrobe, I went up to the attic and set to work. I cleared a path through the boiler housing and, sweating and swearing, tried in vain to make sense of the pipes leading into and out of it. I banged it a few times and twiddled a couple of knobs. Crouching red-faced in front of the stubborn metal box, I didn't notice that my exertions had woken up the kittens, who had been asleep on a blanket near by, and who, too young to have any fear of a half-naked, red-faced man waving a spanner, were now delightedly eyeing the two dangly kitten toys bobbling and jiggling enticingly under my robe. Or testicles, as you and I would recognize them.

As I wondered whether I should keep on banging or try twiddling something else, they pounced. One missed; the other, however, found his target with brilliant accuracy. I let out a yell and leapt to my feet, walloping my head on the cupboard door-frame and dropping my spanner, which would probably have been more use in loosening the grip of the kitten than in anything it had achieved with the poxy boiler.

My head throbbing and my balls in agony, I backed out of the attic with the kitten still hanging there, its tiny claws embedded in my sagging scrotal sac. If you are a man over thirty-five, or know one intimately, you will be aware that it's around this age that over three decades of gravity, combined with general wear and tear, begin to have a lengthening effect on the scrotum. This experience, I can assure you, did nothing to help slow down the process, and now that I'm in my late forties my balls are so low I'm often tempted to tuck them into my socks before playing tennis.

While I'm on this delicate subject, I'm reminded of the time I showed my balls to the Spice Girls. This is back when they were huge (the Spice Girls, I mean, obviously). They had been appearing on Comic Relief where, as part of the general jollity, it was agreed that they would give Griff Rhys Jones and me big, crazy kisses if people rang up and pledged enough money to see it. I can't remember whose idea this was – presumably mine or Griff's. Anyway, to add to the so-called hilarity, I was wearing a kilt. I forget whether there was an actual Comic Relief point to this or whether I was just going through one of my phases where I thought I looked good in something which could quite clearly only be carried off by a chisel-jawed, twenty-year-old male model with a flawless six-pack. But wearing a kilt I was, and with nothing under it, either. I have no idea why, but after the kissing – I think I got Baby Spice, but if my memory hasn't focussed properly then please forgive me, girls – as we left the stage and made our way back to the dressing rooms, all feeling a little cheapened by the stunt, I thought I'd lighten the mood by giving the girls a treat.

'I'm not wearing any pants!' I shouted in a vaguely harassing manner.

'Prove it,' said Scary, I think – if it was one of the others, please forgive me, etc.

So I bent over and flicked up the kilt at the back, expecting an admiring chorus and maybe even to be chased by a bunch of sexually aroused Spices and forced to hide in kindly old Stephen Fry's dressing room or take shelter behind Lenny Henry's magnificent frame. But no. Instead they let out a collective groan of disgust, and Scary – this time I'm positive it was Scary – exclaimed, 'My God, they're droopy!' We then stood around for a short while not really knowing what to say. I blame those kittens.

There's Always Rambo

So far, I've been pretty lucky with the whole inevitable getting-old thing. Still all my own hair, more or less all my own teeth, and aside from a minor injury involving a Frisbee that means I will always see small floating black objects in my right eye, no major accidents to bitch about. My hair hasn't even started to grey yet, aside from a rogue patch on the lower left quadrant of my chin when I grow my summer beard. My left, your right, in case you ever want to verify. I haven't checked my pubes recently so I can't comment on them, but I think they're hanging on in there as well. Certainly they're not falling out, and there's no grey. Do people go bald down there? I suppose if they did they'd keep quiet about it. Maybe there's a special room at the men's hair-transplant clinic where you can go and have some plugs inserted downstairs as well.

I am also lucky – thrilled, in fact – to have got this far in life without ever injuring another human being too badly, either emotionally or physically. I did manage to get both my younger brothers knocked over once, and they both had to go to hospital, but they got to come home afterwards, and what's a broken collarbone among brothers?

Mum made me promise that if I was out alone with the younger boys, without an older person to keep an eye on us, I was never to try to cross the high street with them. But surely she knew it was an impossible promise to keep? After all, the fish-and-chip shop was on the other side of the high street, and if you timed it right and went to the chippie after the lunchtime rush they'd normally be happy to give polite young boys a free bag of 'crackling' – our name for the little bits of batter and tiny, overcooked pieces of potato that gathered at the bottom of the big silver trough they scooped the chips out of. They were especially prone to giving these freebies out to young boys who happened to have even younger, cuter boys in tow, and so, despite my promise, I fairly regularly forced the younger brothers to make the journey.

Nothing ever went wrong when we took the zebra crossing, but that was a good hundred feet away from the chip shop, and on that particular day I suppose I just couldn't be bothered, so we waited for a gap in the traffic and ran over together. No problems getting there. But once we'd got our bags of crackling I tried a new road-crossing method, one that did away with all that tiresome looking-both-ways-for-oncoming-traffic stuff. I steered us towards a reasonable-sized gap between parked cars and told the boys we'd run over on a count of three. With a mouth full of crackling, and not bothering to check if anyone was driving towards us, I counted, and then shouted 'NOW!'

Trusting and fearless, they both ran out into the path of an oncoming Ford Anglia. (I don't actually know what the car was, but I've plumped for the Anglia because there were a lot of them about and I thought it might help to set the historical picture. It seems about right, too, because they weren't seriously injured, and anything much bigger or more solid would surely have finished at least one of them off.)

Much of the next twenty-four hours is a blur. I dimly recall being asked what happened, and I lied, of course. They ran out before I could stop them, I said, and after a while I almost began to believe it myself. They came back from the hospital that afternoon, one with minor cuts and bruises, the other with a cast that covered his arm and much of his shoulder. If they remembered what had happened they never said, but even if they had and I'd been asked to explain myself, I couldn't have done so. I thought about it a little and was never able to understand why I'd been so relaxed about their safety and the Green Cross Code – a lesson that had been drilled into me and my generation by countless road safety commercials, starring everyone from Alvin Stardust to the cast of *Dad's Army* to that rather poor home-grown superhero the Green Cross Man.

Maybe I did it to get back at him. He was rubbish – a dozy-looking bloke with a West Country accent. I knew there weren't any real superheroes out there, but I also knew that if there was one he wouldn't have talked like he'd just finished a cream tea and was off to geld a lamb. 'I warnt be thar when you crozz the road,' he used to say, and he hadn't lied.

One thing I do know, and it rather surprised me, is that I didn't feel particularly bothered, and I certainly didn't cry.

I don't think this was because I was a boy and boys weren't allowed to cry. Along with how to bake conkers and check all hedges and bushes on the walk home from school for hidden stashes of pornography, this was one of the few things I had learnt about being a boy that I knew was adhered to by all other boys. Crying, like skipping and rounders, was for girls. And although I really liked rounders, and liked the look of skipping, I had managed to avoid letting anyone know they appealed, and had been equally successful in not crying, ever. Even the one time I got punched in the face at school, on purpose, by a boy who later became one of my good friends, I held it in. But it makes you wonder, once you get old enough to be comfortable about admitting to liking rounders, where they go to, those tears.

If I've learnt one thing about the universe it's that nothing just disappears – it finds a way of sneaking out via a back route, and although I kept them tamped down for ages, those tears were just waiting for the decade when they could get out.

It was a simple commercial that first made me realize this. One of those mini-films that seem to cram more into their thirty seconds on air than some feature films do in their two-hour-plus running times. And while I'm touching on that touchy subject, why are films so bloody long these days? It used to be that cinemas screened two films, so they had to be no longer than ninety wonderfully economical minutes each. Then they did away with the double feature and film-makers started to relish the extra space, which is fine when you're telling a story as complex as *The Godfather* or *Lawrence of Arabia*. But did the last Batman film *really* need to be nearly three hours long, and so bloody dreary with it? No. So stop it with the too-long films.

Anyway, I was watching TV in America with my wife and the kids, and the adverts came on. This particular commercial started with a nice blonde girl arriving for her first day at her new college. She pushes into her room and sees a little Goth girl sitting there, curtains drawn. The blonde Barbie one opens the curtains and introduces herself and puts the framed picture of her very straight boyfriend next to the Goth's pic of her boyfriend, a Marilyn Manson wannabe. The girls look set to hate each other, giving proper eyes and ting as the kids might say, until they sit down and open up the same laptop. By the end of the commercial the Goth has draped her python around the valley girl's neck and you know they are going to be best friends, for ever and ever. Or until one of them buys a different computer.

Just another commercial, a straightforward piece of sales-manship designed to persuade mums and dads to buy their little girls a computer that will win them friends, or at the very least not antagonize the scary-looking person they may wind up sharing a room with. Nothing even remotely intended to tug on the heartstrings, right? But for some reason this particular ad reduced my wife and me to tears when we first saw it on TV while on holiday in Florida. Big, fat, salty, silly, embarrassing tears. We held hands and laughed, but we were actually, properly, crying. Over a stupid ad about a stupid girl and her stupid computer (a Dell laptop with Intel inside by the way). Of course our kids thought this was hilarious, and started watching us for other emotional outbursts, which seem to happen increasingly often and for increasingly inappropriate reasons.

Is it just us or does everyone get a lot soppier as they get older? Do you cry more? Do you find yourself moved, at times, to excessive displays of emotion over the most pathetic little things? I've noticed it more and more. Some films you expect to get emotional in – *ET*, for example, and I cried like a pinched baby during *Toy Story 1* and *2*. But I think a grown man might expect to feel reasonably safe when settling down to watch the *Sex and the City* film. I welled up repeatedly – not just when Big proposes to Carrie and when he gets the rooms knocked through to make a really huge lovely wardrobe for her. Those scenes are guaranteed, designed even, to moisten the eyes. But when Carrie gave her assistant the handbag she'd always wanted I wept a fresh flood of tears, and it hit me that I had to do something about this phenomenon. It's embarrassing. I even cry while watching films that I only partially engage with, and don't necessarily enjoy that much. The moment I start thinking about how much my kids, or even other people's kids, would enjoy a moment of silly sentiment in, for example, *Horton Hears a Who!* then out come the tissues. It's got so bad that I now make sure I have a small, man-bag-size packet of tissues with me at screenings and near by when watching TV, just in case.

I think I know what started this awkward state of affairs, or at least when the emotional gates began to creak open. It was just after my first child was born. We were in Los Angeles, probably a work-related thing, and I needed to see the newly released Robert Altman movie *The Player*. Great film, and I enjoyed it all the more for not having heard much about it beforehand. But I wasn't prepared for the rather nasty, rather real act of violence in the middle. If you haven't seen it then skip the next sentence. Here's the spoiler: there's a fight, a scuffling kind of struggle, and one of the men involved slips and I think hits his head and dies. Now I've seen a lot of violence in films, and occasionally will deliberately seek out movies with lots of cool, fun fighting in, like the Bond movies or anything starring the great Jackie Chan. But of course that never seems 'real', and you always know when it's going to kick in, and ultimately no one you care about gets hurt – it's always the bad people, or nameless thugs. But this scene seemed rather too real, too plausible, too horrible to deal with. I almost got up and left. I couldn't cope with it. I immediately thought of Jane and Betty waiting at the apartment we were renting and felt I had to rush back there to check they were OK. I didn't – I stayed and calmed myself down and watched to the end.

It's pretty natural that the emotional lurch involved in becoming a father would have repercussions, and although I guess the old 'boy-training' enabled me to keep things in check a little longer, gradually I welcomed the change. I began to feel genuinely connected to those around me in a way I never had before, and if in return I had to show a bit more emotion to the rest of the world then so be it. But now, sixteen years later, still sniffing and snivelling and sobbing my way through commercials for pasta sauce and welling up when I hear any of the songs from *The Wizard of Oz* or catching just two minutes of *Big* when channel-hopping, I'd really like a break.

I'm thinking of starting a group, a sort of Alcoholics Anonymous for the easily moved. We'd sit in a circle in a church hall and, after announcing our age and that we were a big old cry-baby, we'd share stories about stupid things that had triggered us off. To finish we could punch each other in the face and watch the last Rambo movie on DVD and pretend for a couple of hours that we didn't care about our families, or global warming, or abandoned puppies, like in the good old days. Before we became men.

Cheesy Wotsits and Other Looks I Have Worked Unsuccessfully

Over the years I've acquired a reputation as something of an outlandish dresser, which, against all odds, I'm proud of. I've never seen the point in running with the crowd just for the sake of it, and growing up when I did, hitting the latter part of my teens as the punk-rock movement got into its stride, meant my fashion sensibilities were shaped at a time when outside the mainstream was the only place to be. Up till then, my concept of individual style was more of a negative than a positive one, as I tried to live down my parents' laudable attempts to foist an assortment of hand-me-downs and catalogue purchases on to my very tall, very thin and very puny frame.

I know you wouldn't believe it to look at me now, in the full magnificent bloom of middle age, but as a child I was an appalling sight to behold. Trust me, I was monstrous, grotesque, terrifying, like an elongated gargoyle that had leapt down from a parapet to scare the villagers. Strangers would look at me on the streets or the bus and shake their heads, tut-tutting as if this mockery of a young man had been created deliberately to insult them. It hurt at the time, sure, but it has served me in good stead. When I now head out into the world wearing tweed shorts that are clearly not appropriate for a grown man, or a jacket fashioned from plastic with plywood accents, or a tie made of leather and feathers – all actual items I have owned over the years – the reaction from my fellow men and women no longer stings.

There was one incident, however, which occurred at Disney-land in California, that managed to pierce my armour. It must have been around 1989, as I was with my wife but we didn't have children yet. We had both desperately wanted to visit Disneyland as kids, but foreign travel and expensive holidays abroad were not for the likes of our families. So as adults we seized the chance and headed off together. I had no idea what you were supposed to pack for a theme park, never having been to one before, so I did what I normally do when faced with a new experience – I went for the gaudy, dressing-up option.

Day one was fine – we both wore jeans and cowboy boots and cowboy shirts and hats. We thought we were being slightly ironic and cute – everyone else just thought we were from Austin or Dallas or somewhere else in the middle of America. Day two, I pushed the boat out. I wore my finest new purchases from London. Black, voluminous yet somehow also revealing linen shorts, a stripy shirt and – the masterstroke! – black crocodile-skin chisel-toed slingback sandals. I had known they were for meant for me, and me alone, the moment I laid eyes on them in the swanky shoe shop in Chelsea owned by master cobbler Patrick Cox. They were magnificent. Magnificent and insane. Magnificent, insane and rather uncomfortable, prone to chafing around the heel, which resulted in some very painful blisters.

Before you ask, I am not, nor ever have been, a cross-dresser; I'm not remotely interested in women's clothing unless it is being worn by women themselves. Or has just been removed, or tragically is just about to go back on. Women are a vital part of the equation if I am to appreciate stilettos or blouses or puff-ball skirts. I have no desire to see them on me or any other gentleman. So my excitement at finding chisel-toed slingbacks for men was not because I thought I had found a crafty way of buying women's shoes for myself – I just loved the theatrical silliness of them.

So I bought them and had been waiting for the perfect opportunity to parade about in them, and for some reason thought that a day out at a theme park in the sweltering heat of the California summer was the ideal moment. I was wrong. Even sophisticated, educated people might have looked askance at someone dressed as I was that day. But many of these people were from remote parts of America, and they hadn't enjoyed the liberating side-effects of punk and post-punk attitudes. They still thought it was OK to call people names based on what they imagined their sexual preferences might be – preferences they did not approve of. Some merely tried to look as disgusted as possible and drew their children towards them, and away from me. If I had been a predatory paedophile, as my shoes seemed to be signalling to the majority of those in Disneyland that day, would I really have taken so much time and trouble dressing up to look the part? That's what they might have asked themselves if they hadn't been so busy looking around for things to throw at me. If I had been hoping to abduct their sons or daughters, surely I would not have chosen to do so in shoes that I could barely stand up in, much less walk or run in, after just half an hour queuing for Peter Pan (still one of my favourites, by the way). I still have those shoes somewhere, and I hope one day to catch up with Patrick Cox and ask him exactly what he was thinking when he came up with that particular design.

By the age of thirteen, I had shot up to six foot one without filling out in any way – I probably still weighed no more than three, perhaps four stone. As I have described elsewhere, I was also painfully shortsighted, and my hair was still cut by Mum, which, it has to be said, wasn't purely an attempt to economize, although with six kids that must have been a big factor. No, the main reason Mum bravely decided to pick up the scissors and give it a go was that the only hairdressing salon near us – or barber's, as this was in the days when hairdressing salons were the province of women – was a place on the corner next to the junk shop in Leytonstone High Road, owned and run by an elderly Maltese gentleman, a master craftsman who had perfected two styles: really short and horrible or slightly longer and horrible. Eventually he did allow some younger blood, possibly his sons, to come into the business, and they promptly jazzed the place up with adverts for Durex and replaced the pictures of James Mason and Rock Hudson in the window with those of David Soul and Paul Michael Glaser, then riding high in the popularity stakes as Starsky and Hutch. What red-blooded young man didn't want hair and a cardigan like Paul Michael Glaser? None I knew, that's for sure. But by then we'd got used to the passable and free job Mum would inflict on us. Her home cuts looked fine when they were freshly done, but as soon as you washed your hair or slept on it, suddenly it no longer resembled the lovingly shaped halo she'd tried to create, and small bits would stick up and out all over the place, and no amount of patting or slicking down with tap water could make them stay down.

Already you will have formed a fairly accurate picture of my younger self. But now let's put clothes on the mannequin, and let's dress him in cast-offs. To be fair, the stuff available for boys and young men in 1960s Britain, whether new or second-hand, was utilitarian at best. Children's clothes were not miniature versions of adult fashions as they are now. There was nothing flamboyant or fancy.

My mum did her best: she has a photograph somewhere of my two older brothers and me looking very dapper in outfits she was clearly very proud of. She'd managed to get them from a shop somewhere in north London that imported children's clothes from Italy, where kids were dressed with a little more panache. But in Britain, children spent most of their time in either grey or brown until the 1970s, when we were allowed colour for the first time. I suspect that it's no coincidence that kids started dressing a little more brightly at about the time that colour televisions came on the scene and shamed parents into upping their game a bit. My junior school uniform was a dark-grey blazer and trousers with a white shirt, which inevitably turned grey after a number of washes. Jumpers were grey or brown, or, for really dressy occasions, brown with a grey pattern or vice versa.

Even when I moved up to secondary school, which wasn't quite as strictly uniform-based, more or less everything I wore to school was essentially mud coloured. I had a pair of flared herringbone trousers, which you might think would have rather appealed to me, and indeed, for quite some time, while they belonged to my elder brother Paul, I did look forward to owning them. My mum and dad had originally bought a pair for each of my older brothers – both brown, of course – when flares were the latest thing, but not for me. Maybe they couldn't find them in my size or couldn't afford another pair, or maybe I was too young for grown-up long trousers at the time. Whatever the reason, I eventually inherited Paul's, which would have been fine if it hadn't been for the fact that by the time he'd finished with them I'd had a growth spurt and was about four inches taller than he was. So they were hand-me-downs from an older, shorter brother to a younger, taller brother. Maybe that should be hand-me-ups. Either way, they flapped around several inches of exposed ankle.

I suspect they had been bought from a catalogue. In the days before everyone had credit cards, catalogue shopping was a popular way of acquiring stuff you needed or wanted immediately but couldn't afford to shell out for in one hit, because you just paid off a little bit each month. My parents were regular catalogue buyers, and for a brief spell when I was about twelve or thirteen, they even had a shop selling on catalogue goods that customers had sent back.

I've no idea how Mum and Dad made this discovery, but they

found out that the catalogue companies couldn't resell any returns as new, even though there was nothing wrong with them beyond the fact that they didn't fit or the customer just didn't like them, and so all this stuff went to big depots where it was sold off at knockdown prices to other retailers or anyone else who had the necessary credentials or whatever magic wand was required to gain entry. It gave my parents the idea for their shop. With access to the depots, they could buy good-quality stock, for which they knew there was a healthy market, very cheaply, sell it on cheaply and still make a modest profit.

It was a very exciting project, and when I think about it now, I admire my parents hugely for making a go of it. As far as I know, they had no experience of retail or wholesale – or any aspect of the selling or reselling business, come to that – but they set it all up themselves, finding premises in nearby Leyton, equipping the shop and investing their own money in it, and it was pretty successful.

I think my mum, in particular, very much enjoyed the adventure. With all six kids growing up and beginning to do their own thing, she liked having an interest of her own outside the house and family. She was the driving force behind the look of the place. She went for a 1920s ambience (in the early 1970s, when the fashion store Biba was reaching its zenith, art-deco-influenced interior design and anything involving cloche hats or flappers was highly trendy) and came up with the name Anything Goes, which, instantly evoking as it did the Cole Porter song of the same name, cleverly encapsulated both what was for sale there and the period feel she was aiming for. Although they got a local sign-writer to paint the name in art-deco-ish lettering above the front door, the reality was that it was a rather grotty little shop on a rather grimy road in east London.

I remember it being fairly busy, especially when it first opened. Locals thought it was great to be able to get clothes and shoes at such reasonable prices, and all brand-new, not seconds: it was only that the packaging had been opened and the stuff had been tried on. We kids would go over to help Mum out and I spent several afternoons on my own in the shop, which was always fun. Not that you got up to much or anything out of the ordinary happened, but it was surprisingly exciting to feel that you were part of something, on the ownership side of the fence. To be there when Mum or Dad opened the door first thing in the morning or closed it at night gave me a real thrill. It made me feel special somehow, made me think our family were special, and even though the success of the place was rather short-lived as the quality of the stuff they could buy gradually deteriorated, for the first six months or so I couldn't have been more proud if they had turned around and told me we owned Harrods.

Of course, the returned-goods depots were also a valuable source of kit for us which my parents wouldn't otherwise have been able to afford. I have a vivid memory of my mum and dad coming back one day after stocking up with various toys and other bits and pieces, among which I discovered an Evel Knievel stunt-rider set. This was something I'd had my heart set on for ages and I was over the moon. It was one of the must-have toys of the moment, which in my circle at school usually meant we would all talk about it for months without ever actually seeing one up close, then move on to the next object of desire and fascination, which, chances were, we'd also not get to experience until we turned forty and eBay entered our lives. I asked if I could play with it and my dad said yes. I took this to mean that I could have it, so I removed it from its packaging, stuck the decals that accompanied it on to the motorbike and the ramp it would fly over, and put that little mother through its paces. By the time my dad came in to see what all the noise was about there can't have been a patch of wall or an inch of soft furnishing that bike hadn't skidded over or crashed into. He pointed out that by 'play with it' he had meant just that. I shouldn't have put the stickers on and I shouldn't have knocked seven bells out of it.

I was more than a little deflated. Deep down I'd known it was for the shop, not me, though it's rather sweet that my dad hadn't objected to me opening it up to have a go with it. But it was with a heavy heart that I peeled the stickers off and tried to get them to stick back on the decal sheet they had come from. And it was a sad little Jonathan that packed Mr Knievel back into his cardboard bed to go off and be loved, and hurled into windows and over television sets, by someone else's little boy.

Actually, if I'm being honest, I'd have to admit the chances are I ended up keeping that toy, but I like to imagine that I had to give it back, since this is one of the few incidents I can offer as evidence of my heartbreaking formative years in the vain hope of appealing to those of you who enjoy a good misery memoir.

It was mainly clothes that came to us via the catalogue trade, though, and it was rarely stuff we would have actually chosen. Being such an odd-shaped child – I grew into a fairly odd-shaped adult, come to think of it – clothes could not always be found that fitted me properly. Ankles and wrists were normally a little more exposed than was the fashion, and few things I wore ever really looked as though they were intended for me, if you know what I mean. Then there were my feet. They were enormous: size eleven. Now that I'm a powerful and heavy six foot one and a half, they don't seem wildly out of proportion to the rest of me; in fact, I'm quite pleased with them. They're a decent size, not monstrously big and not effeminately small. They give my legs a nice finish and I can wear flares or drainpipes and they look fine at the end there.

But having a pair of size elevens from about the age of ten when you're not yet your full height is no joke, and I was incredibly self-conscious about them. I felt as though all eyes were constantly drawn to my feet. Every time I stepped out of the front door, I imagined people were looking over, seeing a perfectly normal person and then doing a double-take when they spotted these gargantuan plates of meat sticking out of the bottom of my trousers.

My parents were vaguely aware of my discomfort, I'm sure, but it didn't trouble them as much as it troubled me – quite rightly, because it wasn't as if there was anything actually wrong with my feet. One day my mum and dad came back from one of their supply runs and announced they'd got new training shoes for all of us boys, which caused great excitement. This was before training shoes became the footwear of choice for all young men, and they were still something of a novelty. The idea of wearing what were supposed to be games shoes all the time seemed pretty radical.

Personally, I was never a huge fan of the training shoe, from a sartorial point of view, until I recently discovered an eccentric range made by a Japanese company called A Bathing Ape, on which subject I may digress for a moment, because I'm very fond of my Bathing Apes. I have quite a large collection of them, in fact. According to the creator of the brand, the designer Nigo, the name combines a homage to the movie *The Planet of the Apes* with a reference to a Japanese saying about apes bathing in luke-warm water, used to imply that the younger generation is spoilt, pampered, complacent and happy to just copy each other. I think. Anyway, the Bathing Ape trainer is the equivalent of the customized car. Like pimped Nikes, they boast an array of unusual colours, big stars on the side and go-faster stripes. And yes, I know it's hideously inappropriate for a man approaching fifty a) to be concerned about what kind of training shoes he's wearing and b) to opt for the flashiest, most obscure brand he can find, but there you go, that's me in a nutshell.

I think my Bathing Ape habit goes back to this first pair of trainers I had that were designed for daywear. Just as the homo-sexual community has adopted the once cruel slur 'queer' and used it to empower themselves, and just as African American rappers have stolen 'nigger' from the mouths of racists to hurl it back as a badge of honour, so in some small way does my adoption of the brashest trainers on the block as my day shoes of choice redress the shame and pain caused by the events I am about to relate – or am I making way too much of this?.

Anyhow, my brothers and I opened these boxes enthusiastic-ally. We all had trainers in different colours and, though I can't recall now what my brothers' were like, I do remember that theirs were fairly normal and nice. Mine, as well as being, for obvious reasons, the largest of the lot, were also the most revolting bright orange. A luminous, glow-in-the-dark orange.

So orange you could barely looks at them without sunglasses. They were almost identical, not just in colour but also in texture, to Cheesy Wotsits. You know, those snacks covered in an artificial cheese flavouring that look radioactive; horribly tasty things that you should never start unless you're prepared to finish the whole bag – and to have slightly furry, cheese-smelling orange fingers for several hours afterwards.

So imagine, if you will, this kid in trousers ending a couple of inches above the ankle, teamed with giant orange shoes. That was me. I looked like a clown. Flares, drainpipes, nothing worked with them – well, can you think of anything that goes with Day-Glo trainers? No, I thought not. Unless you needed to leave the house dressed from head to toe in high-visibility orange to avoid being knocked over, there was no earthly reason to put these things on your feet.

At school, a kind-hearted teacher who meant no harm took me to one side and asked me what was wrong with my feet. He thought that my trainers were some sort of corrective footwear, and perhaps he was right. Who knows? With hindsight, I'd have been wiser going barefoot. At that age you try to see yourself as a kind of James Bond in the making, picturing in your mind's eye how you might stroll elegantly into a room or a bar in some foreign hotel, and everyone will stop and admire the charismatic, immaculately dressed, sexy stranger that is you. As it was, whenever I entered a room people would glance up, then down at my impossible-to-ignore footwear, and either fall backwards from the glare or just laugh uncontrollably.

I wore those Cheesy Wotsit trainers for about a year and a half. I lived in fear of somebody coming up to me on my walk to school in the mornings and offering me a job with a travelling circus. It was perhaps at this time that I developed the break-neck walking pace that I employ today, much to the chagrin of my wife and kids, who are normally to be found a hundred yards behind, red faced, trying to keep up. But it's not you I'm striding away from, lovely family. It's the past. It's those shoes.

Faster, slimmer, bendier. Working towards a better me

Are you a self-improving kind of person? Don't panic, I'm not judging you, and I'm fully aware that there's no right answer to this question. You say yes and it makes you sound a little desperate, maybe a self-loather, if there is such a term. You say no and you sound lazy and a little smug – what could there possibly be to improve about you? But I struggle with it, because over the years that have whizzed by since I left full-time education I've become increasingly aware of just how stupid and ill-informed I really am, and how little I exploit my full potential.

Of course, I may just be deluding myself – maybe this is as good as it gets. Maybe I am destined to spend the rest of my time on this planet never speaking another language fluently, never drawing gasps of admiration from both men and women and maybe even dogs as I strip down to my Speedos on the beach. Perhaps I should just accept my embarrassing lack of knowledge of world events and my inability to tell you the name of more than one current African leader (and a bad one at that), and resign myself to having no real idea why the Bank of England keeps putting up interest rates then lowering them again. Perhaps this ignorance is just the way it's meant to be, and I should simply settle into the role of happy-go-lucky idiot and enjoy my time.

But I can't. Deep inside me, like a horribly perceptive and honest tapeworm, something tells me I should and could do better. I am driven by an urge, a compulsive desire to be, I don't know, a sort of sleeker, more knowledgeable, more sophisticated and worldly version of myself – the kind of person that I like to think people might imagine me to be if they saw me on a long flight with the right type of luggage and a very smart-fitting suit, my appearance giving no hint of what I actually do for a living but guaranteeing that I am well travelled, well read and great company. There would possibly be sunglasses, maybe a hat of a sort that hasn't been seen for a while, like a flat cap from the fifties that matches my outfit perfectly. But not the kind of hat that suggests I am trying for that look. Oh no, it has to seem accidental and effortless – like speaking another language should be.

I'd love to be able to say more than just hello to the air hostess in her native tongue. Imagine being able to hold a proper conversation in Foreign, never knowing which subjects you might touch on but being confident you had the necessary vocabulary and verbs to carry it off. I can speak a horribly mangled sort of French, in which hand gestures and facial expressions play as important a part in conveying meaning as the words themselves. Even then I often find myself in trouble. On a holiday to the South of France a few years back I managed to exchange a few words with the nice young man who brought drinks out to the sun-loungers. He admired my suit – a nice loose Vivienne Westwood thing in linen that I'd bought on the internet. He was almost definitely just after a larger tip, but I was so excited to be having a conversation in French with someone who spoke next to no English that I blundered on. I have since worked out that I told him I had chosen it especially to wear on the snow, and that I was sorry my children had injured the hotel pigs. That is as good as it gets and probably always will be. I'm pretty sure I'll never be able to hold a conversation about French, Spanish or Chinese politics in any of those respective tongues that is not only knowledgeable but somehow manages to be funny as well as perceptive. But rather desperately, that's the kind of person I want to be.

I don't want to sound too hard on myself here, as I'm pretty certain that the majority of us Brits can't manage more than about fifteen badly pronounced words in anything other than English. But why can't I be more like Stephen Fry? That's who we all want to be, really, isn't it? Slimmer, maybe, and a tiny bit more conventionally attractive, and – in my case, at least – heterosexual, but essentially we all want to be Stephen Fry. And I'm not even close. Maybe that's not entirely a bad thing. In fact, come to think of it, I feel a bit sorry for Stephen Fry – he has no one to aspire to. He is perfect already – his work is done.

For me it's the result of coming from an old-fashioned, working-class background of the sort that you don't see so much any more. Neither of my parents actually finished proper education – they both left school just before they were sixteen. My mum was sixteen when she had her first child and my father was eighteen. That's when my eldest brother was born, on Dad's eighteenth birthday – which by today's standards seems almost illegal, but was pretty much par for the course back then. Now everyone waits until they're about forty-five before they have their first child, especially men, thinking that they're somehow missing out on their youth if they don't still go snowboarding when they are essentially middle-aged.

I'm sure that's one of the reasons why divorce is so prevalent today, because all these twattish forty-five-year-olds can't deal with the fact that they aren't twenty-two with their whole future in front of them any more, so they ditch the wife and kids and all other inconvenient reminders that they're getting on, and swap the Previa for a Porsche, and find a young girl who's too polite to tell them how ridiculous they look, and try to have a second go at life. Which is both greedy and wrong. My parents, however, certainly tried to 'better themselves', a weirdly old-fashioned phrase today. And they wanted us to do better than our circumstances dictated we might.

You would think that with around twenty years of attempted self-improvement behind me I might have achieved something by now, but I haven't, really. I think it's because I try to do too much. Maybe if I had the self-control to focus on one thing, I might actually get somewhere. Proof of just how thinly I am trying to spread my ability to learn is to be found in my loo. This is a list of books in my toilet right now: there is a history of punk, a history of Pinewood Studios, a history of modern Japanese art, another history of punk, this time focusing on the

Roxy Club in London, and then there's *Why Pandas Do Handstands* by Augustus Brown, a sort of natural history trivia compendium, and *Firsts, Lasts and Onlys: Military* by Jeremy Beadle – the same sort of book, but full of strange facts culled from military history. *Utterly Lovable Dogs* is next – not really self-help, I know, but the pictures are so cute that I normally reach for that one first. Then there's a pamphlet that I got from a men's health mag which promises perfect abs in thirty days, right next to four volumes of poetry. *Four.* I don't even like poetry that much. I like a few, the greatest hits – wandering lonely as a cloud, we are hollow men, etc. – but I don't like poetry anywhere near enough to justify four volumes of new stuff, some positively experimental. There's a George Sanders novel, *Steppenwolf* by Hermann Hesse, and finally, minus the cassette it came with, a dog-eared copy of *Teach Yourself German*.

Now the majority of these, especially *Teach Yourself German*, I don't think have ever been opened, and it was wildly ambitious of me to think that even someone who enjoys going to the toilet as much as I do would spend enough time in there to actually learn a foreign language. Anyone straying into my toilet unprepared would be a little worried about who they might encounter in the rest of the house. A gloomy, German-speaking, poetry-quoting punk with spectacular stomach muscles and several cute dogs. Sadly, that perfect man is yet to materialize.

It's not only in my toilet that you'll find evidence of this relentless quest for a better me. If you were to look in what we laughingly refer to as my 'home office' – which in actual fact is just a room where I keep my comic collection, answer my emails and play video games with my kids – you'd find any number of abandoned books and so on. They are always quite practical, though, which I like to think is a saving grace.

You won't find copies of *Men Are from Mars and Women Are from Somewhere Else*, but you will find a collection of cassette tapes – that's how far back it goes – and CDs, providing language courses in a number of tricky foreign tongues. Japanese, for instance. I have three complete and very expensive courses, which, to be fair, I persevered with enough to be conversational at the most basic level with any Japanese tourist. I could ask them where they are from and tell them whether the weather is nice or bad – information that they could probably work out for themselves. How useful it actually is I don't know, but it's very nice to be able to say 'Nice weather, isn't it?' in Japanese to a passing Japanese person, if only to see the look of astonishment that crosses their face because they're so unused to anyone outside of Japan knowing any words other than 'sushi' and 'kamikaze'.

The downside is that I am so excited by this small trick that I will approach anyone who looks vaguely Japanese and ask them how they are and give them a weather report. I have so far embarrassed myself in this way with passing visitors from Korea, China, Thailand and, on one memorable occasion, Wales.

My collection also includes courses in French (I have never even opened this, having mastered how to mangle the language already at school – but one day I might get around to it); German (one of which I bought, one of which I was given and complements the book in the toilet that's never been opened); Cantonese (or is it Mandarin? Anyway, it's one of the Chinese languages – and I've no idea why I bought that one). It gets worse, because on the top shelf I have – only opened once, which presumably seemed like more than enough – a starter course on CD that I purchased for myself in Farsi. Farsi!

Why did I ever think I would want to learn Farsi? Why did I think it was a good idea to spend money, which presumably I'd worked at least a little bit to earn, on this particular CD box set? I've never even met anyone who speaks Farsi. It is spoken by people from the country formerly called Persia and now, of course, known as Iran. Actually, I tell a lie. I did meet someone who spoke Farsi once and she was very nice, but her English was so fluent that the need for Farsi didn't arise between us. So why on earth I wasted my money on a Farsi starter set remains a mystery.

You'd have thought that possibly, while buying self-improvement books, I could have picked one up called *One Language Is Enough: Why You Don't Need to Learn Any More, Just Concentrate on your Abs* and left it at that. But no, I've got the Farsi. And you know what's even more tragic? Several times I've tried to tidy up my room and get rid of stuff that I don't need or which might be of more use to someone else, and every time I've taken down the Farsi CDs and looked at them, and then put them back. That's right, I'm holding on to them because part of me still believes that one day I'll find the time and the necessary inclination and willpower to sit down, put on a headset and 'repeat after me' how to say 'Hello, what lovely weather we are having' to a passing Persian.

Perhaps I shouldn't be so hasty to tar everyone with the same brush here. I don't really know enough about the psychological make-up of women to be sure that they feel the same way.

Maybe having a womb and the birth-giving capability circumvents the need to learn enough to be able to show off in public. However, I can assert with confidence that men (with the exception of Stephen Fry) all feel the need to work on themselves. Essentially, the males of our species are just dogs that have learnt to walk upright.

I'm not saying anything here that women haven't already figured out for themselves or that men wouldn't freely admit to, if they didn't think they were going to be judged too harshly – all we're interested in is eating, sleeping, rutting and occasionally having something not too demanding to divert our attention: you know, a pretty female or a football match. That is where we stand on the scale of things. I'm not saying this to blow our cover, fellas, I just think it's time we acknowledged it, and I think acceptance is a very valuable first step in learning to live with the opposite sex.

I'm not going to get all preachy on you now. I'm not going to start giving you my top ten tips for how to make a marriage last or stay in a relationship, because frankly I have no more idea about that than anyone else. It is a remarkable challenge to put two adults in a confined space, encourage them to breed and then see if they can stay together for longer than about nine months, and I don't know how Jane and I have managed to pull it off. We've been married for twenty years now and I'm still none the wiser. But I do know that every day enough things happen between us as a couple to make us want to stay together. But I'm not going to offer you any advice, so you can relax and rest easy.

Instead, I am going to offer you an observation about the

man-dog similarity when it comes to sex, because short of actually grabbing hold of an attractive woman when she walks past and humping her leg, there's very little to choose between us.

Most men are so easily swayed by a pretty face that that's all they focus on. I know many men who are fairly civilized, urbane, sophisticated and successful, who nevertheless think they would be happier spending their time with a partner who is gorgeous but stupid, rather than someone they can actually talk to. It's a tragic fact that most men are only really interested in the surface.

But there is a cure. Recently, one of our dogs had his testicles removed. He's the youngest of our dogs and, perhaps partly because he's Jane's pet and partly because he's our youngest, we were a little bit more indulgent with him and didn't have the knackerectomy performed quite as speedily as we had done for the others. So Sweeney held on to his little chestnuts for longer. What a lovely little pair they were, really smart and neat. He's quite a dark dog and his testicles were even browner than the rest of his body. Imagine if a top designer had encased some small peanuts, perhaps, in beautiful dark crocodile skin and then given them a lovely, highly buffed wax polish. That's what they looked like, surrounded by a small, spiky bush of pubic dog hair – very attractive, very attractive indeed. Not unlike an hors d'oeuvre I once saw in an expensive restaurant, which might have had something to do with scallops or possibly sea-urchins. It was too pretty to eat, as indeed were this little dog's balls.

Anyway, they were a lovely little set but he was getting a bit too randy, and Princess, the only female dog in the house, was on heat and we'd never got around to having her done and he was bothering her pretty much constantly. She only had to walk within ten feet of him and you could see his little ears prick up and his nose twitch and off he'd go with his slowly emerging lipstick, desperate for action.

Now that's not dissimilar, I'm afraid, to the way I am with my wife. I can't help it, I'm a man. We are hard-wired that way. When she walks into the room the first thing I do is check out her breasts and the second thing I do is try to evaluate mentally, using some kind of ancient masculine arithmetic handed down instinctively from father to son, whether or not the combination of her mood, the look on her face, the situation, the amount of natural cover, and the general wind-chill factor in the room add up to a possibility that we will be having sex in the next forty or so seconds.

Now seeing Sweeney sitting there comfortably, one week after having his nuts removed, completely cured of his terrible compulsion to rut at every opportunity, I can't help but wonder whether I might not be better off without mine. And I'm sure many men have thought about this as well. Little Sweeney just looks so happy with both his exterior testicles and his inner demons removed in one fell swoop. You can even have fake ones put in – they've got these prosthetic ones so you look as if you still have the full package. In actual fact, you could probably choose the size and shape you wanted and actually go one up on what Nature gave you. I've always wanted to have quite large, round, soft ones, rather like peaches. Mine dangle a bit and the one on the left is a little bit lower. This is very common, or so I'm led to believe.

Not having ever spent much time with a lot of naked men, on

a desert island or in jail, for instance, I've never actually had the chance to study anybody else's for long enough to find out just how common it is. But I wouldn't mind mine both hanging an equidistance from my body and being a little bit fuller and a little bit softer. And just think, if you didn't have your testicles any more, you wouldn't flinch every time a ball came hurtling towards you. Obviously a lot of popular American film comedy – especially films involving children – would have to look for a different punchline to those scenes that rely on an adult being hit in the bollocks for a laugh, and *You've Been Framed* would be a very short programme. But surely that's a small price to pay for a saner world. And if they could whip them off and teach you Farsi at the same time, I'd definitely be first in the queue.

A TRULY GREAT NIGHT OUT

It might surprise you to know that I am not a fan of strip clubs. Nor do I frequent or secretly wish to hang out in lap-dancing joints. It might also surprise you to know that this is not because I have had a terrible or shameful experience in one, or that I find the seeming availability of lovely leggy nudey ladies, which turns out to be an illusion in that they are not really available at all, too much to bear. In fact, the first few times I discovered lap-dancing bars – that's right, I discovered them once, then went back and rediscovered them three or four more times just to be certain – I thought they were just about the greatest invention since penicillin or sliced bread. Or a penicillin sandwich made using sliced bread. With the crusts already off.

I can clearly remember filming in the USA back in the late 1980s, away from my lovely child-wife and hence also on vacation from normal behaviour. My working companions and I were very much in love with beer, and would always seek out new bars. This one was opposite the hotel, and it was only because the hotel itself had a very impressive beer-list and did twenty-four-hour room service that we hadn't strolled out before. But on the final night in Baltimore, I think it was, where we were filming an interview with John Waters for a series called *The Incredibly Strange Film Show* on Channel 4, we left the hotel and walked the 150 feet across the street to this late-night bar that also had strippers. It was a memorable and impressive experience.

We were, of course, drunk and everything always looks so much better when you can't really focus on it, which is why as TV presenters get older they sometimes ask for gauze to be put over the lens of 'their' camera, or even, I have been told, have Vaseline smeared on it. I don't think either of those old stand-bys will work in years to come, what with high-definition and all, so I'm buggered. Although I take some solace in the fact that no matter how grotesque, saggy, wrinkled or grey I become, I'll always be beautiful inside because I'm kind to small dogs and ugly children and I never try to upset anyone deliberately.

I was working as a researcher at the time, which is a job that covers any number of requirements, depending on the kind of show you're doing. For example, on a talk show you'd be involved in suggesting guests, then helping to book the guests, then getting as much information as you can find on a certain guest before compiling a list of possible question ideas that the host can consider. Then you'd have to help look after the guest and smooth their ego on the evening they turn up on the show, and then usually forget to write to them and say thank you afterwards. When you're working on a documentary it's a far more interesting and challenging job in some ways, in that you're often trying to source material or come up with facts and information that people aren't particularly keen on giving you, which you then have to find a palatable way of serving up in the finished show.

Now I had a job in the early eighties working for a company called RPM. They were one of the early independent production companies that grew up around the time of Channel 4's birth. More often than not these were run by people who had worked in the hipper areas of television, at the BBC in particular, who had seen a gap in the market and realized they could now make the kind of show that they'd always wanted to, but had struggled to make for the BBC, which was a far more rigid and stuffy organization then than it is today. And so they set up their own little companies and went out, in a rather romantic, noble and foolish way, to try and spread the word. Normally they'd make shows about popular culture, the arts or social issues that they felt weren't being covered properly elsewhere. And this company was one of those. It was run by a very lovely bunch of people, none of whom, it seemed to me, had an iota of business sense.

They were producing various shows, including music-based programmes, and there was also a very early talk show on Channel 4, which was my first exposure to that kind of thing. It was called *Loose Talk* and I was a researcher on it, even though when I got the job I had no idea what I was doing. My brother Paul, the eldest kid in our family, was working in television and he had got in through the proper channels. After leaving university, where he had studied English, he'd worked for a local paper for a while, so he had rudimentary but proven journalistic skills, and he had then found his way on to TV shows that required that kind of talent.

I, on the other hand, rather lazily saw being in TV as a very exciting situation that you could boast about and perhaps meet girls via. And it also seemed to pay far better than any other jobs that I'd heard of. So I was very keen to get in when I left university too and I kind of half borrowed, half stole Paul's CV and applied for various jobs. And the only company that would even give me an interview was this company RPM, who I'm pretty certain knew full well I was lying. But they were the kind of lovely people who were happy to give kids a chance, especially kids with a spark of something approaching genuine enthusiasm and talent, even though they didn't necessarily have the right qualifications.

So they gave me a job on this talk show where I was meant to be booking guests. Essentially, I sat there for the first two or three weeks in a state of mild panic, on the phone to any friends who would give me the time of day or occasionally even my mum, pretending I was speaking to David Bowie's agent or the person responsible for Queen's world tour or the publicist for the exciting group Wham!, who were new on the scene at the time. I was not terribly good at it, although I did book a handful of guests I was quite proud of having got on to television. One of them was the graffiti artist Keith Haring, now sadly dead. Others were Tom Waits, Neil Kinnock, who was just about to be announced as the Labour leader, and Pete

Townshend. Actually, now that I'm forced to think about it, they were all booked by a guy I worked with called Marek, who was far more talented than I was. I think the only person I genuinely booked off my own back was Diana Dors, the busty, blonde screen starlet from the fifties, who appeared on the show one week as a fairy godmother. Oh, and I gave Howard Jones his first TV appearance – remember him?

After the talk show finished I was out of work, and was obviously keen to keep earning, and also to stay in touch with my new acquaintances in the company. They told me that one of their new ventures was to be a co-production with a group called Interface.

Now Interface was a strange company, very indicative of the more overtly political nature of Channel 4 in its early days. The purpose of Interface was to integrate people with disabilities into the media. The idea was a very sound one in theory: to employ a group of people who might not normally be able to get work in a field where they were, and of course still are, woefully under-represented. People who were blind or visually impaired, deaf or hearing impaired, in a wheelchair or walking impaired, mute or speaking impaired – actually there weren't any mute people, I'll be honest with you, but I'm sure if we could have found one we would have employed them, just not put them on phone duty.

That's always a danger with positive discrimination – you wind up employing people for every reason other than their suitability for the actual task. But it was a genuine and laudable effort, and they asked me if I would be the non-disabled person in the team. Not that they needed one – I mean it wasn't like *The*

A-Team, where they already had the tough guy, Mr T, and the explosives expert and the really good-looking one and someone thought, Now let's get a young English kid. The reason for me being there was that I was meant to know enough about the workings of television to help those people who didn't and basically teach them the job, so I could then be edited out of the picture and it would be a company fully staffed by people with disabilities.

So I found myself working for this small company, making two or three documentaries. One was about the state of the compensation system in the UK, another was about disability and religion, though it's all a bit of a blur, to be honest with you. But I quite enjoyed the experience of working there. There was a lovely paraplegic guy. He used to be a tree surgeon and he had gone back up a tree to finish a job for an old lady and had forgotten to put his harness on again and had fallen. He hit a live power wire and bounced on to some solid concrete and snapped his spine fairly low down. He was obviously and understandably severely pissed off about that but he was a lovely bloke, a cheery, thoroughly decent Liverpudlian.

He was a pleasure to spend time with and I had a good couple of nights out drinking with him. One of which finished up with me having to carry him up six storeys to the council flat I shared with my then girlfriend, because the lift was broken. We were collapsing in fits of laughter because he was a fat bloke and out of shape and I'd already lugged his chair up and I now had him in a fireman's lift over my shoulder. It already seemed funny enough, but then halfway up the stairs, the bag which collects a paralysed gentleman's liquids burst all over me. I think it was called a kipper, and it was strapped to his ankle, and he used to wheel himself outside the pub and empty it into the drain. Very convenient. So I've got a fat bloke over my shoulder and I'm now soaked in his piss, and as we're struggling to make our way up the stairs, my neighbour, who always thought I was a little bit on the gay side, walks past. It probably looked like I was just desperate for some action and had dragged a drunk home and was forcing him up to my room. And the thought of how it must have looked as well as his not inconsiderable weight made me collapse, quite literally, in giggles. And unfortunately, quite literally in his piss as well.

I have very fond memories of my friendship with him, but there were a couple of other guys in the group that I didn't enjoy working with so much. One was a blind guy who was OK to start with, but he was quite strange. Years later he went a bit ga-ga – I remember him phoning me up once, claiming that they were talking about him on the news on Radio London. So I tuned in for him to see if I could reassure him, and they were discussing Princess Anne and horse-jumping. I thought maybe I had misheard him and he meant another station, but he was adamant. He told me that Princess Anne was the code word they used for him when they needed to discuss him on the radio.

I often wondered whether I was wrong to dismiss him as being simply unwell. Maybe he *was* being followed, maybe somewhere there's a thick file marked CODENAME: HRH ANNE. Probably not. So he kind of blossomed into full-blown nuttiness, but at the time he was just a little bit mad. And, although this really doesn't show me in a good light, I should own up that when I used to get off the tube for work in the morning, if I saw him walking ahead of me I used to tiptoe around him and run off to the office, because it was very hard work having to sit opposite him all day and listen to his nonsense. Part of me felt bad that I couldn't find it in myself to be more charitable, to find some extra reserve of compassion to draw upon and try to be a good friend. The larger part of me was just worried that maybe he was sighted enough to be able to make out my form as I dashed past him, holding my breath.

But – and the point of this story *is* appearing on the horizon – there was one guy I worked with – let's call him Peter – who was a very sweet guy, really nice. One symptom of his disability was that he tended to shake and twitch a lot, and he seemed to find it difficult to breathe and talk easily, unless he was very calm when he was more able to keep control. Anyway, he wanted to get to know me a bit better and so one day we went out for lunch, along with his carer, a slightly nerdy young guy with a wispy, barely-there beard. Christ, it was a long lunch.

The café we went to did an all-day breakfast, so I ordered the full English and so did he – I think it was partly a kind of matey all-boys-together kind of thing. They gave you a good portion for your money in this café, so there were a lot of beans on the plate, there were sausages, there was toast, there were fried eggs, there were tomatoes, there were mushrooms. It was a big old plateful. And I wolfed mine down in about fifteen minutes. But, of course, for him to eat, the bloke who was with him – the guy with the inexcusable beard who pushed him around and helped him get dressed and so forth – had to cut the food up into mouth-sized portions and feed it to Peter, who would then chew it as well as he could. But that wasn't something he could do easily and it was all a bit slow. On average I think a sausage would probably take about six times longer for him to eat than it would for me.

So I'd finished my meal and we were there for about another hour while he made his way through his. As the sun set at about four o'clock on that particular winter afternoon, I made a mental note to keep it down to just tea and toast next time.

On the way back he suggested we pop into the newsagent's. I bought a couple of magazines and he browsed along with me, and then he asked if I ever bought the top-shelf magazines. I did occasionally, but still felt a bit embarrassed doing so, which is the only sane way to feel. Even today, if I were to reach up and grab one I'd probably make sure no one was watching. Peter told me he wanted to buy them, but his bearded carer, or BC as we shall refer to him, disapproved and wouldn't stretch for them. This was in the heady first wave of political correctness when all liberal men went out of their way to appear as non-sexist and right on as possible, while secretly slipping a copy of *Penthouse* in between the *Guardian* and *Spare Rib* when they picked up the papers. So, to help Peter out, I grabbed one and we paid up and went back to the office.

Then Peter asked me if I would turn the pages of the mag for him because, as has already been established, BC did not approve. So I turned the pages and we were making slightly laddish talk together, praising the fabulous physique of the young ladies in the pictures and thanking their parents for doing a bad enough job of raising them that they would strip off for *Fiesta* or *Men Only* or *Knave*. Peter was clearly loving it, as was I to a lesser extent. We did have work to do, though, so I suggested we put the mag away and crack on, which Peter took as a cue to ask me to wheel him to the loo. Which was a bit strange because that was BC's job, not mine. But then Peter explained that he didn't need to go, rather he wanted me to finish what I'd helped start, and relieve him. Via a hand job. Now, I know I described the researcher's role on a show as being flexible and covering a lot of different requirements, but as far as I knew wanking off the boss wasn't one, so I decided to pass. Peter got rather cross. He felt that I had known where this was heading from the beginning. I had let him buy me lunch, I had harvested the porn, now I had to deal with the inevitable consequences. I try to see both sides of most situations, but I couldn't agree with him. To him, it was as if I had been leading him on. To me, I had merely been doing him a favour. To BC it was a bloody nightmare, because once Peter grew tired of sending me dirty looks he had BC wheel him off to the loo for at least twenty minutes of quality time.

Peter and I never really talked about that again, but a few weeks later, we were working late and he asked me if I ever went to strip clubs. Well, I never did. I once saw a stripper in a pub with my dad when I was a kid and it was quite an unpleasant experience.

I should point out that my dad didn't take me there on purpose. He was self-employed for much of his working life and at this point he had bought himself a Ford model A transit, a flatbed truck which he used to do deliveries and small removal jobs, and he used to employ me and my other brothers as a form of cheap labour. He used to bung us about a tenner a day. It might have been a fiver a day when we first started, but later it was a tenner. So I was working with my dad one day and at lunchtime all the blokes said, 'Let's go to the pub.' And I remember the pub clearly. It was a really rough joint called the Royal Standard in Walthamstow, up at the top of Walthamstow market, which was a big, noisy market, rather like the one you see in *EastEnders* but about twenty times longer and filled with genuine Eastenders rather than faux-enders. We went in there for a pub lunch, which back then meant maybe a sausage sandwich and three pints. If I was drinking, it would have been cider. I was only about fourteen but I was tall for my age, so I could get a drink quite easily without being questioned. Certainly, there were various people drinking in there who seemed younger than me, and I recall there was at least one pram. But to be fair the baby might not have been drinking, or if it was then it would have been a spritzer.

We were sitting there and this lady came on stage who hadn't seen fifty for several years. She was wearing glasses, a fake-leather skirt and some sort of top, which she took not too much time undraping. They say striptease is an art form – one of the great American art forms, alongside jazz, for example. Well, not the way this lady performed it. To be fair, she made a bit of effort, but the audience weren't really there for the act, they wanted skin. There was a bit of music, a rudimentary stab at dancing, and then she turned around, unzipped her top and out came her bosom. She then turned around, unzipped her skirt, and was down to just pants. In an attempt to stretch out the performance she looked out into the room, obviously hoping for a bit of audience participation, and who should her eyes rest on in the front row but me? A lanky, incredibly red-in-the-face fourteen-year-old wearing thick glasses. A gift, in fact.

She walked up to me and went as if to sit on my lap, much to the huge amusement of the men I was with and everyone else in the Standard. Then she took off my glasses, put them down her panties and danced off on to the stage. Now I am a minus nine in each eye, which isn't good. Even when I'm wearing contact lenses I'm only just about legally able to drive. If my eyesight gets any worse, I'll be entitled to a special parking permit. So she danced off with my glasses, and not only was I now incredibly embarrassed but I was also technically blind. And I had the beginning of an erection because, even though she was an elderly lady with no actual stripping skills, obviously she was alive and partially nude and for a boy of fourteen that's all that's required. I was by now in a state of panic. Panic that I had an erection in public. Panic that I didn't have my glasses. Panic that I needed to go to the loo and if I stood up then chances were the jeering, cheering rabble surrounding me would notice my erection, and panic that even if I did summon up the courage to stand up I probably would not be able to locate the toilets without my glasses and might piss in someone's pint.

Finally she came back with the well-travelled spectacles, gave them to me and I put them on. Unfortunately, I was still blind. I'm hoping it was the baby oil she'd rubbed all over herself, but the lenses were quite slimy and greasy. I then fumbled my way to the toilets, slightly crouched, hoping no one would notice my condition. What a terrible way to see your first naked lady.

So back to the anecdote. Peter had asked me if I would care to accompany him to a strip show. I told him that the only time I'd been before was that one time and that it was not a particularly fond memory of mine. But Peter was adamant that in a proper club I'd enjoy it, and said he was a regular at one of the places in Soho and that the people who ran it knew him and he was planning on going anyway but that, needless to say, old misery guts – meaning BC – didn't believe in that kind of thing, so he wouldn't take him. I agreed, providing it was clear up front that I was only going to help him get in the place and out of it again. An executive massage was not on the cards. He said that was fine – and told me he had now got a girlfriend who had moved in with him. So theoretically, Peter was sorted for the evening.

After work we headed over to Soho. There's a mnemonic for remembering the streets in Soho taught me by a taxi-driver: Big Women Don't Fuck Greeks – Berwick Street, Wardour Street, Dean Street, Frith Street, Greek Street. If I've offended big women or Greeks then so be it, but it's quite a useful way of remembering which street lies next to which.

So anyway, we were in the 'Don't' or the 'Fuck' part of that construction, either Dean or Frith Street, and we arrived at the charmingly seedy Sunset Strip, which might even still be there today. It was quite late at night and it was dark outside. Following Peter's instructions, I went into the reception and told them that he had arrived. They told me they'd open the side door, next to the main entrance, which led to a narrow staircase that would take him down into the basement where the action was.

As I bumped him in his chair down the stairs, we went past the changing rooms that the strippers were in. They all looked out as we passed, and on seeing Peter they greeted him by name. He really was a regular. There was something rather wonderful about that moment. The side door, the staircase, Peter in his chair, the semi-naked women in grotty rooms putting on their make-up and powdering their tits with glitter and greeting us warmly. I imagined I was Toulouse-Lautrec sneaking into the Moulin Rouge. Only taller, and pushing a wheelchair. And not wearing a top hat. And not able to paint at all well. Certainly, I was already enjoying the experience far more than that traumatic afternoon in Walthamstow.

We got downstairs, and I wheeled Peter past the audience and over to the back, where there was an area without too many chairs where they obviously accommodated the wheelchair connoisseur. So I parked Peter up there and sat slightly in front of him to his left, and the girls came on. They seemed to be quite happy, healthy-looking young women. They danced up and down, got nice and naked – it was a perfectly enjoyable way to spend an evening. As they got into it, so did Peter, who began to make appreciative groaning noises. He used to make this grumbling noise often, and when the girls were on I noticed that he got a bit louder. But I thought it best not to look round because I assumed he'd found some way of applying friction in the downstairs department to enhance the experience. That theory seemed about right, because the noises grew increasingly urgent and frenetic and loud. So what started as a kind of low-level mish-mash of syllables and vowels, sounding rather like an old Jewish prayer, became louder and louder, and I didn't want to look and spoil what was obviously an enjoyable but semi-private moment.

Finally, when one of the girls had finished dancing, I heard him call out my name quite loudly over the music, which was something of a surprise – I was worried he might have used some fantasy involving me and a full English breakfast to help him go all the way. I turned to find that he had got his little finger trapped under one of the wheelchair handles, and his violent movements, whipped up by the naked ladies, had been such that he had managed to break it. He had snapped his little finger. He had sat there for a good twenty minutes in considerable pain trying to attract my attention, which was difficult bearing in mind there was Abba playing at full pelt and a young Chinese girl showing off her marvellous dim sums. I felt terrible, but probably not quite as terrible as Peter did.

I bundled him back up the stairs, past the ladies in their gloomy changing nooks, who all came out to check he wasn't too badly hurt and to peck him on the cheek or forehead. Outside, BC was waiting, furious with me for not taking proper care of Peter, and I suppose he had a point, but I pleaded circumstantial distractions. Anyway, I said my goodbyes as BC drove Peter off to Casualty. I figured that would be the end of it, but the next time I saw him he had a different carer with him. Old BC had gone. It turned out that just before Peter finally got home to his girlfriend he had asked BC to wipe all evidence of the strippers' farewells off his face – and BC had refused. Peter's comparatively new girlfriend had been understandably pissed off that her boyfriend had come home really late, with a broken finger and covered in strippers' lipstick. She eventually forgave him, but Peter couldn't forgive BC for not wiping him clean, so he sacked him.

I have of course changed Peter's name from his real one for the purposes of this book, just in case he doesn't want whoever he's with now to know about his past. But if you're reading this, thanks for an unforgettably great night out.

Never Mind the Bollocks, Where's a Public Toilet When You Need One?

ow did I become this spectacular example of fully rounded, effortlessly sophisticated, worldly-wise maturity you see before you? It's a question I have never been asked. But if I were, I would offer up three main influences as I grew from boyhood to slightly older boyhood. One, as you already know, was comic books. The next was TV, and the third and probably most influential of the lot was punk rock. Punk was, for me, right up there with the adventures of The Creeper and Dr Strange and Herbie the Fat Fury – all personal comic-strip faves of mine and if you've never read them then do yourself a favour; you're never too old. But punk even overshadowed them for a while.

If you were to view my life as a slice of sedimentary rock, you'd see several years of nothingness: just a bit of general TV-watching and trying to work out if I would ever learn to fly by jumping off the couch. Then, at about eight or nine, when I discovered comic books, you'd come across a fantastic rainbow-coloured layer. That was when everything changed for me, and my monochrome universe suddenly exploded into full technicolour with stereo sound. After that, along came *Doctor Who* and *H. R. Pufnstuf,* and *Star Trek* and *Colditz,* and *Monty Python,* and a bunch of other TV shows that I grew addicted to. Then, at sixteen, it was all blown away by the thrill of punk rock, from which I have never fully recovered. It's slightly embarrassing to have to admit it, but more than anything I learnt at school, or from my parents, or from the day-to-day experiences at work and interacting with the real world, these are the forces that have shaped my malleable self into the man-monster that I am today.

When punk came along I was, of course, the perfect age for it. I turned sixteen in November 1976, just as it all kicked off. Unless, that is, you were one of the lucky few who were involved in the scene's embryonic stages. That was a fairly small group, maybe just one or two hundred people, who knew the bands or already went to the shops or hung out in the gay bars or went to the art schools that all helped to nurture the movement as it spread by word of mouth. As for the rest of us, punk didn't really come to our attention until the music papers picked up on it, usually only to rubbish it. And, of course, when the Sex Pistols made their infamous and unforgettable appearance on the teatime magazine show *Today,* hosted by Bill Grundy.

I remember only a very few key television moments from when I was a kid. One was being allowed to stay up with my dad to see Neil Armstrong and Buzz Aldrin take their first steps on the moon in 1969. For some reason my brothers weren't there, and my sister, who would have been tiny then, was tucked up in bed. We watched it together on a small black and white TV, and I couldn't quite work out whether it was real or not. I also have clear memories of watching *Monty Python's Flying Circus* with Mum and Dad – and, later, a Marx Brothers film with my brothers – and laughing so much I literally fell off my chair. And kept laughing on the floor.

But watching the Sex Pistols being goaded by Bill Grundy, a presenter who must have inspired the creation of Roger Melly in *Viz*, on 1 December 1976 was different. It was like someone had jumped into the television from the real world and shouted out to me to wake up and start living. It was incredible, and all the more remarkable when you look at it now (it's easy to find on YouTube). Rather than mad-eyed harbingers of anarchy and destruction, the Pistols and their fellow punks look like silly, slightly nervous kids having a laugh. It was only because of the dreary pomposity of TV and newspapers back then (as opposed to the desperate desire to appear hip that characterizes both media today) that it made such a splash.

In fact, if the incident hadn't been given so much publicity – *Today* wasn't broadcast outside the London area – punk might never have taken off in the way it did. But the *Mirror*'s decision to put the story on its front page, under the headline 'The Filth and the Fury', spread the word to the whole country. It made those of us who had seen these naughty kids show no respect for an authority that we all secretly knew was lousy and hypocritical feel like fabulous, dangerous rebels.

Nobody used the f-word on telly in those days, let alone before the watershed, which even today would be a bit of an issue. It was as if the Pistols had gone around and emptied a small bag of poo on the doorstep of every boring grown-up in the country. I was amazed, excited, shocked, horrified and, crucially, frightened. These blokes and the weird boys and girls in their entourage were pretty scary. When something both arouses and terrifies you, you're hooked. And so, drawn to this anarchic group of urchins who looked – although admittedly in their case it seemed to be through choice – as awful as I did, I took to reading the music papers avidly, awaiting the latest editions of *Sounds* and *NME* with the kind of feverish anticipation previously reserved for the imminent arrival of another issue of *Fantastic Four*.

It wasn't long before I met a kindred spirit, another Leytonstone teenager, whose imagination had also been caught by the notorious interview. I'll call him Steven. He lived at the end of my road, on the other side, and although I knew him to nod to as we walked past each other, we went to different schools so there was no chance we might be friends – until punk entered both our lives at pretty much the same moment. A few days after that fateful appearance by the Pistols, I noticed he had had his hair cut a bit shorter and looked to be wearing a badge on the lapel of his blazer.

The key signs that you were about to leave the normal world and become a punky outlaw were threefold: one, shorter, spikier hair; two, straighter trousers; and three, badges, possibly but not necessarily accompanied by a skinny tie and a sneer. They couldn't be any old badges, of course. Ideally they had the name of a punk band on them, or a swastika or a rude word. The swastika thing died out pretty quickly, I'm relieved to say. It was never about liking Nazis but about trying to shock people, and even then I thought it was in poor taste. I just didn't have the balls to tell anyone to stop.

I, too, had started wearing straighter trousers and badges, and had just asked my mum for a shorter haircut, and Steven recognized these signs in me. We crossed the road at the same time, met in the middle and became immediate allies. I can't say I ever liked him, to be honest, and I'm sure he felt the same way about me, which is to say he didn't feel much of anything. But you needed someone to walk around with so you didn't feel like a total tit, or risk getting beaten up for being a punk. You also needed to have someone to go to gigs with, or concerts as we rather prissily called them at first.

Until then, Steven's musical horizons hadn't extended much beyond Queen, who ironically had been booked to appear on *Today* that fateful night but had pulled out, allowing the Sex Pistols to sneak in when the producers got desperate. His parents' record collection was well stocked with stuff like the Stones, and I think they might even have had a Velvet Underground album, so they were quite hip, even if they didn't look it. His mum was a plump owlish little thing with glasses and his dad – actually his stepfather – was thickset and balding. He always reminded me of the bloke married to Olive in *On the Buses*. Seeing as his mum looked a bit like Olive as well, I'm sure you can imagine the mixed emotions I felt when Steven took me into their bedroom one day and we unearthed from his stepdad's sock drawer some fuzzy Polaroid photographs featuring his parents engaged in a spot of group sex. Two things of note leapt at me from the pics. Firstly, his mum had kept her glasses on, really old-fashioned National Health jobs, too, but they made the event somehow more absurd and slightly sexier at the same time. Secondly, his stepdad's face could not be clearly seen in any of the photos, but Steven identified him by his socks.

Now, I haven't ever been to a swingers' party, and don't really want to go – like bungee jumping and anal sex, they're OK in theory but I suspect the reality would prove a little too intense and uncomfortable. I was still very much a virgin at the time, and I assumed then, as now, that most people took their socks off before sex. And this wasn't just any sex, this was special-occasion sex. We could tell because they had peanuts and crisps out in bowls. Even if there weren't any house rules written down, you'd assume most gentlemen would take off their socks, if only to avoid looking silly. Steven produced the socks under discussion, a dark-purple pair, and they were without doubt the same as those in the picture. The mystery of why his stepdad kept them on as he entered another lady while his wife kept the nuts and crisps in circulation continues to haunt me to this day. Did he have a toe missing, or perhaps a terrible fungal condition on one foot? Maybe he had hooves, or his feet were an odd colour, or bionic. I shall never know.

Having established we both wanted to be punks, and having shared our dismay over his parents' leisure activities, we got to talking about going to an actual punk-rock concert. This was a pretty big deal because neither of us had ever been to any kind of live show before. We didn't have a clue how you went about it: whether you bought tickets in advance or just wheeled up and paid to get in. We didn't even know what you did when you got there. We had no point of reference: in 1976 there was of course no internet, but also no such thing as music TV. Hardly any music videos were made by bands, and those that were made didn't get shown that often. You could see live performances on telly occasionally, but they were normally shown taking place in pretty sterile environments, like the studio of *The Old Grey Whistle Test*. Even with our limited experience we knew that a punk-rock gig in a London pub or club wasn't going to be anything like that, and we were a bit scared about what it might involve. The music press had begun to write slightly more favourably about the bands, after their initial scorn. But the regular press enjoyed describing punks as little better than animals, and we were worried that there might be some truth in what they wrote, although of course that only served to add to the excitement.

After a few weeks we finally plucked up enough courage to give it a go. Our first gig – sorry, concert – was at the Hope and Anchor pub in Islington: we went to see X-Ray Spex, fronted by Poly Styrene, with Lora Logic on saxophone. It wasn't just how to comport ourselves at the gig that bothered us. We were really anxious about how we were going to get ourselves to the venue, because at that time there was what amounted to a turf war going on between the punks and just about everybody else. The Teddy boys in particular took exception to punks, which I suppose wasn't altogether surprising.

Although the Teds were roguish and had a whiff of the criminal about them, they were very smartly turned out in their Edwardian jackets, with quiffed hair and well-pressed tight trousers, and punks had started wearing a sort of demolished version of their look, including drapes with safety pins attached. They've almost died out now, the Teds, which is a shame. They looked great, in a cartoonish way, but I guess we have as much chance of seeing kids dressing as cavemen as we do of seeing another revival of the Teds.

Steven and I imagined there'd be Teddy boys wielding razor blades round every corner, and there was also a story circulating among the punks that Teddy boys liked to pin you to the ground while the Teddy girls stabbed you in the eye with their stiletto heels. I doubt that ever happened, but to two sixteen-year-old wannabe punks about to head across town to their first-ever punk concert it seemed inevitable. For safety's sake, we resisted the temptation to wear anything that would give the game away, dressing in jumble-sale jackets, with a skinny tie apiece our only concession to punkdom. Once we reached the Hope and Anchor – hopefully without incident – we would go into the toilets and attach the five or six safety pins and handful of badges that we'd carried with us, allowing us to mingle with both eyes still intact.

Of course we didn't see a single Ted, and no one gave us a second glance, but we felt like heroes for having made it there in one piece. The room where bands played at the Hope and Anchor was very small – it probably held only about 150 people – but the gig was just fantastic, it really was. It wasn't that X-Ray Spex were the best band in the world, but they were good, and dressed weird and were *interesting* and swore on stage.

It was also the first time I'd had the chance to try the pogo. This easy-to-master punk dance basically involved jumping up and down on the spot, wiggling your body a bit from time to time like a big fish, and occasionally attempting to spit towards the stage.

Among the tightly packed young blokes down at the front, it was the only form of dancing you could do. There weren't many girls down there. There weren't many girls at punk gigs anyway, and those you did meet weren't all that easy on the eye, it has to be said. But the problem with pogoing in the glorified cellar of the Hope and Anchor was the very low concrete beams in the ceiling. Seeing as I had stupidly positioned myself under one of the lowest, when I launched into my inaugural pogo I nearly knocked myself unconscious. It hurt, and I felt dizzy, and I managed to lose my glasses so I couldn't see, and of course I felt remarkably self-conscious. I had to go and sit down for the first couple of numbers, which I thoroughly enjoyed even though I was afraid I was going to be sick. Overcoming the mild concussion, I waded back in for the rest of the gig and started jumping and flailing for all I was worth.

The best part came on the journey home. Now fully comfortable in our new identities as genuine, courageous, anti-establishment punk rockers, Steven and I entered the old lift at the Angel tube station – one of those great big ones with an iron grille you slammed shut before it would move. Just before we did so, two of the band got in with us. We couldn't believe it. To us, the prospect of meeting someone, anyone, who was actually in a band was so remote it was like encountering a person from a parallel universe. Of course, that was one of the great things about punk: it swept away the barriers between us and them, between those who came to hear the music and those who made it. To make it even more exciting, one of them was

Lora Logic, the sax player. We told them we'd been to see them, how they were the greatest band on the planet, how we would be going to see them every time they played. I also decided that I had fallen in love with Lora Logic and would marry her. Neither of those things came to pass, but at that point it was a dead cert.

As our confidence as punks grew, we began to experiment a little with clothes. Punk turned up its nose at ready-made fashion, especially in the early days. Unless, of course, you had the dosh to buy your clothes at Seditionaries, formerly SEX, the iconoclastic and pricey shop on the King's Road set up and run by Malcolm McLaren and Vivienne Westwood. The punk spirit of improvisation and experimentation suited me down to the ground, as I never had any money and still wanted to spend whatever ready cash I had on gigs or comic books. We bought jackets and shirts from junk shops and ripped them up or customized them with spray paint.

I once only narrowly avoided being beaten up while wearing one of my more imaginative creations. I'd got a white butcher's jacket, or maybe it was a chef's jacket, from a shop that supplied the catering trade, splashed it with red paint to simulate splattered blood, written the words 'Psycho Killer' – taken from a Talking Heads song of the time – in big letters on the back and, the pièce de résistance, adorned it with plastic dolls' faces from a craft shop. These I'd customized by either sewing up the lips or burning out the eyes with a cigarette end. Actually, I probably didn't use a cigarette end because I didn't smoke, but that was the look I was striving for. The result was quite grotesque and I was thrilled. But the first – and last – time I wore my Psycho Killer jacket in public, I got chased for a mile and a half by a bunch of young fellas – not even Teds – who'd seen me from their white van and were so upset that they jumped out to give me a kicking. Fortunately they didn't catch me as I hid behind the bins in the back alley that served the local Southern Fried Chicken shack – the Box o' Chicken, it was called. While I was there I collected a handful of chicken bones, thinking I might be able to sew them on to my next creation. I forgot, and found them in my pocket, covered in a mouldy, furry slime, the next time I put on the jacket.

What I really wanted back then were some plastic trousers. For a couple of months punk was all about plastic trousers and any self-respecting devotee needed a pair, ideally black plastic drainpipes. But black plastic drainpipes cost about twenty-five or thirty quid, and there was no way I could afford that.

One day Steven, who was equally desperate for plastic trousers, equally stupid and equally strapped for cash, told me he'd seen some quite cool-looking angling dungarees for sale up the road. Just as I had been addicted to comics and still loved them but kept quiet because it undermined my punk credentials, so Steven had been a keen angler, and I suspected he still secretly went fishing at the weekend while I catalogued my X-Men. So off we went to check them out in the local angling store, and they weren't cool at all. For a start they were a dull, dirty blue colour. Presumably this was to confuse the fish, if you were wearing them while standing in a stream. The plastic they were made of wasn't nice plastic either, not at all like proper latex. It was thick, not especially shiny stuff. And they were baggy.

'We can't wear them,' I said. 'They're the wrong colour, the wrong shape and they've got a bib on them.'

'Wait,' he said. 'I've got an idea. We could put big white shirts on over the top, instead of underneath, so you can't see they're dungarees.'

I liked his thinking. Then I suggested we could use my dad's staple gun to staple them down the insides of the legs till they looked like drainpipes. It seemed a brilliant plan and, seeing as these dungarees were only £1.99 a pair, definitely worth a try. So we bought them and stapled the legs, and put them on with shirts on top to go out for the evening. Our legs looked like a couple of giant powder-blue sausages, and the shirts over the top gave the outfit a slight maternity vibe – but, delighted with our reckless brilliance, off we went into town, to the Marquee, to see an as-yet-unsigned band called Generation X.

It wasn't long before a basic design flaw in our faux plastic drainpipes became apparent. If you wanted to have a widdle, you had to take the whole lot off – remove your shirt, undo the straps of the dungarees, wrestle the stapled trouser legs down to your knees – and then put it all back on again.

The real trouble started when I realized that the toilet cubicle in the Marquee, as a result of being stuffed with beer containers, loo paper and other foreign bodies, had completely flooded. That meant having to pee at the urinal right by the door. Or it would have been right by the door if there had been a door, but the door had been smashed off and nicked. So having a pee would involve going through this performance in full view not only of everyone else who happened to wander in to take a leak, but also in front of the audience on the other side of the doorway. I decided this would be too shameful, and resolved to ignore my full bladder all evening. I wish I had that sort of control today, as I must have drunk seven or eight pints of lager before heading home.

Not surprisingly, once the night air hit me, the situation got rather desperate. I couldn't find an open toilet anywhere, so I just had to keep holding it in. Eight pints! I have no idea how I did it, but I managed. All the way home on the Central Line, and then a good half-mile jog from the station. I didn't want to stop and pee in an alleyway because I knew that occasionally they arrested people for that, and my anti-establishment stance was really just a front – I was still a bit scared of policemen.

When at last I reached my front door, hopping from one foot to the other, I discovered I'd forgotten my key. I rang the bell as loudly and insistently as I could. Everyone was asleep. I rang again, and again, and then because I really couldn't hold it a second longer I ripped off my shirt and dragged the dungarees down around my ankles. I couldn't wee in the street, so I flipped the lid off one of our dustbins and let it flow. Ah, the relief. I must have stood there peeing in the bin for about twelve minutes in total, and that was the sight that greeted my dad, woken from his slumber, when he finally unlatched the door. He looked out blearily, shook his head in a mixture of resignation and disgust, and left me to get on with it. I knew then, without any doubt, that I was a proper punk.

Daddy really doesn't know best

I first became a dad over seventeen years ago. First one tiny, scrunchy-faced, crying, scrabbling, needy little Rosslet, then three busy years later another, this time with a bit of jaundice thrown in for good measure, so he looked like a creased yellow muppet. Three years after that, out popped one more, back to the regulation shrimp-pink this time, and so far that's our lot.

It's a surprising experience. Not the birth particularly, though that's tiring and emotional and wonderful and, if you go to the hospitals we did, bloody expensive. And it can be just as expensive for pets.

Recently we paid the vet to give my daughter's chihuahua a Caesarean – giving birth can be pretty risky for such tiny creatures – and that cost us over two thousand quid for four puppies, which were lovely, but why it's as expensive as coming home with a small human I don't know. Perhaps because the work is more fiddly – although if doctors started charging on the basis of the size of the bits involved then the whole system would go tits up. Men would be forever boasting about the size of their bill, even offering to be charged more, while women would probably give the whole topic a wide berth. But money aside, the surprises of fatherhood are many.

When we had our first, I remember the sheer horror and panic I felt when the nurses told me that we could all go home. We'd spent a couple of nights in the hospital with this little baby that we'd made, and every half an hour or so these lovely, kind, knowledgeable ladies would come in and make sure everything was OK and then go out again.

But on the third morning they came in and dropped the bombshell, 'OK, you can go home now.'

Even though I was thirty by then, I still felt like a kid, and there was no way I considered myself anywhere near ready to look after a child. Jane was only twenty, which by today's standards seems frighteningly young. When my eldest brother was born my dad was eighteen and my mum seventeen, and youthful parenthood was far more commonplace. Nowadays most men seem to leave having a baby until they're about fifty-four and most women seem to be around forty-two. But we were youngish, and certainly felt too young to be heading home on our own with little Betty all wrapped up, hoping for the best.

We'd bought a new house but hadn't yet moved in because it still didn't have a finished roof or central heating, thanks to the builders that my wife's dad had recommended. Don't worry, I've nearly forgiven him. The couch at our old house had been commandeered by the cats and, delightfully, the cats had contracted fleas, so we brought our baby straight into a flea-infested home. She immediately came out in a rash, prompting the first of dozens of trips to the doctor in her first fortnight. Eventually we decided we'd had enough and, seeing as it was summer, went off on holiday to France, failing to factor in that 101-degree heat isn't really the best environment for a new-born.

But although we weren't ready for the experience of parenthood, you gradually relax into it, and three or four months down the line you realize it's the same for everyone. Blind panic, sheer terror, sleepless nights. And then it dawns on you that maybe you can do it after all. There are a few basic rules, of course, about not breaking the baby, not dropping the baby, not overfeeding the baby, not underfeeding the baby and keeping the baby clean, but beyond that, if you just dollop a little bit of love into whatever you do, you'll be fine.

In fact, once I'd got the hang of it, I found the whole process far easier than I'd feared. The worst thing – and no, curiously enough, it wasn't changing nappies – was trying to get the babies dressed. I marvelled at the way small infants seem to be permanently in motion, their hands and feet whirring and kicking and grabbing, their little heads twisting while they gurgle and burble. I always panicked that I wouldn't be able to get arms in sleeves or T-shirts over heads without causing an ear to fall off or a limb to get twisted in the wrong position and left there, and that my children would grow up hating me because as a result of my clumsiness they walked with a terrible limp or could never bowl a cricket ball.

Aside from changing nappies and getting the baby dressed,

my next big concern – and I'm being very honest with you here, so please don't judge – was that our sex life might suffer. As you've probably worked out by now, a regular dose of legal intercourse is pretty important to me. As soon as our first little babby had popped out, I wanted to know how soon after the birth you are allowed to get back into the saddle.

I would like to make it perfectly clear that when I say 'saddle', there's no actual saddle involved. I've no doubt some people enjoy that kind of thing in the bedroom, but I find it hard enough just keeping up with the outfits. I once had a frilly shirt my wife quite liked me to wear. I think it made me look a little like a Mills and Boon hero – either that or Jane just liked it because it disguised my paunch. She never said. Anyway, she was fond of it. But keeping that clean and in the right drawer was enough of a drag. As for these people who have cupboards full of vibrating toys and lubricants and whips, and possibly saddles, I don't know how they manage. We don't go in for role-playing at such a dramatic level.

Anyway, the right time turned out to be fairly soon after the birth, but not as soon as some. If my memory serves me correctly, the great J. G. Ballard confesses in his autobiography that he made love to his wife almost immediately after she'd given birth. Well, not only have you got to take your hat off to the man, but the pair of them should be congratulated on their courage. Frankly, that's way too early. Christ, not even the next day! I mean, you might want to wait until you'd got home, or had a shower at the very least. But I suppose you don't want to leave it too long and risk getting out of practice.

Jane, I must say, was always very tolerant and obliging. As

long as the kids were either asleep or in another room she would let me cop a feel of some description. I remember having a delightfully frenzied love-making session on the stairs. Although the children were safely tucked up in bed, she seemed a little distracted throughout. It didn't bother me: like most men I'm mainly concerned with how much I'm enjoying it myself, but afterwards, as she stood up and we were rearranging our clothing, I noticed that there were two big Sticklebricks stuck to her buttocks. These spiky relatives of Lego are not nice things to tread on, let alone sit on, but, God bless her – and this is a sign of real devotion to spousal duty – she'd kept schtum about it the whole time I was enjoying myself. It's a sacrifice that still fills me with admiration.

There are other changes as well, of course. Time to yourself, for a start. What did you do with all that spare time you used to have before a small, violent, hungry stranger came home to live with you? All that available, disposable time, which used to stretch out in front of you like acres of open countryside, just disappears. As do those splendid Saturday mornings spent indulgently nursing a hangover, before a lovely late leisurely lunch and an evening of marginally less extravagant drinking than the one before, knowing you can spend Sunday in bed to recover, the recovery aided by the Sunday papers and a spicy Bloody Mary before lunch/ a stroll/ a nap/ *The Antiques Roadshow*/ dinner/ a little drink/ a cuddle/ bed. How lovely to waste the weekend doing nothing, rather than scratching around on a rainy Sunday with three kids who are developing cabin-fever, trying to work out where to take them all for some 'family fun' – a phrase which strikes me as being inherently contradictory, as anyone who has spent a Sunday morning in the soft-play area of one of those indoor adventure playgrounds will join me in testifying. It might be fun for some of the family, but rarely for all.

Of course, memory has a way of condensing those long stretches of tedium, those hours spent watching a child on a swing or in a pond filled with brightly coloured balls, or sitting in a draughty church hall with a bunch of equally bored parents at a ballet or fencing or judo or drama class. At the time, despite loving the odd moment, I can remember finding the experience less satisfying than I'd always imagined. Several years on, however, I am able to persuade myself that those moments were the pinnacle of my life thus far, and that maybe I should shoot for a fourth kid before I get too old to hoick one into a swing unaided.

On the subject of those indoor play areas, I once went diving into the ball pond myself, to frolic with the kids. This was after an exhausting half-hour spent chasing them through those infernal plastic tubes that criss-cross the ceiling. After getting stuck in one of the tighter corridors and having to enlist the help of a couple of teenagers to simultaneously push and pull me out, while they helpfully remarked that I was fatter than I looked on TV, I decided that the ball pond offered less potential for embarrassment. But diving underneath the grimy balls to hide from my six-year-old son, I felt something squidgy under my hand. Another parent had clearly flouted the no-toddlers-in-the-ball-pond law, despite many signs posted around the area, and a nappy-wearer had parted company with his or her fully loaded undergarment, which was now stuck to my right fist. I chose to assume it belonged to a child because the possibility that I was now attached to a nappy that had been filled and discarded by an incontinent adult is the stuff of nightmares.

That particular place was shut down by the council shortly afterwards; the rumour circulating among the local parents was that several dead rats had been found in the kitchen and one in that very ball pond, so perhaps I got off lightly.

As a parent you do find your freedom curtailed, no two ways about it. Once upon a time we might have decided on a Friday to go away for the weekend, and on Saturday morning wake up in Amsterdam. Fast-forward a year and you'd find us lounging around at home with the baby, and one of us would say, 'Shall we go out?'

'OK, let's do it.'

An hour later, we'd still be indoors, searching for either the nappy bag or the bibs, the nappies, the dummy, the baby, the baby's gloves . . . and then, just as we were heading for the door, we'd remember we needed some milk warmed up just in case. And maybe I should get out of my pyjamas if we were really going to hit the park.

Out we'd go, finally, to endure another half-hour of preparation – 'Have you got the car seat ready? Is it strapped in? Did you remember the wet wipes? Have you got the Disney singalong tape?' And so on and so on and so on, until they hit about fourteen and only want to stay indoors in their rooms or sneak off without you to drink cider and suck on other teenagers' necks.

And this was despite the fact that I am married to someone who could quite easily be a five-star general when it comes to planning outings. On the few occasions when it was left to me I would usually leave the house without any of the 'essentials', including those bloody nappies, and have to try to make do with something I found on the floor – like a leaf, or a newspaper or a crisp bag. The way things are going with recycling and all, maybe that kind of improvisation is to be encouraged. Actually I wiped my bum on a leaf quite recently, and it didn't do anywhere near as good a job as double-ply Andrex, which surprised me. I was playing tennis with my friend David Baddiel and had one of those sudden, desperate urges to go that hit maybe once a year or so. There was no time for niceties, so I wandered behind a shrub and unloaded, grabbing a handful of broad, hopefully non-stinging leaves to tidy myself up. They did the trick in a rudimentary way, but rather than feeling fresh and outdoorsy I imagine I smelt like a panda with diarrhoea.

Despite the struggle involved in leaving the house with children in tow, we have always tried to carry on with something of a normal adult life, even taking the kids out to restaurants with us. They are surprisingly well behaved and so it's never caused too much of a problem. The worst place for trying to eat with kids was San Francisco, where we all stayed once when I was filming. When we wanted to go out for a meal we'd ring round several restaurants to double-check that it was OK to bring the kids (we had two at the time). The phone would invariably be answered by a charming young gay guy, or possibly even a straight guy who had adopted the standard San Fran accent so as not to be outed as hetero. They would always be bemused as to why we would want to bring children to a lovely expensive restaurant in the first place, and concerned about how we would control them once they were there. Nearly all these conversations went like this:

'Hello, we'd love it if we could get a table this evening for three or four people.'

'Why, certainly, sir.'

'Great. But can I just check with you whether children are welcome?'

'How old is the child?'

'We have one who's three and a one-year-old.'

'Oh my Gaad. Hold on, please.'

Then there would be a long pause while he tried to calculate the ramifications of this terrible information, and sometimes he could be heard conferring with the rest of the staff.

'Well, it's unusual, but it should be OK. How can you be sure they'll stay quiet?'

'Well, we can't – that's why I'm asking you whether it's OK to bring them along. But if they do start to kick and scream, I promise I'll take them outside.'

That normally ensured that the restaurant was, after all, fully booked for the foreseeable future.

I don't entirely blame them. Jane and I went for a lovely meal with Tom Jones once in Los Angeles. I had just interviewed him, and he offered to treat us at his favourite restaurant of the time. Matsushita, I think it was called, on La Cienega Boulevard. Like a lot of LA restaurants, the place itself was quite unassuming, although the food was spectacular. It was a tiny place, and we loved it, so we arranged to come back for lunch the following week with the kids and some less famous friends. Again the food was great, and after asking for the bill and signing the credit-card slip, I popped off to the loo. While I was away one of our children – and the guilty party has asked me not to be too specific here – exploded all over the table. This little treasure managed to poo with such force that it shot out of both the legs and the waistband of the nappy, landing on the floor and the table and completely filling this tiny eatery with a lingering smell that clashed terribly with the day's special.

Understandably the waiters weren't pleased, and we hurried off, apologizing. But they chased after me, furious, not least because in their haste to throw out the tablecloth and chopsticks and dishes and anything else that my precious little angel had managed to launch a dirty protest on, they had also thrown out the credit-card slip. I had to return to the restaurant and walk the gauntlet of glowering Los Angelenos trying to enjoy their sushi in a baby-created fog. Even though that was fifteen years ago, I bet they'd remember my name and refuse to have me back, with or without children.

I was very much a hands-on dad during the kids' early years, and enjoyed being able to divide the responsibility with Jane. She did the lion's share – or lioness's share – of course, but I tried my best, even in the face of some good old-fashioned sexism. I remember going to those Gymboree-type set-ups down at the local library or church hall, where they'd have a Mother and Baby Hour – a concept that always annoyed me, seeing as I was trying to be just as hands-on as a mum. I imagine now they'd call it Parent and Baby Hour, but back then it was always Mother and Baby, and though most of the other people there were indeed mothers with their babies, it didn't exactly put you at your ease. Everyone was always very nice to me, so doubtless I was just being paranoid, but I couldn't help wondering whether they thought I'd borrowed the baby just to try to get some hot-MILF action.

Once the suspicious sideways glances have died down and the mummies begin to accept you, you realize just how competitive they are about their babies, always comparing what age they started walking at and when they said their first word and whether or not they know who is the president of Uzbekistan.

I've worked with competitive people and performed in front of some tough crowds in my time, but nothing compares with a roomful of young mums all trying to best each other in the Baby Einstein stakes, all desperate for their little bundle to be the smartest, the most developed, the best dressed.

Jane and I lived in New York for a few months once, and we took the kids to a baby play place on the Upper West Side. There are few less restful ways of spending a few hours with your kids than in a room filled with a bunch of snooty, Waspy mums in immaculate outfits with their children beautifully kitted out in little Ralph Lauren Polo suits. They'd look on in horror as we rolled in, in slightly crusty tracksuit bottoms, trailing three rather diseased-looking north London children. They'd visibly shudder as Harvey wiped snot down a slide or Honey sneezed into the face of a mini-Manhattanite. Happy days.

Despite all that, I really miss having small children, and I know Jane does as well. I don't miss them waking up at all hours. I don't miss them being illogical and not understanding when they need to go to bed or why it's not OK to do certain things. I don't miss changing them. I don't miss panicking that they have meningitis every time they cough or run a temperature and rushing them off to the doctor. I don't miss any of that stuff. And whenever I hear a child screaming on a plane or in a restaurant these days, I'm delighted, absolutely bloody delighted, because I know it's not mine making the racket. I just sit back and enjoy watching someone else deal with it. That's a bonus I never anticipated would give me so much pleasure. But what I do miss is that unique sense of connectedness between a parent and a very young child, which you lose something of as they grow up to become fully formed personalities with sophisticated little minds and clear wants and opinions. In the early years parenthood really is as uncomplicated as holding a puppy on your lap. Your babies look up at you adoringly, and if they're safe, warm, dry and not hungry or suffering in any way, then all is right with the world and it's a lovely, lovely feeling.

I never doubted that I would have kids. I always wanted children and luckily my wife agreed. We have quite different backgrounds: Jane comes from a small family, just her and her parents, surrounded by a network of relatives, whereas I was brought up in a large nuclear family, very much created by my parents, in which other relations – cousins and uncles and aunties – really didn't feature much at all. I have wonderful memories of my childhood, with my mum, my dad and us six kids in a big, busy, noisy house, so I guess I wanted to emulate that. I didn't want to go quite as far as having six children, though, and Jane and I tentatively agreed that three would be a nice number. In fact, I think Jane agreed with herself on that question – I don't actually remember being consulted. But I was perfectly happy with it.

Eventually I learnt not to go around being too evangelical

about parenthood, much as I love it personally. When I was younger, before it dawned on me that the world was a shade more complicated than I realized at the majestic age of twenty-three or so, when I first started to work, I would rattle on about children to child-free couples. 'Yeah, you should have kids . . . You'd make a great father [or mother] . . . Don't you want children? . . . I'm surprised you haven't had children . . . When are you going to have children? . . . Why not go upstairs and make some babies? . . . Babies are great.'

I must have sounded like a nut, but I really wanted to see everyone make babies, so I could play with them and help look after them until I finally found someone to make some of my own with. And they would politely deflect my comments or change the subject. Finally, someone took me to one side – he was a very nice man, a reasonably well-known comedian – and said, 'Look, it's very sweet that you keep asking, but actually, we can't. We've been trying for years and years now, and it's not biologically possible, so please, please stop saying that every time you meet us.' I felt awful. It had never occurred to me that some people didn't have children because they couldn't. My remarkable insensitivity still haunts me, and the fact that Jane and I were lucky enough to have three so easily seems like a miracle.

Of course, there are some folks who make a deliberate and conscious decision not to reproduce, and that's fine. Better that than make kids they don't really want or know what to do with. I met someone once who was as pro staying childless as I am on the side of breeding. I interviewed this fellow, a terribly grumpy old American comedian, on my radio show. He's a very famous and (in my personal opinion) somewhat overrated ancient borscht-belt type. Much of his material is about the difference between being Jewish and being Gentile, and although there's some humour to be had out of this, I find those kind of jokes rather mechanical and obvious and consequently they don't really work for me. On the show he was funny enough, I guess, as I chatted to him between records, but then he enquired whether I had kids. When I said I did, he asked me if I regretted it.

'No, not at all,' I said, a little taken aback. No one had ever asked me this before or since – why would they? If one of my children had gone on a shooting spree or appeared on *Big Brother* then I might have understood it, but none of them had brought shame on the family – and he'd never even met them.

'I'm sure you do, if you're being honest,' he continued.

At first I thought maybe someone had put him up to it, or maybe he had some material on the subject and was laying the foundations for a couple of killer punchlines. But nope, he just insisted that, in his experience, if you kept pushing long enough, every parent would eventually crack and admit that, yes, their life had been made exponentially worse by the arrival of kids, and they wished they hadn't had them and they would have preferred to spend all their time and money on themselves and their partner. I can only guess that most people gave in and agreed with him just to get him to shut up and take his creepy opinion and go away.

I was so intrigued by his weirdness that when I went home afterwards I Googled him to try to find out whether he'd channelled his energy into some marvellous charitable pursuit or helped save a small Third World country or something – anything that might have convinced him that his childless time on the planet had been somehow extraordinary. But nope, he was just your common or garden miserable old fucker. Perhaps he had a miserable time of it as a kid. Maybe I wouldn't have been quite so certain about wanting to be a dad if I hadn't enjoyed being a kid so much myself. It's only the experiences you love and want to repeat or share that you recommend to others, after all. Very rarely do I come out of a bad movie and say to somebody, 'Yeah, I hated that, you must go and see it.' I only do that when I feel a film is so awful it defies belief, thinking that others might want to see it for themselves just for the experience. Normally, though, it's the exhilarating things – rollercoaster rides, delicious meals, sexual positions – that you pass on with glowing praise, telling your friends they might want to give them a go. And so it is with being a dad.

One of the less selfish benefits of having children is that your parents and in-laws and various relatives all get so excited about having grandchildren or nephews and nieces to spoil. On my side of the family there are a lot of kids, but as Jane is an only child, on her side she has been the sole provider of a new generation.

We've had a lot of very enjoyable and fondly remembered family days, and none more so than those involving Kinny, who really sums up for me the pleasure the young and the old can bring each other. Kinny is not actually a blood relative, but a wonderful woman who not only looked after Jane as a baby, but her mother before her. She still comes over to see us regularly, joining us for lunch once every week or so, and even though she's in her mid-eighties now, she has such a great spirit. You'll still find her sitting on the floor playing on the Nintendo Wii with the kids, or out in the garden messing about with a water balloon, or perched on the swings in a pair of totally inappropriate sunglasses that one of the children has forced her to wear.

On one occasion – I think it was Kinny's birthday, in fact – we were sitting round the table playing that game which involves adding to and remembering, in sequence, a long shopping list. You know the one: the first person says, 'I went shopping and put in my basket a cup,' and the next person adds another item: 'I went shopping and put in my basket a cup and a robot,' and round and round you go until somebody forgets, and then they're out. We were all playing with Jane's mum and Kinny, and things started out calmly enough, with sensible choices like a newspaper and a puppy. But the kids were at that age – I think Honey, the youngest, was about seven – when they were highly amused by some of the rude words they'd picked up, and we soon realized that they were trying to slip in some off-colour options to see if anyone noticed.

Before long we had a newspaper, a puppy and a thong, and the list grew saucier and saucier. With about ten or twelve items in the metaphorical basket, one of the kids selected an item I suspect doesn't even exist, unless Elton John has been keeping quiet about his birthday gifts. A diamond butt plug. It seems to me rather a waste of a good diamond, because who's going to see it up there?

Anyway, the diamond butt plug was added to this imaginary shopping list. None of the grown-ups wanted to make a big issue of it, and of course it was very funny, and the kids were killing themselves laughing, but we were all a touch embarrassed about what was going to happen when Kinny's turn came round. Was the octogenarian at the end of the table going to have to announce to the assembled company that she'd acquired a diamond butt plug? We were also pretty curious about what she might think a diamond butt plug was.

We needn't have worried. When the list got to Kinny she began: 'I went shopping and I put in my basket a newspaper, a puppy, a thong . . .' She reeled off the items that followed and as she counted down towards what we were all waiting for there was an audible intake of breath. Finally, the moment arrived. 'A Bagpuss, a hat made of cheese, a picture of David Dickinson and' – we were on the edge of our seats – 'a diamond bus pass.'

It just goes to show that the gradual hearing loss associated with age really does have a silver lining.

You've Done It Again

Ooh, it's a minefield, having famous friends. If you work in television you can't help but acquire a few over the years. You meet people and you get on well and you become mates – it's the same as any other job in that respect, really. I've still got a couple of friends from before I was famous, but not many. But that's got more to do with the fact that I didn't have a lot of friends back then, than with me changing, or them changing because of me changing, if you know what I mean. But it's tricky, being friends with famous people. There are hidden dangers that you rarely encounter with people who have normal jobs.

I have a friend who works with computers. He does OK for himself and he knows his stuff, but he never asks me to check out a new office he's just equipped with Apple Macs and tell him what I think. I've never had to sit through a film he's made on the subject or read a novel he's written set in the fast-paced and ever-changing world of information technology and offer an opinion as to whether or not he might get shortlisted for the Booker prize.

But famous friends need to know what you think, all the bloody time. At the very least you have to be aware of their work and acknowledge what they've done. And occasionally they'll do a show or bring out a book or be involved in a movie which isn't particularly good, and you face that terrible quandary – do you lie, or do you lie? This happens no matter who you are. I've made my fair share of rubbish on TV, as well as putting in a couple of guest appearances in movies which aren't very good. It's always me playing me, but I'm not even very convincing at that, so I've learnt to give acting a wide berth, and I've also stopped asking my friends what they think. So why can't they afford me the same courtesy?

Over the years friends have announced endless new projects, or even come to me directly with new ideas, and I'm dangerously close to running out of ways to sound impressed and delighted when I'm not impressed or delighted at all. But there's no alternative. No matter how close you are to someone, they don't really want to hear the truth from you.

One thing that I've found works with people you don't know that well, if you're called upon to pass judgement on their new movie or West End performance, is to merely smile, nod meaningfully and say, 'Well, you've done it again' – a phrase which is *so* brilliantly open-ended that it covers just about every eventuality. That normally satisfies people.

Another way of getting around the problem is to find one or two small things within what may well be a steaming dung heap of awfulness that you didn't find as objectionable as the rest, and focus on those. So in the case of a movie you could say, 'I loved that bit where you were walking along the street and you looked up at the sky. I thought that was tremendous – that walking/sky-looking sequence was fabulous. And all the door-opening you did was tremendously natural. Brilliantly done. No one opens doors like you.' That tends to work, or at least gives them a polite clue not to press you any further.

The hardest people to avoid being honest with are ones who've written a book. You can quite easily say, 'Oh, I didn't get to watch your programme' or 'I'm terribly sorry, I haven't managed to see your movie yet, but I will get around to it.' But when someone's given you their book it is more embarrassing to say, 'I haven't read it yet. It's on my pile of books to read.' You can only keep that up for so long. I know – I've tried. You've got about five weeks, maximum, before they start hating you for not making the effort. And neither can you manage to talk about it without being specific.

With a movie you can just pick out a couple of moments, but with a book you have to talk about the characters, the writing, and it's so much more of a personal creation as well. With a film or a play you can always pick on someone else in the cast who maybe didn't pull their weight. That's a great way of deflecting your general disappointment. And let's face it, most of us like to hear that someone else did a slightly shittier job than we did. But a book – that's tough.

There are probably only one or two really super-close friends who I would be totally honest with regardless of the conse-quences, because I respect and like them too much to lie to them.

Whether that's more for my sake or theirs I don't know. But there have been a couple of times over the years when I've been subjected to something on stage or I've been handed a novel and read it, or tried to read it, and I've said, 'You know what? I didn't like it.' You come to realize as you get older that just because you don't like something doesn't necessarily mean it's bad, it's just not for you.

The only sensible way to proceed is to tell people you can't read or listen to or go to see things made by friends. As a default setting it saves you a lot of emotional wear and tear in the long run, but it's a bit like forcing them to acknowledge up front they *might* have made something rubbish, so whether it really helps is debatable.

Bad reviews are pretty horrible, regardless of whether they are accurate or not. A friend of mine once told me something that someone else had said: that when he receives a bad review it feels a little bit like someone has put a large wet blanket over his head – it's like you are carrying something thick and damp around and although you know it will dry out eventually it seems to take for ever. To be honest, I've been pretty lucky with the press. I tend to get good reviews or no reviews, which is in some ways pretty much the same thing, and most recently people tend to review my wages rather than my shows. But I've come to the conclusion over the years that if I'm doing a show and enough people are watching it then it's a good show, regardless of reviews. If I'm doing a show and people aren't watching it, then it's probably not such a good show, again regardless of the reviews. However, there are exceptions.

Probably one of my all-time favourite programmes was a

profile I helped to make of an obscure Finnish film director called Aki Kaurismäki, which when it went out on a Friday-night slot on Channel 4 was universally ignored by the critics and only reached an audience of around 200,000 people. Obviously a profile of a heavy-drinking Finnish art-film direc-tor is never going to take on *Coronation Street* as an audience pleaser. But we weren't helped by the fact that Channel 4 broad-cast it the same night that the very first Comic Relief went out, which was a very big deal, if you can remember that far back. And even if you can't, I'm sure you can guess that it was quite an exciting event in British television history. I co-hosted that evening with Lenny Henry and Griff Rhys Jones, and it was ter-rific fun, and of course helped pave the way for the many years of Comic Relief and the huge amount of money it has raised ever since.

I've met just about every famous person I'd care to meet. There are only a few who have eluded me and they tend to be the sort of people who just don't do talk shows – Jack Nicholson being the primary one. I'm a huge fan of Nicholson as a screen actor and I rather like what I sense about his personality and his free-wheeling approach to life, but I've never interviewed him because he doesn't do talk shows. At the risk of putting myself out of business, that's probably a smart decision. He's been quoted as saying that if you appear on shows like mine, people think they know you, and when they think they know you, they try and factor in what they think they know about you when they watch you in a movie, to see how much of it is you and how much of it isn't you. That sense of knowing someone, even when you don't really, only tends to happen on television. You don't get the same feeling from a radio appearance, or from reading about someone in a magazine interview. You only get it when you see them and hear them on the small screen.

More often than not, when I get to meet famous people I've admired, they don't let me down. I'll be mentioning my affection for Tom Cruise later, who is always remarkably forthcoming in interviews and just terrific fun to be around. Will Smith is equally great value. Jim Carrey is a dream to have on the show because he treats each appearance as a job to be done – he has to come on and entertain and earn his position on the show – and he's fabulous. Harrison Ford – I've heard people say that they find him a bit cold and distant and a little bit difficult to interview, but I think that's just his manner. I find him great. He's charismatic, a terrific actor, of course, and I enjoy his company – not that I know him socially, but I've enjoyed the times I've spent interviewing him.

I've always loved having Johnny Vegas on the show. Ricky Gervais, who I count as a friend, is a tremendously funny interviewee and I love having him on the programme because he has no respect for me whatsoever. Maybe in real life he has a little, but certainly when we're out there doing the show he acts as if he thinks I'm a gibbering idiot. Russell Brand is another person I love having on because the to-ing and fro-ing that goes on between us is great. David Baddiel is another friend of mine and that also works on screen – which is unusual because it doesn't always. In the past I've sometimes had friends on and I've found it a bit tricky because I'm always so aware that I don't want it to seem like some sort of chummy showbiz club, which is a difficult thing to avoid, especially if you get on well. And then there have been one or two people I've met who have been difficult.

A couple of times it's because they've been drinking heavily – that's always a problem – and once or twice they've been on drugs – I've had people on the show who are clearly off their tits on substances and that's never easy because I always feel I'm talking to the drug rather than the person. And you have to factor in that even celebs and popular stars with a comedy bent sometimes have a bad day, as we all do.

I like to think that I'm fairly approachable when I'm out and about, but if someone comes up to me for an autograph when I'm in the middle of a row with the wife or if I've just been telling one of the children off about something, obviously I'm going to try and smile and be nice to them but it's going to come a little less readily. Ditto with the guests on the show – sometimes they've just had a really bad day.

There's one very popular female actor in this country who is more of a comedienne, very well known, she's been in any number of shows from the sixties onwards. She's a lovely woman and a great storyteller and I'd been a huge fan of hers for years. I finally got her to come on one of my programmes. She'd always been the sort of guest to have appeared on Parky or Wogan, not the new kid on the block, which I suppose is what I was seen as – a bit of an upstart. At the time she was more famous for a series of television commercials than anything more substantial, but I was really keen to meet her. She came on the show and it was dreadful, just horrible. She was unhelpful, she was truculent, she was difficult. I got the feeling that she didn't like me and didn't want to be there. It turned out that her eldest daughter had received her examination results that day and had done far less well than she'd expected, which explained her foul mood. At least that was the explanation she gave me afterwards. People are people, no matter how famous they get.

I spent some time backstage once before appearing at a Royal Variety performance in London. I was due to introduce some youngsters who'd done quite well on a talent show I'd been hosting for ITV called *The Big Big Talent Show.* I was delighted to be on the Royal Variety. I'd never been on one before and it was, weirdly, quite a thrill. Since then I've been on it a couple of times but it's still a thrill. I've still got the keyring that was given to me to commemorate that first appearance – the date has faded a bit but I think it was 1997.

Anyway, it was at a strange theatre over near Victoria where *Starlight Express* ran for about seventy-five years, and I shared a very, very small dressing room backstage with – get ready for some world-class name-dropping – Joe Pasquale . . . Michael Ball . . . and Jim Davidson. The four of us squeezed into a room the size of a large coffin. None of whom I knew, none of whom I was, at that time, a particularly huge fan of, but all of whom I found to be very pleasant company. You might think that I wouldn't necessarily get on with Jim Davidson because he comes from a different comedy and political perspective from me, but he was very charming and I liked hanging out with him.

He turned up last and was in a foul mood when he arrived, and we were all a bit worried and a little bit intimidated, especially as we were sharing such a tiny room – and none of us are small fellas. Michael Ball leaning out of the window smoking, Joe Pasquale changing his shirt and wondering whether he could get his trousers ironed, me sitting there trying to read a book, and Jim Davidson saying what an awful, awful day he'd had and how his wife was a terrible pain in the arse. About an hour later a bunch of flowers turned up for him from her, so presumably he was in the right that time. We ended up going for a walk around the block and chatting to each other, and I was amazed at how decent he seemed, if a little messed up. But Jim Davidson went on stage that night and killed, he was terrific, as was Michael Ball. Joe Pasquale didn't do as well, and I died on my arse, completely and utterly and painfully. But when I came off they all smiled at me and said, 'Well, you've done it again.'

ABLE TO LEAP TALL CHURCHES
WITH A SINGLE BOUND

Famous people are naturally cleverer and better informed than non-famous people. This must be true, or why would we get asked to talk on TV and the radio on every subject from marriage to gardening to travel to drugs? Why would we offer up our opinions on modern parenting, eating disorders and how best to dress your dog if we didn't have something vitally important to pass on?

I myself have been asked to talk on subjects as diverse as gardening and the Boy Scout movement, despite the fact that I've never been a Scout. That wasn't a deal breaker, either – quite the opposite, in fact. They felt I could offer a fresh, new, non-Scouting perspective. In the last twelve months I have been approached to sit on panels focusing on British sausages, how best to maximize the positive impact of the 2012 Olympics, and wind farming as a viable energy source for the next hundred years, none of which I know any more or less about than the average ill-informed schmo.

My services have also been requested to help judge modern literature, horses, cars and young fashion designers. Clearly I have no real expertise in any of these areas, and with the exception of the sausages, very little genuine interest either. Being aware that at best I could only offer my opinion, somehow elevated in importance because I gently tease celebrities on a Friday night, has given me the wisdom to say no, and to avoid sticking my oar in where it doesn't really concern me. But that's not to say that I don't enjoy holding ill-informed opinions on matters of great importance.

Religion, for example, is a subject which every sensible bone in my body tells me to avoid. The best-case scenario is that you mildly upset whoever you're talking to. The worst-case scenario is that someone puts a bomb in your car or chases you down the street with a knife or asks fellow devotees around the world to try and hunt you down and remove you from the planet.

As a matter of fact, I have actually been chased down a road by a knife-wielding person who I'm pretty sure meant me no good whatsoever, and although it makes for a memorable anecdote, I wouldn't recommend the experience. Although we didn't stop to chat, I'm pretty sure he was of a different faith, although the knife-wielding and chasing had nothing to do with religion and everything to do with drugs. It was the first time I'd gone on holiday outside the UK, having bought a cheap package deal to Tangiers, which happily coincided with the Muslim month of Ramadan.

I had spent the day trawling the bazaars with the rest of the tourists in my group, but then decided to go for a little walk on my own. I realize now that it must have looked like I wanted to get high, something young fashionable types often head off to North Africa for. That wasn't, in fact, what I was after, as I told the young man with astonishingly bad teeth who started following me and offered a bag of hashish. Even though I did not doubt it was 'top top quality get you high for long time English boy', as he loudly advertised. I politely yet firmly said I wasn't the dope-smoking type, didn't have any money, didn't want to get high just now and so on. Maybe it was my annoying face – and it was quite annoying back then – or maybe it was the fact that during Ramadan no one eats until the sun goes down so tempers are easily frayed, but he whipped out a huge bloody knife and chased me down the road. It was a proper scary Arab-looking knife with a curvy blade and I imagine a rather nice handle. I'm thinking ivory perhaps, with some carvings. I didn't get too close a look, because when you are running from a knife-wielding person who you assume is hungry and you can see has started foaming around the lips, which are pulled back, the better to frame his monstrously bad teeth, you don't hang around.

To avoid him I took refuge in a little shop selling tourist crap – small camels made from that nondescript pale leather you see everywhere there, and models of mosques, and stuff that didn't really look like anything. The shopkeeper was very nice at first, but when she saw the foam-flecked nut outside, waving his scimitar at me, and realized I was there to hide, not to buy anything, she shooed me out with a broom. I managed to hang around long enough for the dope-pushing loon outside to leave, but the experience didn't overly endear either the people or that region or North Africa in general to me.

I'm certainly not anti-religious in any way and, like most people, I like to think that I'm spiritual. What that means is I like to think I have a little depth, and am not merely interested in how many exciting features my new mobile phone will have and how long I can spend on holiday next year. Spirituality seems to be a catch-all for people who can't be arsed to actually commit to a religion but who want to feel they've got some connection to the bigger picture.

Years ago, I was interviewing a bunch of people for a job, and in order to get a clearer idea of what they were like, as well as to see if we would have to buy in any special milk or avoid making jokes about sacred animals while they were around, I asked if they were religious. Well, not one of them was, but they all said more or less the same thing – that although they were not really religious as such, they were spiritual. Which means, of course, absolutely nothing.

A big part of me would love to be religious, if only because it's so bloody predictable being an atheist. Recently it's become oddly fashionable to adopt a sort of aggressive-atheist pose and knock all religions, especially Western ones. I think most people are too scared to come out against the stricter Eastern gangs. Richard Dawkins would probably happily accept the blame for much of this. If I've read him right – and I'll admit I got a bit bored and gave up on him once I grasped the gist of what he was saying – his theory is that religion, which relies on a belief in the supernatural to explain who we are and why we are here, is simply incompatible with the rational, scientific conclusions we must draw from the more or less incontrovertible proof that we evolved rather than magically appeared. Which is fair enough, but I always thought the whole point of faith, the thing that made it such an attractive and wonderfully human characteristic, was that you believed in something without needing any proof. You put your trust in something bigger than yourself, outside of yourself. Sure, there's a very good chance that a lot of people are going to turn out to be very disappointed when all's said and done, but still it's a rather beautiful and fragile idea, and it doesn't need to be squashed down by scientific bullies, however well meaning.

I'm certainly with Dawkins all the way when it comes to the spread of pseudo-science – people who have put forward various New Age ideas – at least I guess they were once New Age but are now middle-aged – about time and space and vibrations and the inner harmony of bodies and how you can change a glass of water's molecular structure by writing the word 'GOOD' or 'LOVELY' on a piece of paper and sticking it on the outside, as some Americans seem to believe at the moment. All of this, of course, is absolute nonsense, and damaging nonsense as well, and people who believe this stuff and teach it to their kids deserve a good old Middle Eastern beating with a stick in a public square and should then be consigned straight to an Old Testament-style hell.

There are any number of different practices that are supposedly beneficial – like reiki, for example. There are so many reiki masters out there you can't move for them. These are people who claim to be able to help you by giving you a kind of massage without touching you, and it's complete and utter bollocks. It's all born out of a desire to help, I suppose, but it's so depressing. Our friends the reiki masters may want to be seen as being special, but rather than spending a bit of time helping out at a local church fête or doing something useful, they go off and listen to some complete and utter twat teaching them to hold their hands six inches above someone's body and move them over mystical points.

My wife made several TV series for a cable channel, called *Jane Goldman Investigates*, in which she went off with a very open mind, hoping to find something of interest in the world of the supernatural and the mystical, the world of modern faith-healing, aromatherapy, holistic stuff and so on and so forth. She met a lot of very nice, very sweet people. People who are doing what they do for the right reasons, because they want to help and they believe there's something in it. They're not all con-artists, although there are more than a few of those out there. But whatever the reason for their alternative beliefs, they are all bloody annoying.

I went to see Barbra Streisand at the O2 Centre here in London, and I had my lovely eleven-year-old daughter Honey with me. In her excitement at getting a closer look at Barbra Streisand, whose legendary voice and nose I had described in exquisite detail, she tripped and grazed her knee on the steps. One nice lady there offered to fetch the first-aid box, while another, equally nice but horribly deluded, offered to perform reiki on her. Even at eleven my daughter can spot a nut, and politely declined. But honestly. Who in their right mind would try to heal a kid's knee by waving her hands over it when a plaster and a hug do the job perfectly every time?

We had contact with a definite flake once. She was a reflexologist by trade – a form of massage that focuses on your feet as a way of dealing with all other internal ills. I'm happy to concede that there could be something in that, seeing as the body is connected on the inside, via tubes which I believe are called veins. That's about all I remember from Biology at school. That and some absolutely terrifying pictures they showed us during the sex-education part of the course. Older boys had whispered of this particular lesson, buried away in our Religious Education period for some reason, during which you would be shown photographs of an actual, real man and woman, in the actual, real nude, actually and really going at it. There are no words to describe how eagerly we all looked forward to this particular lesson, nor words of sufficient power to describe the revulsion and disappointment we felt when the pics we had so feverishly built up in our imagination were shown, and turned out to be of a middle-aged nude man and woman with their faces completely smoothed out. Featureless, smooth-faced monsters with sagging, aged bodies. It was like looking at screenshots from an especially disturbing episode of *Doctor Who*.

Anyway, this reflexologist – who lived on the south coast – was a friend of my wife's mum. At the time Jane had a bad back, so her mum paid for a session with the reflexologist. Jane was grateful, but pointed out that travelling from London just to have her feet rubbed for an hour seemed a bit much. But the method to her mum's madness was that the reflexology lady practised a form of transcendental healing, which is to say she claimed that by using the power of her mind alone she could visit the astral plane which hovers above or alongside us all without being seen. Once on or in this plane her astral self could visit other astral selves, and do whatever it needed to do, including stroking Jane's feet, before going back to her body. For a fee, of course. You'd think it wouldn't cost a lot; certainly there weren't any travelling expenses.

Jane suggested that while this lady was hovering around in spirit form she might perhaps be able to look in on Dave, our iguana, who was sick at the time. This was, of course, a joke on Jane's part, but her mum didn't realize that and phoned the lady and asked if she did iguanas. She said she would look in on Dave at no extra cost, which was nice of her. Whether she ever visited or not we don't know. Certainly Jane's back didn't get better in the immediate future and neither did Dave, who only recovered after being taken to the vet in one of those boxes that you normally carry cats in. After reassuring several rather startled old ladies in the waiting room that this wasn't a very scary new breed of pussy, I left the vet's with a small jiffy bag filled with penicillin and hypodermic needles. Twice a week for the next month I had to inject the antibiotic just under the iguana's armpit. It's a tricky procedure, trying to creep up on a more or less fully grown female iguana and stick a needle under its armpit, especially after the first few visits when she knows what you're up to, but it's a lot more fruitful than relying on some loon by the seaside dozing off and charging thirty-five quid every time she has a nap.

And that wasn't a typo, by the way. The iguana's name was Dave because we believed her to be a boy until one day she laid some eggs. We stuck with Dave because we'd had her for several years and had all grown used to it, and I doubt if iguanas are that bothered about gender-specific tags. They're more advanced than we are in that way. I don't think you can really tease an iguana by calling it gay. Not that I've tried.

It might surprise you, but I am far less scathing about Scientology than I am about all the 'you will live for ever and you can change the world with the power of positive thinking' claptrap that seems to appeal to celebrities, primarily, but all people who have an illogical fear of death – illogical in that it's inevitable. I suspect most people think Scientology is the absolute be-all and end-all of celebrity religious nonsense. And if you want to pick it apart, you're fully entitled to do so.

I should point out that I have absolutely no intention of ever becoming a Scientologist, so there's no vested interest here. But I don't think Scientologists get a fair deal. I don't know enough about the religion itself to be able to say whether, as a belief system, it's any more interesting or useful in helping you get through life than being a member of the Church of England or a born-again Christian or a Baptist or a Muslim. But I do know that the handful of people I've met who've happened to be Scientologists have been some of the nicest and most courteous of any it has been my pleasure to spend time with. I've met the three highest profile Scientologists that I can think of – Tom Cruise I've met several times, Will Smith I've spent quite a bit of time with over the years, always in a professional capacity, and John Travolta I've met once or twice.

Let's do them in reverse order. John Travolta seems to be not only very happy and stable and together, but for someone who's been famous for as long as he has, he seems to have maintained a real sense of playfulness and fun. Now you might think that's a given, bearing in mind the amount of money the man has earnt and where he is in the world, but I've met far more miserable millionaires than happy ones over the years. In fact, I've not done badly myself, but sometimes I start and end the day as just another grumpy old bloke. So it's great to meet someone who not only has earnt his dough but really knows how to enjoy it, and seems to have got the right balance between his family life – whatever that might be, because obviously people love to speculate about that kind of thing – and his professional life.

Will Smith is number two on my hit list of Scientologists, if indeed he is one, because I don't know if he's actually gone on record about it, but everyone seems to think he is and that's good enough for me. Likewise, he seems to be not only remarkably focused on both his career and his family, but completely certain about what he wants to do with his life and where he wants to be at any given time. And you have to admire that. In this day and age, when most of us spend far too long scratching our arse and wondering whether or not we're doing the right thing at work, at home, for ourselves, for our friends, for our partners, it's refreshing to find someone who – presumably thanks to this particular creed or religion, call it what you will – has got that level of focus and achieved what he wants in life.

Probably the most high-profile scientologist, and the one who gets the most flak for it, is Tom Cruise, 'the Cruise-ster'. But here's a guy who I've met many times over the years, including when he was at the very height of his fame – about the time when he'd just started filming *Eyes Wide Shut* with Kubrick, and before he started getting some of the knocks he has recently for his admittedly crazy behaviour, jumping up and down on the couch on *Oprah Winfrey* and saying how if he saw a road accident he'd know he had to stop to make a difference – that kind of crazy. But whenever I've met him he's been incredibly down to earth for a star of his stature. When he walks into a room, he pays attention to everyone. He says hello to everyone, no matter what job they're doing on a shoot – getting the coffee, doing the make-up, lugging the camera or sound equipment around – he doesn't differentiate. He goes up to them and shakes their hand and looks them in the eye and says, 'Hi, I'm Tom Cruise. Pleased to meet you.' He's one of the most famous people on the planet and he knows that when he walks into a room people are going to look at him, and that they'll all have some kind of preconceptions about him, not always favourable. But he comes right in and goes on over and makes friends with the lot of them. It is rather exhausting to watch, I'll give you that, but when he leaves the room everybody loves him. So, as long as you can get past the stuff about aliens and volcanoes and avoid reading any of L. Ron Hubbard's bloody awful science-fiction books, Scientology doesn't seem much sillier or more harmful than any of the bona fide longer-running religious games in town.

Here's what I like about the olde-timey religions. I love the way the people dress. I mean, who came up with their outfits? They are, more or less without exception, fierce, as I believe young people say nowadays. Who doesn't smile when they see a nun coming down the road? And not just because they're usually friendly old ladies. I'm sure that if you had the kind of Catholic upbringing that many people I know who were brought up in Ireland in the fifties and sixties did, when nuns seemed to rule almost like General Franco and his Barrista – no, hang on, they're the people who make cappuccinos, aren't they? Well, whatever Franco's bullies were called – then you won't have fond memories of nuns and you probably don't smile spontaneously when you see one. You probably feel more tempted to tip them over, like bored teenagers in rural areas do to cows on farms at night. But I was raised godless, and I like the look of a nun. For a start, you never know what they're wearing under that outfit. Sometimes I like to think that maybe something saucy is going on under there, or they're nude, or maybe they're like little stacking Russian dolls. Wouldn't it be fabulous to lift up a nun and find another one underneath, exactly the same only slightly smaller? Then under her a smaller nun and then a yet smaller nun, until you get to the very middle and there's a little toy like a Kinder Surprise. Or a nun the size of a Malteser, made of marzipan that you could eat.

I also like the way that priests dress. Purple is a great colour and a sash is a great accessory. To top it off, anyone who wanders around with a little hanging basket filled with incense in front of them and smoke coming off it – that, my friends, is attention to detail.

Other religions have caught my eye on the fashion front as well. I've always been very fond of a turban, ever since I saw James Coburn wear one in the second of the 'our man Flint' movies – those Bond spoofs he made in the sixties. He wears a white one and it looks spectacular on him. I hereby vow that I will one day wear a turban-and-Nehru-jacket combo on a big night out. I suppose I had better do it fairly soon, so people at least know it's deliberate and don't think I've just had a shower and forgotten to take the towel off my head before leaving home. But it won't actually be the first time I've taken the plunge on the turban front.

Way back when, I spent a brief period hosting the Virgin Breakfast Radio Show here in London. This was after Chris Evans had managed to get a group of businessmen together to buy Virgin and he was pretty much in charge of it, and he encouraged me to come back to the radio. I'd done a little bit of radio years earlier – for one stint he had actually been my producer, but it didn't really work out. Two big egos both trying to come out on top didn't make for an easy working environment or particularly memorable radio. Anyway, Chris thought that my career was not where it should be – and he was probably right – and he very kindly and generously encouraged me back in. The money wasn't particularly good but it was OK, more than you'd get for working those kind of hours in the real world, and so I took over a Sunday-morning slot which was popular, and then when Chris was going away he wondered if I'd stand in for him on his morning show. Which I did.

One thing I did on the show was to try to run a kind of multi-ethnic week – mainly because I wanted to get free food sent in from different local restaurants. I've always loved Japanese food, and at the time the papers were still banging on about the Japanese treatment of prisoners of war in the forties. Atrocious stuff, I'm sure, but eventually we have to move on, so I called one Monday's show Forgive and Forget, It's Jap Day – probably not quite sending out the message of tolerance and forgiveness I had hoped for. Nor did we get any free sushi. Tuesday we did Italy – nothing.

On Wednesday we sent out the call for Indian food, and we were delighted when a couple of young Sikh listeners offered to come in and promised to cook something for us. Of course they arrived fully turbaned, as befits members of the Sikh community. And we got chatting about turbans and my desire to wear a turban, and they happened to have some spare turban equipment with them, if that is the correct phrase, and they duly turbaned me up at the end of the programme. I am assuming that the art of turban-tying is passed down from father to son, in much the same way that I must remember to teach my boy how to do up a tie and shave properly before he gets too old and starts to improvise. But if you join a religion late in life, I wonder how they teach you. Classes? Or do you get a starter kit with basic instructions?

Anyway, I was very receptive to the idea of becoming be-turbaned, not least because although this was early in the morning, I was quite delightfully drunk, or at least tipsy. At that time at Virgin there used to be a large fridge near the studio which was filled not only with Richard Branson's own brand of Coca-Cola – which I always found a little on the sweet and sickly side, frankly – but also with free beer, which was sent in on a regular basis. I can't remember the name of the lager supplier, but someone obviously thought it was a good idea to ply Virgin DJs with free alcohol, and so we had a permanent supply of lager chilled and waiting.

Initially, working in the mornings, I didn't have a drink until at least twelve o'clock, and on Sundays we'd maybe have one at lunchtime – that seemed fair. But by the time we'd started the morning show we had become rather fond of it and would generally start the day with a bowl of cereal and a lager. I wish that was an exaggeration, but it isn't. In case you're curious, lager doesn't go too well with the really sugary cereals like

Crunchy Nut Corn Flakes or Coco Pops. But with the maltier ones, like Shreddies, it's terrific. Just don't tell the kids.

Boozing first thing became the norm, and on that particular day I was definitely half cut and easily persuaded by our friendly Sikhs to try on a turban. It didn't really suit me, to be honest – I'm a little on the jowly side, with rather podgy features, so I looked more like Beryl Reid than James Coburn. But then, in what I thought at the time was a flash of magnificent inspiration, I remembered that Sikhs didn't need to wear crash helmets whilst on scooters or motorcycles, because their turban was an outward sign of their religious faith and consequently it would be wrong to insist that they remove it. So they were allowed to ride scooters etc. helmet-free, as long as they were wearing their turban.

I've always been a fan of the scooter as a mode of transport and it just so happened that I'd ridden my scooter into work that day. And so, partly because I was excited at the wearing of my first turban, and partly because I was half drunk, I decided to hop on the scooter and ride home. I'm surprised that I wasn't pulled over, but what a spectacular and lovely sight that must have been – a middle-aged, slightly overweight white bloke, wearing a turban, driving a scooter while under the influence. I'm not proud of it now, obviously, and am amazed that no one got hurt. And I apologize if anyone saw me veering up a hill towards them and thought that I might be about to run them over. But fortunately I got back uneventfully, and I like to think that I've learnt my lesson, and that this will serve as a cautionary tale to all other radio professionals that lager and turbans and scooters do not mix.

But I wasn't actually heading home that day, I was heading off to a local nursery where my little boy, Harvey, who must have been no more than four or five at the time, was due to be a tiger in a small production of a bunch of fairy tales and nursery rhymes. My wife was waiting outside for me. She saw me riding up on the scooter more or less on time, no crash helmet, wearing a turban, slightly flushed in the face, put two and two together and realized that I was a waste of time. She pretended that nothing was too amiss and just checked that I had remembered to bring the video camera, which I had. But in my excitable turbaned and drunken state I forgot to press 'Record' and just held the camera to my eye, looking through it, watching my charming son rolling around pretending to be a tiger in a scene which I'd hoped to be able to watch many times over the years, but which due to my terrible lack of self-control, louche behaviour and bad parenting is now lost for ever and exists only in our memories.

I'm not one for regrets, and I've learnt over the years that living in the moment is a far more satisfying way of enjoying your family than trying to store experiences up for the future, but I do occasionally flush with shame and embarrassment when I remember what a stupid, pointless man I was for a few years. That then was my sole experience as a Sikh, and although I'll concede that I didn't give it my best shot, I have still concluded that, like the rest, Sikhism isn't for me.

I have, however, considered starting up my own religion – and why not? My religion would be very specific – I would base it on my many years studying that great pantheon of characters that exist in the world of the superhero. It's not such a silly idea.

OK, I know you're probably thinking, Who wants to go to a church where the priest is wearing a red cape and a mask? But is it really that different from what you get when you go to a Catholic service at the weekend? Is it that far away from what you see on TV when a bunch of clerics out in Iraq wearing tall black hats are laying down the rules for how people should behave thousands of miles away at a certain time of day? Really, what's the difference between Batman's cowl and a sheikh's turban?

My religion will be based on the teachings of Marvel comic books specifically but a little bit of DC as well, and maybe some of the lesser-known publications over the years. Let's face it, they've always had a very strong moral code. Look at Superman, for example – it doesn't take a huge stretch of the imagination to see the parallels between his story and that of Jesus, although I assume this was only a subconscious thought when he was created by two young Jewish men, Jerry Siegel and Joe Shuster, in the late 1930s. Someone comes from a faraway place that we can't know of, lands here and is adopted by an earth-bound couple, who raise him as best they can. When he reaches maturity he has to wander off and sort out what he wants to do with himself, and then he comes back and realizes that he must sacrifice his own needs and desires and use his incredible powers to do good for the humble men and women of the planet. There you go – same story. Superman doesn't die on the cross, but I suspect that's because it's a monthly comic book and it would have been a bit of a challenge finding an interesting and believable way to resurrect him every thirty days.

Take Spiderman, too – here you've got someone who is a

regular, selfish young man, gets some power and initially decides he wants to use it for his own ends. He soon learns that's wrong, adopts the maxim 'With great power there must come great responsibility' and spends the rest of his life looking after those less fortunate than himself, while wearing one of the best costumes ever designed. How cool would the Church of Spiderman be? Webs everywhere, and the sermon delivered by a bloke hanging from the ceiling.

So my religion – and I don't know what I'll call it yet, but you'll be one of the first to know – would be based on those superheroes in particular. Some of the other characters might have to be pushed to the wayside a little bit. You wouldn't want to go down the Hulk route, obviously – you know, when you get very angry you're allowed to smash everything in sight and then afterwards everyone chases you. That would be wrong. And some of the others . . . I mean the whole Batman and Robin thing is a bit dodgy, Batman being essentially a lonely psychotic older man who has a penchant for young boys in costumes. Which brings me back to Catholicism and all those stories about priests and altar boys, which is not really the best advertisement for a faith. Although it doesn't seem to affect the number of parents, particularly in the London area, who are desperately keen to get their children into Catholic schools. It seems that they don't mind if their kids get buggered as long as they wind up with really good grades at the end of it.

You might be wondering where all this leaves me. I can't be doing with the Kabbalah and I've passed on Scientology, I've decided that the Muslim life may well be a little bit too strict for me, and I'd need daily help with the turban if I joined the Sikhs. I've fought my urge to dress as a priest and I would have a problem, frankly, with the no-sex rule there. Is there any religion apart from my yet-to-be-founded Superhero one that can offer me anything?

Well, yes, there is. There's one I've encountered several times that actually does make some sense of how people should live their lives on the planet, and which might offer something to me as an individual, and that's Shintoism. You may not be familiar with it, because it's a little off the beaten track. But Shintoism was at one time the state religion in Japan. It was big there before Buddhism started nudging its way in from China a couple of thousand years ago. And now most Japanese folk seem to divide themselves between a little bit of Shintoism and a little bit of Buddhism – as far as I can work out anyway from my trips to Japan.

I've taken the trouble to look into Shintoism a little. Essentially, as far as I can work out, it is a pantheistic religion that allows its followers to confer the godhead on to more or less anything. You can worship whatever you wish, providing you think you see the spark of spiritual life there. So if you want to worship rocks, you can worship rocks. If you want to worship rivers, you can worship rivers. If you want to worship women – and who doesn't? – then you can worship women. You can worship trees, cars, anything you want. And I think it filters down into everyday life in that we-are-all-connected way that they seem to favour in Eastern religions more than Western ones.

I just love the idea that you don't have to go to any particular church unless you want to, you don't have to observe any set of rules unless you want to, it's OK to live your life however you like, as long as you do no harm to others. Ultimately, that seems to me to be about the most grown-up of all religions.

You don't need an old bloke standing in a pulpit telling you what to do, then handing out a little tray that he wants you to put money in so that he can spend it on something which you don't have any say over. And with Shintoism there's none of the status or pecking order involved with being a priest as everyone's pretty much on a level pegging, and there's none of that terrible tyranny of information that people seem to love exerting on each other – you know, 'I know more about God than you because I've read the book', 'I know more about the Kabbalah than you because I've spent more money at my Kabbalah centre', 'I know more about reiki than you because I'm a reiki super-duper master.' This sense of superiority has got to be wrong. Whereas a religion which just enables you to make sense of why you're here and calms you down and teaches you not to be mean to other people – surely that's where it's all at.

So if I do leap, feet first, into Shintoism I've already given a little thought as to what I'd like to worship. I will set up a shrine to the Marvel comic books of the 1960s and early seventies and maybe another one dedicated to my wife, even on those days when she's being especially unreasonable and doesn't agree with me on everything. Small furry animals of the cuter variety – they should be worshipped. Babies, obviously, should be adored and worshipped and cherished by all that pass them – even really ugly ones. You don't see that many super-ugly babies, and when you do, politeness dictates that you shouldn't point it out to the parents. But, in a way, the ugly babies need more of a shrine than anyone else.

And I think, ultimately, my favourite shrine will be dedicated to that moment at the beginning of a movie when you're sitting in your seat and the lights go down and you've got your popcorn and your giant carton of drink and you know that for the next hour and a half or so you can stop worrying about global warming and whether your mobile-phone bill is going to be huge or wars in other countries that you really hadn't thought we should be involved with or the fact that you need to lose maybe fourteen pounds and shouldn't be eating the M&Ms you've just purchased or any of those other petty concerns you have – you can leave all that aside and hope that with any luck this will be the greatest movie ever made. That's what I'd like to worship – that moment just before you get to see a new film by someone who might be as great as Sergio Leone or David Lean or Alfred Hitchcock or Federico Fellini, or even Stephen Spielberg or one of the new guys. That's my favourite thing, probably, and that's where I find a little bit of peace.

The War To End All Wars

Like many men, I'm sure, in my youth I felt I would do something of great worth with my life. I would leave a lasting legacy, an achievement of some kind that would have future generations talking about me with respect and possibly even admiration and awe. I went through all the usual phases – wondering if I might be Jesus, dreaming that I could well be the next James Dean, hoping that I might accidentally find the cure for cancer without really having to work too hard at it.

As those dreams all dwindled away, I began to focus on smaller, altogether more attainable fantasies. Perhaps I might rescue a family of important people from a burning vehicle or a hotel that was about to collapse. Ideally, there would be at least two or three very hot young women in there, all desperate to show me their gratitude in the most straightforwardly physical way – once I'd given interviews to all the news channels, of course. Naturally, I would rise above such base temptation and show my true colours by saying, 'I want nothing in return – put your breasts away, madam.' Thankfully, my resolve has never been tested.

But if I'm to take a step back and look at my life objectively, I can see that there has been one heroic struggle in which I have played a prominent, if far from decisive role. The war against nits. I can guess what you're thinking. That sounds feeble compared to the war against terror. That doesn't have anything on the war on want. It might not even compare that favourably to the battle to get a bikini-bod back after giving birth that so many female celebrities are keen to share with us in glossy magazines. But it has been a very real, very passionate struggle that I have devoted a considerable amount of my limited time on the planet to, so show a little respect, please.

Yes, my sworn enemies on Earth are head lice, or *pediculis capitis* to give them their proper name: those revolting, blood-sucking little parasites that set up home and lay their eggs – which are the actual nits – in your children's hair. The wretched things walk from head to head wherever children gather so persistently that for the last ten, maybe twelve years of our lives, I can't remember one sustained period when we haven't either been suffering from a full-blown nit invasion, recovering from a lengthy bout of combing out, or girding our loins for a renewed attack.

I think my daughter Betty first got nits when she was about six or seven. Back then we were blissfully unaware that they were going to loom so large in our domestic life. I remember going to a school play in which she had something approaching a starring role. She had to play a little girl in some comedy turn in which she recited a poem and got dizzy and passed out, and she did very well, but of course I would say that. Anyway, for the rest of the show she was standing on the stage, in front of all her classmates and their parents, furiously scratching and rubbing her head and pulling at her hair. In our ignorance, we thought it was quite cute, just some kind of tic attributable to nerves, but later, when we were informed that she was playing host to a whole army of nits, we realized what the more experienced parents present had immediately known – she had been colonized. It was only when we tried to comb the nits out that we began to appreciate just how nightmarish it is to get rid of the tenacious little fuckers.

Every time we dolloped conditioner on her hair to loosen the eggs' grip, dragged the fine-toothed nit comb through it and wiped off the comb on a tissue, out would come what seemed like hundreds of grown-up head lice and the baby nit egg things. The tissue would be black with them. It's really quite stomach-churning the first time you see it. We worked our way across the whole of her head, sweating and moaning and taking the occasional break, and wondering what we had done, or failed to do, that had caused this horrible state of affairs.

Still, we finished the job, congratulated ourselves and went to bed, feeling exhausted but noble, safe in the knowledge that we had cured our child of this terrible affliction, and agreeing never to speak of it again. What we didn't know, in our nit naïvety, was that you have to repeat the whole procedure two or three days later, and then again about a week after that, because if you miss one or two eggs and they hatch and breed, suddenly you have another whole regiment. And of course they spread from one child to the next, and can live for days on pillows and towels, just waiting for the chance to hop back on board and start the population explosion all over again. And the grown-ups in the family get them as well, although personally, I got off lightly, because they seem to prefer women and children – they don't like the testosterone that grown men produce, apparently, or they prefer oestrogen, or maybe they just don't like me much. But it's a blessing, as my wife almost always gets itchy once we find them on the kids.

Betty got them first, but we've all had them now. My son, Harvey, is a delightful boy in every way, and is blessed with long, very thick hair, rather like his disconcertingly youthful father's, and the nits just love him. His head is Disneyland for them. There must be dozens of them on every bloody strand. We would spring-clean him regularly, apply the nit-killing juice, then embark on the long, conditioner-based comb-out, and repeat it a few days later, and once more after that, and hope and pray that was going to finish them off. Six months later he'd be scratching away again and we'd be back to the same hellish routine. It's like a really depressing real-life version of the movie *Groundhog Day*, but instead of falling in love and learning to play the piano and becoming better people, we just fight off wave after wave of unwanted head lice.

Honestly, though, my wife does most of the grunt work. I'm more of a general, overseeing the campaign from a safe distance. I try to help, I really do, but I don't have anywhere near Jane's patience or attention to detail. I'll comb through the child's hair, comb it again, then make a rudimentary inspection and have one last go at it. Jane, on the other hand, will divide the head into sections, tying up the hair in elastic bands, a bit like those people in the Bahamas who do holidaymakers' hair in corn rows. Which is all very well if the holidaymakers are Afro-Caribbean, but unfortunately they tend for the most part to be very large white women who come home, bright red from the sun, resembling overweight lobsters with a game of noughts and crosses taking place on their head. Not an attractive look, really. But Jane deals with those nits with such remarkable thoroughness that I have decided she's better equipped for the task than me, and seeing as it's one of those jobs that, if you can get someone else to do it, you will, she's stuck with it from now on.

Honey, our youngest, doesn't suffer quite as badly as Harvey, but, having the longest hair of all the children, when she does succumb, the little monsters seem to find it easier to hide from the comb, leaping from lock to lock like tiny bloodsucking Tarzans on vines. Maybe I'm crediting them with too much intelligence, but by God, they're a hardy breed. And what I've found out about head lice – which you may, or more probably may not, wish to know – is one of the reasons why they're so hardy (in addition, of course, to their craftiness in developing immunity to insecticide, which often only kills the adults in any case, as it doesn't always penetrate the shells of the eggs). The female head louse needs to have intercourse with the male just once in her lifetime to produce any number of babies. Apparently, when the male has had his pleasure, run away and decided never to speak to her again, the lady louse stores his sperm in a little bum-bag or rucksack or something, which she can dip into whenever she fancies making another batch of nits.

I don't like to be defeatist, but at times I think we're fighting a losing battle. We were just about to give up and shave all our hair off and think about joining a cult so we didn't stick out so much, when we discovered a service in London called Hair Force that will comb out the nits for you. That's right, the cavalry have arrived.

So we took the kids along and found that, for cash, some lovely ladies in white uniforms, wearing white leather holsters that contain all manner of nit-killing combs, devices and potions, would attack the nits on your behalf. The kids don't mind too much, because they're given a portable game machine to play or a DVD to watch while they lie face-down in a sort of massage chair and the ladies set to work, following a very similar method to the one my wife employs with the rubber bands and the sectioning of the hair, and with an eye for detail found only in ladies and male surgeons. They also have marvellous little Hoovers that suck off all the nits. It's quite a nice sensation, having your hair vacuumed, and I can now see what rugs get out of the experience. It's still a long and boring endurance test, but on balance, we all prefer being nit-free, even if the kids claim they miss them a little bit.

When the children were fidgeting and begging us to stop after a couple of hours of prolonged, tedious combing, during which our tempers would inevitably fray slightly and they would start to fidget and whinge and plead to be set free, I would take one of the bigger, hatched lice and show it to them under a magnifying glass. Hoping to persuade the children that the boredom and discomfort and general dreariness of sitting still and being groomed like a baby chimp was worthwhile, I explained that the horrible creature under the glass thinks of their head as home, and their blood as supper. These monstrous things, I'd say – and if you've ever looked at one under a magnifying glass you'll know why Disney have never tried to turn one into a lovable cartoon hero – these things have sex on your head. They make babies up there. They are throwing big nit parties while you sleep. Given the chance, they will build nit schools and roads and office blocks, and keep breeding until you can no longer see your hair, but instead go through life wearing a huge nit-and-louse afro, which in turn will keep growing until you have a nit beard, then a hairy nit chest, and then you disappear under a writhing nit mountain, which will spread and join together with other nit mountains until finally the whole planet is one big nit ball floating in Space. So sit still and let your mum keep combing.

This worked for a while, until Betty, who's a very sweet-natured girl – at one time we believed she might well be the next Dalai Lama – asked why we couldn't live in peace with the nits and the lice, maybe even save them and keep them as pets. But this is war, I'm afraid, and I cannot tolerate pacifists or collaborators, so the nits are always flushed away, and anyone found trying to keep one hidden in a pocket or the palm of their hand is threatened with baldness. This may well be a war we cannot win, at least in my lifetime. But there is a sense of victory in never giving up, and although I might be imagining it, I think I can sense something akin to respect in the lice I encounter these days. And for that alone, I think I deserve to be remembered.

MIDDLE-AGED MAN SEEKS PERFECT HAT FOR LONG WALKS, MOVIES AND LONG-TERM RELATIONSHIP

On the clothing front, my idea and your idea of what looks great on a man probably differ. I like combos that cause a small start of shock when first spotted, which then settles down into a slow burn of admiration. I suspect that I've pulled this off maybe two or three times over the last twenty-five years of dressing myself. Not bad, eh? Which means I've inflicted a considerable number of fashion disasters on innocent passers-by, many of which I remember with a certain nostalgia. Others I will have forgotten about completely until somebody shows me a slightly dodgy photograph from an old teenage magazine like *Just Seventeen*, which took a fleeting interest in me when I first appeared on TV. I popped up in *Smash Hits* once or twice as well. And there I am, preserved for posterity walking out of some über-eighties bar in a bowler hat with a spike on thetop, or flared trousers with an embroidered inset and a high cummerbund waist, or velvet harlequin sleeves. All actual items I have owned and worn, and not for a bet.

Even now, I have several outfits in my wardrobe which I am convinced look absolutely splendid on me, but which I have been made to promise I will never, ever wear when taking the children to school or collecting them afterwards. My personal favourite is a Vivienne Westwood original buffalo-boy-style hat, like a kind of overgrown bowler someone has sat on. I have that in two colours – camel and a dark-chocolatey brown. I have to concede that the dark-chocolatey brown doesn't quite work – for some reason it makes me look a little bit like Chip, or maybe Dale, from the Disney cartoons. But the light one I'm very fond of. I wore it on TV once: as I recall it was on *They Think It's All Over*, the sports quiz on which I was a regular, and about a week later, when I took the kids to the circus that sets up on Hampstead Heath once a year, their professional clown, a performer of some repute, asked to speak to me after the show. He came up to me after a splendid performance – unfashionable though it is, I really like circus clowns – ruefully shaking his head. 'I saw you on TV last week, wearing that hat thing,' he said. 'People like you are making my life very hard. How can I get a laugh dressing silly when people like you dress even sillier? Can't you please stop?'

I tried to persuade him that I had been wearing it as a style statement but he refused to believe such nonsense, convinced it was fancy dress designed to make me look like an idiot. By insisting it was a collectable designer piece from the eighties and not a comedy prop, I was adding insult to injury. But I needn't have bothered, because the answer to his question is simply, 'No. I can't stop, God help me.'

That particular hat brings me to one of the thornier problems addressing the ageing male in post-twentieth-century Britain. What to wear on your head. It seems to me that in the forties and fifties it was easy. Once you hit adulthood in those golden years of the hat, you started wearing a trilby, which you wore all your life, rain or shine, hairy or bald, until you died. You didn't have to look for the right sort of hat, you didn't have to worry about what it might be saying about you or whether you looked right in it, whether it suited your face or personality. It was like an arranged marriage. Like it or lump it, you two were going to be together and you had to try and make it work.

But what a challenge it is nowadays to find something that doesn't make you look stupid, American or pretentious. I've tried them all, more or less. The baseball cap is not an option unless you are actually playing a sport that requires the sun and your hair to be kept out of your eyes. There is absolutely no excuse to wear one at any other time. Americans can do it, but they enjoy spray-on cheese and Billy Joel, so I rest my case. The denim variety are also popular with East Europeans, I've noticed, and I'll admit they do go well with stone-washed denim, but only if you want to look like a low-level thug in a James Bond or Jason Bourne movie.

The trilby is a no-go because of fashion. It doesn't go with most modern clothes, and unless you have a really thin face, like David Bowie, you look like a rent collector in one. A comedian friend of mine who started dabbling in serious acting took up with a trilby at the same time. He looked fucking ridiculous, and I toyed with a number of ways to break this to him. I suggested that the great tragedy of hat-wearing is that the person who goes to all the effort never gets to enjoy the end result. You take all the risk in walking out with it, and then it's a free show for everyone else. But he only stopped when his wife told him that no one was going to take him any more seriously as an actor just because he was wearing one of those on his head.

The cap is a bit odd unless you're Terry Scott dressing as a schoolboy, an actual schoolboy, or you belong to a cricket or rowing team. The beany looks bloody awful, and so does that weird new hat that youngish people like Russell Brand wear, like a sort of knitted head sock. It just makes you look like you've suffered a head injury. Which in Russell's case may well be true.

Maybe it's me, though. Maybe it's just that my head doesn't suit hats, it's too doughy and lopsided and jowly and creased. Although I did find one hat that seemed to work. It was a doughy, lopsided, heavily creased fez I bought many years ago to wear with a monocle bought at considerable expense at the same time. The monocle was needed because I'd always wanted to have one to pop out of my eye when a comely young lady walked past. It seemed funny at the time, but I now realize it was just creepy and weird and pointless, like a lot of things I did in the nineties. In case you're wondering, I've also tried both the bowler and the top hat as possible accessories, and both make me look even more ridiculous. I wore the bowler to a premiere with the family one night and I looked like an Oliver Hardy tribute act. The top hat has only been worn twice. Once when I went to Buckingham Palace to collect my OBE – that's a nice day out. The second time was when I performed as the Fat Controller from *Thomas the Tank Engine* in a rather strange show put on for the Queen's eightieth birthday in the grounds of Buckingham

Palace. Wearing it, my resemblance to the Fat Controller was so alarming that I was faced with the choice of either sticking with the top hat and going on a crash diet to negate the Controller vibe, or never wearing it again. The hat looks perfectly happy on the top shelf of my wardrobe, so I think I'll leave it there.

I suppose this pathological and rather tiring need not to dress like everyone else began with punk rock. It happens to be punk rock because that was what was happening when I became a young man, keen to style myself differently from the way my parents had dressed me, their choices being predominantly governed by whether something was cheap, durable and inoffensive. That's not to say they didn't indulge us when they could. My brothers and I all had matching flared jeans which my mother had painstakingly hand-embroidered with the word 'Wombles' on one leg. To be honest, I never really liked the Wombles – I always felt slightly depressed when they came on. Even as a kid I knew that an animated adventure about tidying up a common was never really going to get the pulse pounding. Tom and Jerry or the Clangers would have been a much better bet, and I'd even have preferred Hector from *Hector's House*, but it was the Wombles my mum went for, without thinking to consult her little fashion victims. But most often it was cheap, durable and inoffensive clothing they went for, although they were prepared to sacrifice the last criteria providing the first two were met.

So, striking out on my own, it dawned on me that how you looked, how you dressed and how you did your hair was the key to the way the rest of the world identified you. Straight trousers suggested you were forward-thinking, and a skinny tie showed you were hip and not some old bloke, just as spiky hair made it clear that you weren't still listening to Fleetwood Mac albums. All of which were important distinctions to make at the tail end of the 1970s. But it wasn't really until I finished school and university and started working full time that I began to get it right when it came to clothes. By which I mean getting it right for me, not the rest of the world, who often wonder out loud why I don't invest in a light for my dressing room. Philistines.

At the time I started working for a living, around 1981–2, there was a growing awareness among men in the media that it was perhaps a good thing to pamper themselves and preen a little bit, like women did. And by the mid-eighties, men's grooming was becoming so de rigueur that you could hardly open a magazine without seeing an article on men's fashion or moisturizers or gels. Hair products for boys seemed to take up more shelf space in chemists and supermarkets than ever before in the history of mankind. We're paying the price now, living in a world inhabited by young men who almost all end in pointy bits. If you squint next time you walk down the high street you'll find it easy to imagine that most of the lads are wearing crowns, so prevalent is the spiky head/too-much-gel look. But in the eighties it seemed daring and exciting, and the old brands tried to jump on board as well. Tru Gel and Brylcreem even made a brief comeback at one point, which is weird because if you've ever tried them then, like me, you will have wondered exactly what they were meant to do for you. Apart from leave a nasty stain on your pillow.

So it was the post-punk years, and we'd just swaggered

through the New Romantic movement, at the height of which it wasn't out of the ordinary to see a bloke walking through the West End of London dressed as a pirate. That was a fun time. All bets were off and you were allowed to step out in fancy dress any night of the week, regardless of where you were going.

I was now working, so I had to think about buying clothes that did more than just make people look twice and get you into the right club. As I began to earn a bit of money I tried to buy the type of suits that would carry you through a working day and then, hopefully, with some slight adjustments, take you into the evening as well. There existed a real shopping Mecca for the cash-light, style-heavy shopper back then, a place called Hyper Hyper which I used to frequent. It was a kind of deranged Top Shop where individual stallholders rented space to sell all kinds of weird clothing: garments that looked like a bunch of underpants sewn together, or giant zoot suits with big chains, or outlandish pirate hats, or clothes that looked like they belonged in *Doctor Who*, or decorators' boiler-suits sprayed in alarming colours, all of which were mainly nightclub wear. I loved Hyper Hyper, but across the road, among the funky stores of the marginally more sedate Kensington Market, a store called Rock a Cha specialized in really quite cheap but very well-made slim-fit 1950s suits. They were the business.

Another favourite was Johnson's, at the end of the King's Road, just before the Vivienne Westwood store that occupied the site of the infamous Seditionaries, formerly Sex. I don't know what is there now – possibly a shop selling upmarket hair products or an employment agency for Filipino nannies – no doubt something rather soulless compared to the fabulous Johnson's.

It had been set up and was run by its namesake, a cool cat called Lloyd Johnson, and it was a real magnet for people who were into fashion, but into fashion in a peculiar way. People who were into fashion without being fashionable. They liked clothes but they didn't want to wear what was dictated to them by magazines. So Lloyd always kept in stock drape jackets, baggy rockabilly-style shirts, tight jeans and ludicrously voluminous jeans, and bizarre shoes. His rails bulged, especially downstairs where the older stock went. I don't remember him ever having a proper sale. Instead the old stuff got squeezed on to the already overcrowded rails at the back of the basement, until people started buying those sorts of shirts or jeans again. I first bought clothes from him in about 1979, just as punk began to fizzle out. I remember going to a party kitted out in a Johnson's jacket patterned with huge black and white diamonds, big, baggy, ill-fitting jeans that didn't do a lot for me and shoes that looked as though someone had taken a ruler to them, divided them into quarters and painted each section in alternating black and white, which, with my enormous feet, was a ridiculous sight. If only I'd had that Vivienne Westwood hat back then I could have skipped going home and gone straight to the Big Top, where I like to think I would have married the tattooed lady and lived happily ever after, with the patter of tiny feet echoing about our caravan. That's if we shared with the dwarfs, of course.

Undaunted, over the years I bought any number of things from Lloyd, including a leather jacket festooned with chains, which I still have in my cupboard and which I once wore when pretending to be a Tom Jones backing singer. I also bought a number of fantastic crushed-velvet suits in a variety of garish colours, which, I very, very strongly suspect, I would not squeeze into now. The trousers had a fairly unforgiving 32-inch waist but the fabric was brilliant – a lush, shiny material that really caught and reflected the light and looked great in the studio. I did a whole series, called *Mondo Rosso*, for BBC2 in those suits.

The programme wasn't seen by too many people, but was one of those shows that was thoroughly enjoyed by all who did watch it, and by me. It was one of the best experiences of making a TV show I've had because the end result was exactly what I wanted it to be. And wearing flashy, trashy, sleazy clothes from Johnson's was part of that. The shop closed down, unfortunately, with very little fanfare, towards the end of the 1990s. At that time Las Vegas was reinventing itself as a place where younger people could go and waste their money, and I believe Lloyd rode the crest of that wave and went out there for a while to sell his louche rockabilly bowling shirts. Wherever he is now, I hope he realizes how fondly he is remembered by everyone who passed through the door of his King's Road emporium.

Contrary to the normal pattern, I've grown to prefer louder and trashier and weirder-looking outfits more as I've got older, rather than less. When I first started on TV I just wanted to look smart and maybe a bit cool. Modern European designers were becoming popular in the UK, the likes of Gaultier, Armani and Versace (back then Dolce had only just met Gabbana and Viktor and Rolf were still in short trousers).

When I saw magazine photos of Jean Paul Gaultier's huge suits, with their big, sloping but baggy shoulders and low-cut collars, it was love at first sight. I thought they looked great, but I couldn't possibly afford them. Even in the mid-1980s they were £500 or £600 each. That's a lot for a suit even today, but back then seemed almost surreal. It was like having the choice of a new flat or a new suit and settling on the suit.

If you couldn't stretch to that – and no one I knew could – there was a larger-than-life character who had come down to London from the North to set up shop as a tailor, and who, for a small consideration, would meet you outside one of the bijou stores that sold these very expensive suits, like Bazaar on South Molton Street, which was a particular favourite of mine that I would drop into occasionally to check out the clothes and marvel at the prices. You'd go into the shop and, while you distracted the sales guy by discussing with him whether or not you were minded to purchase the Jean Paul Gaultier medieval-style sackcloth doublet, or perhaps the all-in-one catsuit with cape attached, my tailor friend would quickly sketch the suit you really hankered after and make you a knock-off for about seventy-five quid.

I still desperately wanted to get my hands on a gen-u-ine Gaultier. When I got the chance of hosting my own show for Channel 4, it was all I needed to throw caution to the winds. For the pilot of *The Last Resort*, I blew the entire wardrobe budget, plus every last penny of the presenting fee I'd allocated myself, on three expensive suits. It wasn't actually as much as it sounds – the clothes budget was three or four hundred pounds and my fee was probably only five hundred, if that – but it all went on the purchase, in the sales, of two Alfredo Dominguez suits from a store called Woodhouse, and, finally, my very first Jean Paul

Gaultier from Bazaar, accessorized with a vintage hand-painted silk tie I got from Paul Smith. Oh, what a joy it was to wear! I never felt as good wearing anything else as I did in that suit.

After that I always made a big effort to get hold of suits I liked and wanted to wear. The confidence I gained from looking good, at least in my own eyes, made up for the nerves I felt going out and presenting a live TV show with next-to-no experience and very little material to call upon. That was the start of my love affair with the slightly more eclectic fringe of modern menswear.

I have strayed once or twice, and even tried designing a few of my own. That's an easy trap to fall into. After you've bought a few suits from all the more way-out designers, you begin to think this suit-designing lark can't be that difficult. It's just a matter of tinkering with the size of the lapel and deciding where to put the pockets and buttons. Next thing you know you're sitting with a tailor working on your very own bespoke masterpieces. In my case, that idea was prompted as much by becoming friends with Vic Reeves and Bob Mortimer as anything else. I'd noticed that Jools Holland always wore suits of a unique style and cut, but it was only when I started hanging out with Vic and Bob that I realized you really didn't need to worry about what other people were wearing, you could incorporate any features you liked into a bespoke suit. You could say, 'I once saw a collar on a jacket worn by Patrick McGoohan in a film made in 1962 and I'd like you to copy that for me, please.' So I happily jumped on that bandwagon for a while, having suits made with flared sleeves and buttons on the trouser turn-ups and different-coloured lapels. I had a light-blue one, for example, with a black-velvet trim on the collar. I can see now that it made me look like a ticket collector, but at the time I thought it was pretty damn swish.

That style of suit never really worked for me anyway – it always looked a lot better on Vic, partly because he dyed his hair black and fashioned it into a quiff and partly because, frankly, back then he was a far more handsome man than I was. Now, of course, I am the better-looking one and he is grotesque, but at the time he was a very attractive young television newcomer and he carried off a suit possibly with greater aplomb than any-one before or since.

The other downside to bespoke suits is that it's just so *boring* getting them made. All the measuring and fitting and going back time and again for another fitting, then another fitting, then another bloody fitting. Aaaargh! All to wind up with a suit that won't be anywhere near as nice as one you can buy off the shelf from a proper designer.

It's a lot like getting your hair cut and styled. If you go in with too high an expectation of what can be accomplished then you are bound to be let down. You are, in the words of Elvis Presley in the marvellous movie *Roustabout*, 'cruisin' for a bruisin''. Many is the time I've gone for a trim, walking in look-ing just the way I do and imagining that, in the hands of the right hair artiste, I will emerge looking like that cross between George Clooney and mid-period David Bowie that I feel more than capable of pulling off. Imagine my disappointment when I come out looking like myself, with shorter hair. I did once have a haircut so terrifically unflattering that I locked myself in the bedroom of the hotel we were staying in at the time and told

Jane, through the door, that I was either going to wait until it grew back or throw myself off the balcony. In the end I calmed down and we agreed not to talk about it, but I was mistaken for Curly from *Coronation Street* at least three times in the following weeks.

My attempts to get the perfect suit made for me have never quite panned out as hoped. The biggest error of judgement came when I decided I would start dressing like the young Cary Grant. I fancied myself heading towards middle age with a whole new and altogether more appropriate look, perhaps classically fashionable in a timeless way. So I went to another reasonably well-known young tailor, then based in Soho and equally at home in the company of wealthy young posh types from Chelsea and the local ladies who offered intimacy for cash – brasses, he called them. I showed him a picture of Cary Grant in just the sort of immaculate suit I was hoping for – a one-buttoned jacket, with that slightly drapey style to it that they had in the 1940s. Nothing too extreme: broad shoulders, longish but quite thick lapels, pegged trousers, but not too narrow nor too wide at the bottom.

'This is the suit for me,' I said. 'I am positive this is the suit that will make me look fabulous. If it does, I'll probably wear nothing but this style for the next ten or twenty years. So let's keep it simple, keep it plain. Let's get it right.'

'Absolutely,' he agreed. 'But do you fancy trying it in velvet?'

'YES!' I shouted. 'Great idea, let's go with velvet.' And for a week or three while it was being constructed, velvet seemed like the greatest idea either of us had ever had. Until it was finished.

Part of the problem was the colour. I'd asked for green velvet, which I thought of as being quintessentially forties. So the guy brought in some samples, one of which was a dark green, or more of a peacocky green really, I suppose, and it could not have looked more beautiful to me. I almost cried, it looked so perfect. I had one set of measurements taken, went back another day for a second lot, and then had to go in a third time for more measurements and alterations, by which point you've forgotten what kind of suit you asked for in the first place. Finally you get to put on something that looks like a suit made by a partially sighted child for homework, with tattered bits of paper and chalk lines all over it. Then they take that away, and back you go again, hoping you're getting somewhere close to having this bloody suit finished.

Anyway, when this green-velvet wannabe Cary Grant suit was finally unveiled, it looked predictably appalling. My tailor – and I use the term sneeringly – had been very excited to inform me that the velvet he had found for the suit was, if not actually from the 1940s, certainly not new. He had managed to find several bolts of vintage stuff in a warehouse outside Leeds. But what he had either not noticed or not even known to consider was that the velvet he had bought and fashioned into the cruel parody of a suit that I now stood before him wearing was upholstery velvet. Thick, durable, hard-wearing, fucking scratchy upholstery velvet.

I am exaggerating only slightly when I say the feel of the fabric was closer to a Brillo pad than the soft, plush velvet that Cary Grant would have worn. And because the fabric was so thick, by the time he'd put a lining in, it could virtually stand up on its own. I suspect it would have been perfectly capable of getting itself round town without me inside it at all. It was a dreadful-looking thing. I did try to wear it once or twice, but it was not only ugly but also phenomenally uncomfortable. Sitting down in it placed a great strain on the knees because the material didn't really take to being bent. It was like wearing a roll of carpet on each leg. You had to sort of snap down smartly and catch it by surprise, then force it to bend to your will. All the time you were in a sitting position you could feel this ancient, tough couch velvet straining to spring you straight up again.

I soon gave up on that velvet suit and for many years it either hung or just stood up in my wardrobe, gradually being pushed to the furthest recesses where I keep suits that are no longer in favour, while I toy with the idea of giving them either to friends or possibly to a charity auction, where quite a lot of them have eventually ended up – usually raising dispiritingly small sums. I didn't donate this one to a charity auction, though. I gave it to a small Indian gentleman who came round to help me with my plumbing one day. He was admiring my suits and I mentioned that from time to time I cleared some of them out. His eyes alighted on the peacock-green velvet. He was nowhere near as tall as me, nowhere near as well filled, probably about a foot shorter and about three stone lighter, and yet he clearly coveted this suit. I said, 'Well, if you really like the look of that one, you can have it. Have it as a tip.' He was absolutely over the moon, this little fellow. He said, 'I'm going to get it taken in, taken up – it's going to look great.' And he left, wrestling with the green-velvet suit like someone learning to dance with a shop dummy in his arms.

Needless to say, being ever optimistic about how much better each new outfit will make me look has meant that I have owned any number of proper designer outfits that were just appalling. Probably the single worst outfit I have ever owned was a Jean Paul Gaultier single-breasted suit with a double-breasted-style collar and panelling under each arm in a kind of pleated elastic. The trousers had a flat front, rather like 1930s sailors' trousers, and flared out somewhat oddly below the knee. If ever a suit was trying too hard to get noticed, this was it. And just to make sure that this suit could not under any circumstances be ignored, it was made from a shiny, silky fabric that came pre-creased. It looked as if someone had slept in and on the material for months before deciding it looked just horrible enough to be worn.

Obviously, I was thrilled with the effect I thought this suit might have on less fashionable, more timid souls. Let's call them sane people, shall we? Boring old non-mental dressers. I was very pleased with this suit and wore it on my very first trip to New York. I'd been invited there by the *Mirror* newspaper, in the days when it was owned by the late, not-so-great Robert Maxwell, to judge some sort of beauty competition to find them a new page-three girl. Embarrassing, I know, but they were offering a free trip on the *QE2* and then a flight home on Concorde. I jumped at the chance so quickly that I didn't realize the invitation was for me plus one. So when I turned up alone at Liverpool docks in the car they'd sent for me, the *Mirror* people were a little surprised I hadn't wanted to bring my mum, at the very least, if not a close friend or nubile young lady. Which I could easily have done, had I realized it was part of the deal – I was already dating Jane, who was both a friend and a nubile young lady.

As it was, I had a rather dreary time crossing the Atlantic on my own. My cabin was just above the engine room, and I was kept awake for the whole four- or five-day voyage by this pounding, rhythmic banging beneath me, thinking regretfully that I might have created the same effect in my room if I had invited Jane along. She probably wouldn't have enjoyed it much, though, as the journey was as rough as I imagine it can get without the boat actually tipping over. Luckily for me, I don't suffer from any type of motion sickness, so I was one of the few passengers who didn't go green and start chucking up once we hit stormy weather and high waves. Now unless you've been across the Atlantic on a boat in bad weather you won't know what I mean by high waves. These waves appeared to my naked eye – and obviously, I'm not a sailor, I just occasionally dress like one – to be about three hundred feet high. They probably weren't quite that massive, but when you're on a ship the size of a small town and it is rocking violently, it feels as if they are. So the good news was, I didn't get sick. The bad news was that the doctor's medical room was on the same deck as me, and on the second night of bad weather I opened my door to be confronted by the longest queue of queasy people I've ever seen. Actually, it was the only queue of queasy people I've ever seen, before or since, but it was a big one.

The line stretched from the medical room, which was at one end of the deck, all the way down to my cabin at the other. And even though I was feeling quite jaunty and not at all nauseous, as I made my way past the queue the smell of partly digested food and bile was so strong I almost succumbed myself. People were clutching buckets and carrier bags and hats into which they had thrown their lunch. There was puke all over the floor, sloshing around with the movement of the ship, not quite ankle high but hard to ignore. Thank God for the bingo on the main deck. There's nothing like a bit of bingo to take your mind off hundreds of people vomiting outside your bedroom.

Despite the puke, arriving in New York by boat was very exciting. I was looking forward to tracking down the B movies and grindhouse films I'd always dreamed of going to see in the States. I wanted to catch some kung fu, maybe some blaxploitation pictures – those 1970s movies that were much the same as regular films but – and here's the novelty – starred black actors and actresses. Occasionally they were also written or directed by African Americans, but a lot of them were made by white people just cashing in on the trend.

As well as the big films, like *Shaft* and *Super Fly*, there were lower-budget gems – *Coffy*, with the wonderful Pam Grier, springs to mind – and some that had branched out into other genres. The black Dracula film *Blacula* was popular enough to spawn a sequel, not to mention a black Frankenstein film, called *Blackenstein*. No, I'm not making this up. The monster itself owed little to the conventional interpretation, to tell the truth, apart from the square head, which they achieved by shaving the actor's afro into a high flat-top rather like a trimmed hedge. Scary. Apparently, *Blackenstein* didn't do too well at the box office, because there were plans in the works for a black mummy film which, had it gone ahead, would have been called *The Blummy*. I would have been more than happy to buy a cinema ticket just to see the word 'Blummy' in big letters on the screen, regardless of how good or, as was much more likely, bad the film itself turned out to be. I could quite happily have got up and left after the opening title and still felt I'd got my money's worth.

By the time I'd checked into the hotel, changed into my elastic-sided, flared-trousered Gaultier suit and wandered down to 42nd Street, it was already evening. I was thrilled by the atmosphere – this was when 42nd Street was still deliciously sleazy, before Mayor Rudy Giuliani cleaned up New York City to the point of Disneyfying it. Obviously, it's better in some ways today. It's nice that people aren't getting stabbed and that you're not tripping over junkies every few seconds. Yet I can't help but feel New York's lost a lot of its character. Where, now, can you go downstairs and see a transsexual strip off for a dollar? Nowhere. Or at least, nowhere I know of. By the way, when I paid my dollar I was under the illusion the she was still a he, and although it wasn't an entirely pleasant surprise I was glad to have seen one up close.

There was only one cinema that wasn't showing porn, a glorious old grindhouse with a kung fu film showing. I can't remember which one now: it might have been *When Taekwondo Strikes*, and then again, it might not. When I bought my ticket and I went into the place I was the only customer. I was very happy, sitting there waiting for the film to start, my feet up on the seat in front of me to avoid the many cockroaches running around and copulating on the sticky floor. And then, just as the credits started to roll, a gang came in. An actual New York-style gang. There must have been about fifteen or twenty of them, all youngish men, all heavily muscled, all sporting a strange kind of top like a karate top with the arms cut off, and all wearing headbands. I was convinced that I was going to die that night.

Back then New York had the sort of reputation that London has worked so hard to achieve. A scary, lawless place. A place where you'd get mugged if you walked anywhere on your own after dark. You were warned not to go near Central Park unless you were keen on being raped or murdered or both, and hanging around 42nd Street unaccompanied came a close second on the list of incredibly stupid things overdressed tourists really shouldn't do. So I sat there in a state of absolute panic and heightened awareness. Every time there was a rustle I'd jump, thinking, Oh my God, one of them is getting a knife out. And every time I heard the scuttle of a cockroach on the floor I told myself, That's it now. First they'll kill the cockroach and then they'll start on me. But of course they didn't. I'm pleased to say that, such is the power of kung fu, they watched the movie, hooting and hollering through the fight scenes and chatting through the rest, and when it was over, they very politely got up and filed out. They hardly even looked my way. In fact, they were one of the nicest bunches of people I've ever sat through a movie with. Possibly they saw the suit and were more scared of me than I was of them.

In case you're wondering, the suit and I finally parted company in Hong Kong. I took it with me to film an interview with jackie chan, and decided to get it cleaned by the hotel. They must have washed rather than dry-cleaned it, and when it came back to me it was several sizes too small and every designer crease had been pressed out of it. If only I had kept the address of that Indian plumber I could have sent it to him as a gift.

Consider the Alternative

I t's great to be alive, isn't it? Especially when you consider the alternative. I love life, which is not as stupid a statement as you might think, because on any given day I meet people who clearly don't feel the same way. I bump into them all the time, shuffling around with long faces, scowling when they see someone wearing a hat for no reason or singing out loud. Everyone has the occasional off day, sure, and I probably meet an equal number of people who deserve to be scowled at, but there definitely comes a stage in your life when you have to decide which side you are going to be on. Choose the wrong one and you'll wind up with one of those downward-turning, deeply lined faces that only come with many years of visible disapproval.

I know I've been lucky. I have a wonderful and fabulously well-paid job, and a loving wife and three adorable children and seven very special dogs, a tremendous comic collection and a snake, but those aren't the only reasons why I love being alive. I just love the experience. I like what every day brings; even on bad days, I quite like it when I go to bed at the end of the day. When you're in bed, nothing else can go wrong. Unless you can't sleep. But that's why we have TV. And masturbation. There's always something you can find to watch or do that will cheer you up.

But I admit I've never had a really bad day. I haven't had a day when my house has blown up and I've had nowhere to sleep at night. I've never had to hear the words 'Dad, I'm calling from the police station' or 'Welcome to Iraq', and I've never been stuck in a lift with Michael Barrymore or Abu Hamza – although both at the same time might be fun. But I've certainly had a few rough times in my life, and even with those, when you look back, you generally realize that you learnt something, and rarely is anything *all* bad.

If you were to ask me what's the one thing I'd miss most when I'm dead, it would simply be being alive – I can't think of anything I'd single out. I like to approach my life in this manner, like a happy idiot, and in that spirit I try to find something to enjoy in a small and Zen-like way about everything. Washing up, making the bed, hoovering. Not that I do much of any of those things, and I'm sure if I did I might run out of things to appreciate, but even if it's just the end result, you can generally find something to like.

Going to the dentist is a tough one, of course. I like my dentist and even play tennis with him, but there are few highlights to lying back with your mouth wide open while another man crams his hand in while holding something small and sharp. But the stuff you rinse with at the end is nice, and it's great when it's over.

Other chores are easier – the optician's, for example. When I was a kid my optician was ancient and rather terrifying. In fact, he was probably only in his late fifties or thereabouts, but when you're ten that's unimaginably old. He also had the bushiest white hair sprouting from his ears and his nose – it surprised me that he could breathe or hear anything. You used to see a lot more of that sort of thing back then, before Trinny and Susannah and Gok Wan and all the rest of the TV makeover crowd started to gently bully us all into over-grooming. I miss those days. Bearded ladies, men with bug-red noses dotted with blackheads like ants on a jam spill, bushy eyebrows that touched and occasionally even grew into the hairline, long broken fingernails. Now I think about it, my childhood seems to have been populated by hairy pirates and gypsies and malformed goblins. The world was a little smellier back then, for sure, but perhaps it was more interesting too.

Anyway, my young eyes were just as bad as they are now, only these days I wear contact lenses to correct my incredible short-sightedness. And I really am very short-sighted indeed. It's something that I'm perversely proud of. You would think that an affliction which verges on a major disability wouldn't be a source of any kind of happiness in my life, but I like telling people, opticians in particular, that I'm a minus 9 in each eye with slight astigmatism. That means that, without glasses or lenses, I can't recognize anyone or anything unless it's about three inches from my face. Even when I'm looking in the mirror I am sometimes a little scared that it might be a stranger staring back. So far, I'm relieved to say, it has always turned out to be me, but I do need to pop my glasses on to check. Because I wear the soft type of contact lenses which are thrown away at the end of the day (a marvellous boon to mankind), I have to go in for a fairly thorough eye test before I can order a big batch of new ones, to make sure that I can still see clearly through them, and also to check that they're not damaging my eyes in any way.

But when did going to the optician's get to be such a time-consuming deal? When did eye tests become so complex? It used to be that you sat down, they shone a torch in each eye, got you to read some letters on a board and sent you home. But these days it's not just a matter of going in and reading a few numbers off the chart. They still make you do all that old stuff, but then you have to embark on the thing with the variable lenses in the giant glasses that look like something Mr Magoo would wear if he ever became a rapper. They should just let you take those glasses home with you, so you could sit around at your leisure, popping them in for yourself and going, 'Is that better? . . . Is that worse? . . . Can I see better now . . . or now?' Hours of self-made fun to be had, and they'd look quite cool too – they have a kind of über-nerd vibe about them.

Before we go on, another piece of optician's equipment that I have a bone to pick with is that silly device where you have to rest your chin in the plastic cup and your forehead against the top bit. I have never liked doing that because I always think I can feel the sweat of the previous occupant. Maybe they give it a little wipe down between customers, but in these days of MRSA and salmonella and botulism and weird diseases flying through the air and zombies rising from their graves, I really don't want to put my chin on a chin rest where possibly a large bearded gentleman or even a bearded lady has been before me. What if they had beard nits, or bits of old cheese and Marmite panini lodged in there? But I'm not one to complain, so I endure the lengthy test, which now also entails looking at a moving dot of light for about twenty minutes with each eye, pressing a button each time I see it reappear. And they blow a puff of air right on to the eyeballs, and make me do eye aerobics, looking up and down and diagonally and side to side. It's exhausting, but at least you can help pass the time by chatting to the person who's giving you the test, which is not really an option at the dentist's.

Last time I went in for the eye-test marathon there was a new person in charge of all this marvellous equipment – a young lady. I am never at a loss for things to say, because I find other people's jobs in life quite interesting. In fact, I'm quite nosy, which I think is a good trait in anyone. As soon as you lose that interest in other people and what's going on around you, you might as well be in an urn somewhere.

So I was asking this young lady the usual stuff – where she came from, why she had become an optician – and we were chatting away and she was perfectly nice and I was only lying a little bit about how long I wear my lenses each day and how often I clean my hands and so on and so forth. And then it occurred to me, because she was a very pretty young woman, that opticians probably have to deal with more than their fair share of sexual harassment, and wouldn't it be terrible if a man was in a room like this and he suddenly lunged at the optician. Obviously it's a fairly intimate situation – you're in the dark, you're a man, she's a woman, she's touching your face and speaking to you in a soft and slightly concerned way, there's a certain tenderness involved, and let's face it, a lot of the time men are thinking about sex. I know I am. So I asked her. I made the mistake of saying out loud, 'Have you ever had a man lunge at you when you're in the dark like this?' and I noticed that she backed away slightly, presumably thinking that my asking the question was a precursor to going in for a grope.

I don't blame her at all. She had a large, partially sighted middle-aged man sitting maybe nine inches away from her in a darkened room, asking her if she had ever been grabbed in just such circumstances. Of course I didn't mean it that way at all.

I immediately reassured her that I was not planning a lunge. Perhaps I stressed it a little too strongly as I think – though I may be imagining this – she seemed a little disappointed. I don't for a second think she had really wanted me to lunge, but as soon as I made it clear that the thought hadn't actually crossed my mind she looked a little offended. Or maybe that involuntary shudder she gave was one of relief. Either way, I immediately regretted the forcefulness with which I had pointed out that I had absolutely no interest in lunging at her, so I tried to redress the balance by saying, 'Not that you're not perfectly lungeable. You are very lungeworthy indeed. I am sure you have been on the receiving end of many lunges in your social life and long may that continue.'

Really I should have just shut up, but I am so convinced that I can salvage most situations with words that I pressed on, and at this point made matters slightly worse by saying, 'If it does happen at work then I suppose you shouldn't be too flattered because, of course, the person doing the lunging is having his eyes tested, so presumably he can't really see what he's doing in the first place.'

By now she had realized I am an idiot and had decided not to take offence, which was good news for me because I then got to discover the following bombshells. As I suspected, quite often men will reach out and try to cop a feel or a squeeze or even brush against the young lady accidentally on purpose as she's fiddling with the silly glasses on their face. In particular, she said, it happened when she was working in the City, where the financiers hang out, and where young men who earn far too much money and as a result behave rather badly are particularly lecherous. She said she got quite adept at spotting the type and heading them off at the pass. Who'd have thought this would be one of the regular hazards of working in the field of sight-correction? But it gets better. She went on to inform me that apparently young female opticians don't have to endure any-where near as much lunging as young men. You might find this hard to believe, but I have it on good authority, straight from the optician's mouth, that sometimes a male eyeperson – I've got bored writing optician – might pop out for some reason, just to see if they've got lenses in stock or whether or not they can get those Armani frames in pink, only to discover when he comes back into the room that the lady in question has undressed herself and is sitting there, bold as brass, waiting for the next step with her threepenny bits hanging out. I asked how the men deal with it and was informed that normally they just back out of the room and ask one of the ladies in the shop to go in, or offer the amnesty 'OK, I'm going to go out again and we'll pretend this didn't happen' – crushing words for anyone to hear when they've just laid their intentions out for all to see.

I was raised in more modest times, when ladies would attend dances once a year in the hope of meeting a young man with good prospects to make a life with. I don't think I am quite prepared for a world filled with fumbling molesters and middle-aged exhibitionists stripping for action in small rooms just yards from the pavement where the rest of us are traipsing past. But part of me is secretly thrilled. It means that all those letters I read as a kid in *Men Only* and *Knave* and *Escort* in which lucky window-cleaners or plumbers or gardeners were offered a little extra something by the lady of the house weren't necessarily just made up by losers, for losers.

Because I have discovered – late in life, I know – that up and down the country in the small, dark, cosy, womb-like interiors of opticians' cells, women are taking off their brassieres and waiting for some poor young bloke, who's probably only a year out of optician school, to come back in and deal with their matronly advances. And if you don't think that's a good reason to love life, then I'm giving up on you.